Homeless Lives in
American Cities

Homeless Lives in American Cities

Interrogating Myth and Locating Community

Philip Webb

First published in 2014 by PALGRAVE MACMILLAN® in the United States—a division of St. Martin's Press LLC, 175 Fifth Avenue, New York, NY 10010

Where this book is distributed in the UK, Europe and the rest of the world, this is by Palgrave Macmillan, a division of Macmillan Publishers Limited, registered in England, company number 785998, of Houndmills, Basingstoke, Hampshire RG21 6XS.

Palgrave Macmillan is the global academic imprint of the above companies and has companies and representatives throughout the world.

Palgrave® and Macmillan® are registered trademarks in the United States, the United Kingdom, Europe and other countries.

ISBN: 978-1-137-37422-6

Library of Congress Cataloging-in-Publication Data

Webb, Philip, 1971–
   Homeless lives in American cities : interrogating myth and locating community / by Philip Webb.
      pages cm
   Includes bibliographical references and index.
   ISBN 978-1-137-37422-6 (hardcover : alk. paper) 1. Homeless persons—United States. 2. Homelessness—United States. 3. Cities and towns—Growth—Social aspects. I. Title.

   HV4505.W33 2014
   305.5'6920973—dc23   2014004216

A catalogue record of the book is available from the British Library.

Design by Scribe Inc.

First edition: August 2014

10 9 8 7 6 5 4 3 2 1

Contents

Introduction

The lyrics of Billy Joel's 1989 pop music song "We Didn't Start the Fire" string together a list of historical figures and events of the preceding four decades. In his brief summary of the 1980s, Joel touched on geopolitics, pop culture, and prominent social problems, like suicide, AIDS, and crack. Stuck into the middle of the litany was the simple line— "Homeless Vets" (written to rhyme with the preceding foreign debts and the following Bernie Goetz). Homeless vets were emblematic of that decade, which saw homelessness rise onto the national stage in a way never before seen. Men and women across American cities were increasingly seen sleeping on sidewalks and warming themselves on exhaust gratings. Congressional hearings and news shows focused great attention on this "new" urban problem. When a study a decade later compiled data to find out how many of the homeless people in the United States were vets, it was discovered that one in every three homeless men (and nearly one in every four homeless people) were veterans.[1]

When inverting these numbers, it becomes clear that two-thirds of homeless men were not vets. However, an enduring 1980s image of the homeless popularized in Joel's song or in the small-town wanderings of vagrant John Rambo in *First Blood* (directed by Ted Kotcheff, 1982) was a veteran. Veterans came with a ready-made explanation or etiology of their homelessness; post-traumatic stress disorder could easily account for the mental health and substance abuse problems commonly thought to be at the root of homelessness. The veteran could also be a sympathetic figure—one that homeless advocates could easily invoke in requests for funding and services. While the veteran was a popular image (among many) of displacement in the 1980s, this decade was not the first time that the two categories (displacement and veteran) were connected. After wars, veterans have long had difficulty integrating back into their mundane home lives.

Following the American Civil War, disbanded groups of soldiers often found it difficult to integrate back into domestic life.[2] Many availed themselves of the spreading of rail lines across the countryside to travel. They combined the new technology with their newly acquired wartime skills of foraging through fields and forests for food and shelter; this practice (called tramping) was developed by Civil War veterans.[3] By the end of the nineteenth century, those who went from place to place without working took their name from this practice—they were called tramps. They, along with hobos and bums, were grouped together by social activists and sociologists to form nascent categories of the socially displaced—those with no permanent ties to integrate them into society.

In the latter decades of the nineteenth century, terms for social displacement rose and fell, remaining in a state of flux as commentators grappled with how best to represent these problems. The category of the homeless man eventually replaced talk of these veterans who tramped, hobos that roamed, and bums that lazed.[4] While each of these terms signified distinct connotations, they eventually were all subsumed under the rubric of homelessness. The Civil War vets who were later represented as tramps would just over a century later come to be understood as Billy Joel's homeless vets.

The theme of a veteran returning from war—and thus upending the home life of his family who had moved on in his absence—is quite old. In Aeschylus's *Agamemnon*, the eponymous character returned home victorious from the decade-long Trojan War only to be killed by his wife, Clytaemnestra. She had in the intervening years started a relationship with her paramour, Aegisthus, and resented her husband for their daughter's death. Returning from the same war, Odysseus wandered and experienced travails for another decade before approaching his home in Ithaca, where suitors clamored for his wife Penelope's hand. The term *homeless* first appears in the English language in a famous translation of Homer's account of the itinerant veteran Odysseus. It was coined in George Chapman's seventeenth-century translation of *The Odyssey* (now most famous as the namesake of Keats's poem "On First Looking into Chapman's Homer"). Though dating to this early modern period, the term was not used with regard to urban poverty until the middle of the nineteenth century.

In Chapman's coinage, the term initially described a veteran who was both unable to return to the land whence he came and unable to reunite with his family. This dual idea of place and family are at the core of the concept of homelessness. Home is not merely a place for family residence, formation, and nurturing. Overlain with discourses of gender and labor, the home is initially the representation of a critique of the anonymity of urban life; it embodies the sense of a place to which one could retreat from the vagaries of the modern world. It was, in Christopher Lasch's phrase, a haven in a heartless world. The "homeless" concept arose with the perils of the industrial city, which was thought by many to embody every conceivable threat of the modern, heartless world.

By the time Billy Joel sings of homeless vets, the term has been sanitized into a legal category; a homeless individual had become one without a fixed place to stay. In this new legal instantiation of homelessness—the one that still governs social science, social services, and social policy—the idea of homelessness appears to be merely about a place. But as I shall show over the arc of *Homeless Lives in American Cities*, the family lingers as integral to the category of homelessness. It took another couple decades after the 1980s legal shift to even begin the process of expunging the discourse on homelessness of its proclivities for framing social problems in terms of its impact on and relationship to family ideals.

Here I shall demonstrate that current social policy and social science are predicated upon older cultural attitudes about the city and the family. I shall trace contemporary political, legal, sociological, and social service definitions, categories, and assumptions to nineteenth-century responses to urbanization that both drew upon and acted out of these older cultural attitudes. Fin-de-siècle activists, sociologists, and critics deployed mythic tropes, which consolidated these responses. Invocations of Cain, the Wandering Jew, or Rachel weeping for her children distilled an argument about homelessness—these tropes articulated a reaction to the city, immigrants, and the poor. These adverse responses coalesced in mythic tropes, which embodied the bourgeois cultural attitudes in a simple picture; they made an argument about the homeless figure. But these tropes used to describe the homeless were only part of the response. The responses that usually accepted older cultural attitudes as a given included both these mythic tropes and analyses of changes in urban life and the middle class family. In *Homeless Lives in American Cities*, I interpret the different responses to the city, the distinct modes of representation, and how different attitudes are mediated through these modes. In the discourse on homelessness, I argue that the homeless man represents anxieties about the city and its impact on the bourgeois family.

To fin-de-siècle commentators, this homeless figure came to represent the other of the bourgeois family. The invocation of mythic tropes was initially only used in the negative process of othering; it was the underside of attempts to protect the family in response to the onslaughts of urbanization. This bourgeois response to the city primarily had two mutually constitutive parts: (1) positively, there was a literature of family, and then (2) negatively, there was a discourse of the other, which pathologizes those socially displaced persons who were thought to be threats to the family. The other in this polarity—an emerging homeless figure—became a repository for critiques about urbanization.

Modernization and, in particular, urbanization became principle forces for ongoing transformations of American social life. Nineteenth-century urbanization brought millions of people from far-flung places to settle in such close proximity that new spatial arrangements for society developed haphazardly.[5] Older modes of design, which had carved out spaces for private family life, fell to the wayside; the virtual public/private split ceased to exist in the fin-de-siècle slums. The anxieties that manifested (and continue to manifest) as concern for the family as an institution ultimately reflected great uncertainties about the ways the modern metropolis completely changed the bases for social relationships. Longtime ties to the same town, the same community collapsed with the new mobility and the ever-new spatial arrangements necessitated by urbanizing capital. Yet the American city has continued to change since its Victorian explosions, and with these changes, the discourse on homelessness has continued to evolve. Certainly rural homeless exist (and at certain historical moments, like the Dust Bowl migrations, have been rather widespread); in fact, the relative invisibility of the rural homeless populations results from the urban assumptions of the discourse. As a discourse, homelessness developed as a critique of the city and continues to remain intertwined with urban changes. With most of the globe's population now living in metropolitan areas, the city has become a dominant determinant of how people live and arrange their daily lives. As the spaces of the city change, relationships to the space experience a lag; a new development—like the advent of slums or the later exodus of industry from city centers—takes time to be negotiated so that it can be integrated into broader social life.

The discourse on homelessness has taken a major role in bringing semantic order to the city. It encompasses both the positive encomiums on the family and the negative othering of the homeless figures and their social lives. This negative process includes both the deployment of mythic tropes and the broader analyses of changes in urban life. In the nearly century-and-a-half arc of this project, I shall demonstrate that social activists, journalists, and academics cease using the mythic tropes in those periods when the family is understood to be secure. In those periods when the family is perceived to be under greater threat—times of more intense social and urban change—activists begin to again deploy mythic tropes in their responses to the changing city. For instance, in the 1980s, displaced families began to appear in social service agencies. Representations of family were already becoming problematic; this trend was already under way after Daniel Patrick Moynihan had pathologized the African American family[6] and after divorce rates in the nation had begun to rise. With the appearance of the homeless family, activists reverted to mythic tropes to rhetorically separate this newest group from the homeless individual.

The bourgeois family—particularly its Protestant incarnation—was elevated by fin-de-siècle reformers to a social ideal. The city is, after all, the space of the burgher or bourgeois; that is, the city dweller, the spaces, and the norms were ultimately consolidated to ensure that it remained so. Because urbanization and immigration changed social life so much in the waning of the nineteenth century (a point explored extensively in Chapter 1), commentators developed new ways to discuss these shifts. The family came to represent the last bastion of a simpler time and place, of a community in which people lived in the same place for generations. In short, it became a remnant of a supposedly collapsing *Gemeinschaft*.[7] The term *homeless* rose in popularity in tandem with another idea, a commonly proposed ideal for a social foundation and the utopic locus for the family: the Christian home. This family ideal was developed in theological tracts and in treatises of domestic science; it was invoked by journalists and social commentators as the answer to urban problems. In these articulations, the Christian home was an ideal for the family—it was a structure for what was later called the *nuclear family*. In this representation, the immediate family was to provide emotional support and be an enclave into which to retreat from the ostensible threats of the world outside. According to these commentators, urban life was becoming fast and crowded, and the Christian home was to be a haven from its vicissitudes.

The Christian home became a model for the ideal family at a time when society was in flux. In this model of private life resisting the modern world, the perils of the city and their supposed threats to the family came to be called *homeless*. Fin-de-siècle social commentators used this language of homelessness to represent to their bourgeois audiences a lack in both places (the residences of the poor) and relationships (family and social life). In this early stage, homelessness did not represent a condition of living on the streets, staying in shelters, or curling up to sleep in a car, though in Part IV these conditions become the preoccupation of policymakers and social scientists. Homelessness at this time was a much broader concept. It was used to refer to living conditions, social practices, and family structures that failed to measure up to the Christian home ideal. Slums, tenements teaming with boarders, multiple generations under the same roof, unclean poverty, and darkened, soot-stained stairwells and hallways were all signs of homelessness. The profusion of slums in a New York exploding with new people—both domestic migrants and international immigrants—precipitated several social commentators to call it the "Homeless City."[8]

The early formation of American homelessness is tied to the city and the changes in social life brought about by its expansive rise. The initial connections with the ancient veteran Odysseus and the subsequent popular image of Billy Joel's homeless vets were not part of the fin-de-siècle formations of a discourse on homelessness. The early framers of this discourse began by juxtaposing the middle class family with the urban tenement. The bourgeois family was central to the foundation of the discourse and has remained so, even though the rise of legal categories seemingly sets aside the role of family and social relationships in defining homelessness.

The Idea of Homelessness

In this study of the discourse on homelessness, I chart a story of the American city and the middle class family. Because these are never static, the idea of homelessness shifts as activists, journalists, sociologists, and policymakers renegotiate urban change and social life. In the early stages, those figures, whose writings analyzed and documented homelessness, explicitly redressed the explosive rise of the city and changes in family life. Over time, such direct connections are not always made. Yet many assumptions, definitions, and categories continue to implicitly perpetuate the social and political anxieties and critiques whence the commentary on homelessness began. In this book, I uncover how the assumptions and social norms that informed the fin-de-siècle rise of homelessness are continuously shaping and reworking the sociological literature and social policies on homelessness.

I look at how our ways of talking about Billy Joel's 1980s homeless vet derive from analyses of 1890s Lower East Side immigrant slums. I look at how the New York Draft Riots of 1863[9] and even the Paris Commune of 1871[10] stoked middle class fears of urban life and provided an impetus to anxious social critics to develop a language, which brought a semantic order to a city that reformers and politicians were trying to order institutionally and spatially. The move from a Victorian critique of immigrant slums to 1987's Stewart B. McKinney Homeless Assistance Act (later amended as McKinney-Vento) is not immediately self-evident.[11] An immigrant family stooped over the kitchen table of their tenement flat working hard in a cottage industry of tailoring or cigar rolling is not easily seen as the same problem as urban camping. Exploited labor and the panhandler do not appear to be the same social problem, but the implicit norms of our current language of homelessness began long ago with that immigrant family. *Homeless Lives in American Cities* looks at the discursive negotiations of the modern American city to better understand how the current constellation of policies and structures of social service programs came to be.

Homeless Lives in American Cities outlines how the idea of family became integral to the discourse on homelessness. I argue that the American discourse on homelessness arose from Victorian social and political anxieties about the impact of urbanization on the middle-class Protestant family. The fact that contemporary social policy has Victorian roots has become part of conventional wisdom, as has the role of religious charities in giving rise to social work and social science.[12] Here I am teasing out the implications of these claims; I am fleshing out the story beyond institutional connections. I shall look at the stories told by activists and reformers—the ways in which they described and diagnosed social problems before they developed institutions to redress these problems. By looking at the writings of activists in different eras, I am able to see how each incarnation of homelessness was understood before missions, shelters, or policies intervened. I am able to uncover the cultural roots of many policies or the narratives adapted by social scientists to form definitions and categories of homelessness. As I shall show in different periods, social activists' responses tell a story about the homeless whom they are confronting; sometimes, these stories invoke mythic tropes to explain or articulate their understanding of homelessness. I shall show the invocation of these tropes in multiple periods. These illustrations placed the modern homeless figures within a larger story. They provided a moral valuation, a social assessment—in short, an argument about homelessness. And I am interested in the significance of this argument.

Homeless Lives in American Cities is a study of the cultural arguments that gave rise to sociological and policy responses. I shall show representations that articulate arguments about the family's role in social life, the pitfalls of the modern industrial city, and the proper forms of associational life. By looking at these arguments (which are antecedent to institutional interventions with homelessness) and tracing these through subsequent permutations, I show the connections between the poor tenement dweller and the panhandling vet. I shall demonstrate how our current policies and social services came to be. I show that our social services and policies are grounded in the deployment of mythic tropes whose invocation tells a story about the pitfalls of the modern American city.

From Myth to Social Services

This project grew from my encounters with both services and policies as a one-time homeless service program director and current executive director. Running homeless services is one part compassion, one part realist toughness, and one part regulatory enforcer. While the first two define interactions between social workers and their clients, the last part occupies much of the time and attention of a program administrator. Regulatory enforcing ensures continued lines of funding, one's ranking in the local continuum of care, and smooth audits. The audit by an official from the regional office of the Department of Housing and Urban Development (HUD) will include questions about finances and accounting, case notes and outcome measurements, and most importantly, the required verification of homelessness (and the supporting documentation) for each service recipient funded by the government.

Any program director knows there is a range of documentation and forms of verification. Sometimes the caseworker may know that the applicant is homeless, but the supporting documentation is wanting. The balance between compassion and realism enters here and determines if the applicant can access the services, is denied them, or is sent upon a Kafkaesque journey through the bureaucratic underside of social services to find someone willing to state in writing (on letterhead) that he or she is indeed homeless. One family shelter with whom I collaborated started to only take referrals from other agencies rather than allow families to apply directly to them; they wanted someone else to spend his or her time verifying and documenting the family's homelessness.[13] ✓

The proving of a lack or an absence is always difficult. In this case, the applicant must prove the absence of a particular material asset—a fixed place to stay. With the 1980s rise of this legal definition, the idea of homelessness has come to be almost coextensive with houselessness, or an unsheltered state, and especially so with the advent of Housing First emphases in social services. But these are not the terms used to describe the situation. The negation of home evokes far more than merely being without shelter; this narrow sense of homeless as unsheltered is very recent and tied to the McKinney-Vento Act, which both funds and regulates most homeless services.

But these regulations have only redefined the now dominant term for *social displacement*. The term *homeless*—or at least its deployment in contexts of urban displacement—dates to the late nineteenth-century rise of the modern industrial metropolis. The term is a way to represent displacements that arose during this time.

A basic premise of this book is that social displacement has always been with us, while homelessness has not. Homelessness is that particular form of displacement that arose with the American industrial city. Displacement is not new to the collapse of feudalism, the rise of industry, the Protestant Reformation, and colonizing imperialism. From Exodus to Ovid, the *Odyssey* to the *Mahabharata*, displacement appears to have plagued the ancient world. Exile and banishment were such superlative punishments that they were the first two meted out by the Jahwist god of Genesis—the banishment from Eden and Cain's exile from both the soil and his family. But these were individual acts and individual punishments.

Social displacement is the unmooring of an individual from the broader society; homelessness, however, is a particular way to represent social displacement in the modern city. Before those displaced by urbanization, there were those displaced from land by the collapse of the feudal system; they were called vagrants and vagabonds. In twelfth- and thirteenth-century Europe, there were groups of beggars wandering as a religious vocation; they were called mendicants. Homelessness is not a category to represent all people displaced throughout history but a new term to describe a modern, urban displacement. Homelessness is a term to represent a type of displacement that arose through processes of urbanization in the last decades of the nineteenth century—one that slowly became the dominant category of displacement in the New Deal and Eisenhower years and came to national attention in the 1980s.

Now in twenty-first-century America—nearly 25 years after Billy Joel's homeless vets—homelessness has come to be a minor social and political concern. We now live in an era in which domestic concerns are dominated by immigration, energy prices, and family values issues like gay marriage. Homelessness's relatively contemporary heyday as a concern of American political life has waned since the passing of the McKinney Act. Since this federal legislation and the funding that it authorized, the problem of homelessness has lost a central role in debates about the American city, family life, and social order. The act and the ensuing adjustments by social scientists mark the unwinding of this discourse on homelessness. The displacements this category was developed to represent were no more. People are still without shelter, but their displacement is not the homelessness that arose at the end of the last century. The term lingers on and so carries traces of the nineteenth-century critique of the city.

Because homelessness has moved to the periphery of social policy, and even discussions of urban life, we are able to approach it with a greater level of calm than we would have just a few decades ago. Pitched battles of advocates versus corporate leaders or street dwellers versus shop owners have subsided. With this distance, we can take a long view to better understand the cultural history—not only of the policy but also of the assumptions on which this policy (and social science) is grounded. We can identify how that policy grew from earlier decades of social services, social commentary, and social science and how these arose from cultural responses to Victorian social changes.

Homelessness as a Cultural Problem

Homeless Lives in American Cities is a new history of the study of homelessness, looking at homelessness as a cultural problem; it covers the entire arc of homelessness in the United States from its beginnings as a vague category to represent fin-de-siècle urban threats to family life to our current Housing First emphases. Many histories have a propensity to either ahistorically collapse distinct categories of social science—like the hobo and the homeless—or anachronistically project the category of homelessness back onto historical periods before it arose.[14] I solve these problems by locating the rise of the category of homelessness within the context of nineteenth-century urbanization's supposed threats to the ideal of the Christian home. I begin where the term homeless first becomes connected to the city and show how this idea has transformed over time to demonstrate cultural roles of homelessness in American history.

Telling people who live on a subway grating or in the back seat of a car that their plight is a problem of culture can seem, at best, insensitive and, at worst, inhuman. Intellectually, it smacks of an abusive idealism. These allegations would be true were *Homeless Lives in American Cities* about the individual holing up in an alley at night. It is not. Rather, I study homelessness as a discourse, a set of unspoken norms about a particular form of social displacement. Homelessness is not a category for all displaced through history but a new term to describe a modern form of displacement.

Homeless Lives in American Cities analyzes homelessness as a particular way of talking about displacement and a particular constellation of concerns. As we shall see, the form of displacement shifts, but the discourse maintains some important continuities while adapting to these changing urban conditions. The continuities all stem from anxieties about the middle class family. A discourse on homelessness does not exist without an overweening concern for the bourgeois family. These concerns have in multiple eras been mediated by the invocation of mythic tropes. These representations both grew from Victorian cultural assumptions about the family and the city and also subsequently codified these as social scientists took up categories and terms from the activist commentary.

The discourse on homelessness is central to the American response to and negotiation of urbanization; this discourse helped to bring a semantic order to a city newly teeming with people and problems. This semantic order established the parameters for what was considered homelessness. The modern metropolis brought unprecedented changes and in just a period of decades completely transformed American social life. While the city was temporarily reined in by processes of rationalization in the early decades of the twentieth century, the discourse and the constitution of the homeless figure continued to shift with ongoing urban changes. In *Homeless Lives in American Cities*, I identify four primary stages in the formation of the contemporary homeless figure.

In Part I, "Formation of Homelessness," I look at material from the 1890 publication of Jacob Riis's *How the Other Half Lives* through the First World War. I find that the homeless city emerged; the place and, subsequently, its population were considered homeless. Next, in Part II, "Consolidating

Homelessness"—from the 1923 publication of Nels Anderson's *The Hobo* through Theodore Caplow's 1960s Bowery Project—I argue that with the social (and discursive) stabilization arising from the political and rhetorical efforts of Progressive Era reformers, the sociological category of the homeless man is consolidated. This homeless figure is defined as a disaffiliated man—a man without family connections. Then in Part III, "Fragmenting Homelessness"—from the early 1970s emergence of the bag lady until 1987's Stewart B. McKinney Act—I argue that the midcentury consensus on homelessness as disaffiliation frays with broader changes in the nuclear family and changing demographics in the homeless population. Finally, in Part IV, "Transforming Homelessness"—from the McKinney Act to the present—I chart how the homeless figure was redefined on the basis of a material condition of where one stays at night, and social policy and services slowly adapted to this new idea of homelessness, as part of a larger process of the neoliberalizing of social services.

In each section, I trace how the preservation of the family continues as the often unspoken leitmotif of the discourse on homelessness. Nineteenth-century urban changes provoked anxieties about social life. Because metropolitan life changed so quickly, older ways of talking about social life became quickly irrelevant, yet new ones had not yet developed. Writers turned to mythic tropes to represent urban life; their invocation began to effect a consolidation of arguments about the people and practices being othered—set apart from the presumed bourgeois norms. The deployment of myth enables the social engineering and cultural attitudes to remain explicitly unspoken. Many of these unspoken attitudes were codified through these mythic tropes only to be subsequently taken up by social scientists who later evaluated displaced populations. Social science analyses of the displaced shift with changes in urban life but continue to work from the Victorian attitudes codified through mythic tropes.

In *Homeless Lives in American Cities*, I contextualize the discourse on homelessness and contemporary family values within reactions to problems of urbanization. I analyze the roles of myth in furnishing discursive fixes for these modern problems, and through this process, I explore how contemporary American social science and policy emerge from Victorian cultural attitudes about the family, the city, and social life. This project reveals the diverse forms of social displacement and the inadequacies of our current ways of representing them.

Homelessness from Past to Future

The prominence attached to homelessness as a social problem in the 1980s has waned. Urban life is now quite orderly. The contemporary American city has little resemblance to the fin-de-siècle homeless city with its throngs spilling from sidewalks into the streets. The discourse on homelessness arose through problems in establishing the American city as the primary locus of production; the homeless figure remained a problem as the city became primarily a locus of consumption. The city of consumption has to be kept orderly to abet the movements and safety of the consumers. American cities have now been thoroughly rationalized, and even more so, they are sanitized.

Laws and American cities have changed. HUD's realignment of program and funding priorities with the advent of the Homelessness Prevention and Rapid Re-Housing Program (HPRP) consolidates the move away from the lingering traces of the earlier discourse on homelessness. The shifts in policy and services to Housing First emphases and programs mark the institutionalizing of this discursive shift—homelessness is in the first instance addressed as a material problem. Social services are beginning to internalize the new framework that began with the McKinney Act but is only now normalizing into an assumption of programs and services. After decades of advocates making the case, the National Alliance to End Homelessness's first principle of housing first—"Homelessness is first and foremost a housing problem and should be treated as such"[15]—appears to be gaining a wider acceptance.

Now that shifts in attitudes and assumptions seem to have consolidated, perhaps there will be an eventual semantic change to signify this termination of the discourse on homelessness. The language of homelessness is laden with so many judgments, so much history, and so great an engagement with problems of yesteryear to continue to effectively function. The term *homeless* must go. Before the discourse was codified, Children's Aid Society founder Charles Loring Brace floated the term *houseless*.[16] While it is an improvement over the current term, it still problematically assumes the proper domestic space to be a house and not a multiunit dwelling, a bias that we shall again see with William Dean Howells's Isabel March—the flat was an inadequate space for a home. No, houseless will not do. Something as antiseptic and boring as the twenty-first-century city is becoming is probably most appropriate—undomiciled, unsheltered, or shelterless come to mind. The term should reflect the materiality of the current definition. The term for a material condition should not evoke as much affect as does *homeless.* The cultural logic of homelessness was completely integrated with family legitimation—the homeless man was the other of the family. The *raison d'être* for the discourse no longer exists. The discourse cannot be put away until we shed its signs from our language of social displacement. In *Homeless Lives in American Cities,* I make the case for such a change by starting where this affective investment in home and this process of encapsulating threats to the family begins.

PART I

Formation of Homelessness

In Part I, we look at the emergence of the American industrial metropolis and the social displacements that both gave rise to the city and resulted from it. Primarily focusing on the New York City of the long fin-de-siècle period, this part analyzes responses to urbanization and its migrations, including overcrowding, inadequate infrastructure and housing, and cultural mélange. These historical changes were the object of much contemporaneous commentary as well as policy and institutional responses. I argue that this urban commentary brought a semantic order to the chaos of late Victorian New York by, on the one hand, legitimating the bourgeois, middle class family and its Christian home ideal as the proper foundation for social order and, on the other hand, othering the spaces, individuals, and social practices that failed to conform to these norms. These responses to urban changes by writers and scholars, service providers and politicians began a process of semantically ordering the city—which precipitated spatial, political, and institutional processes of ordering—from which arose the incipient rhetoric of homelessness.

This initial rhetorical response to the city furnished representations of urban life that first brought order to the city and then later to those residents whose locations, family structure, and living arrangements did not conform to the Christian home ideal. Early social activists and journalists, whose rhetorical efforts usually intertwined with their activism, began this process of ordering urban life by developing terms and categories for representing new conditions. It was only later, when some basic assumptions of what was meant by homelessness were established, that the term *homeless* began to appear in the work of social scientists. In its early usage, the term only represented vague connections between discrete categories of displacement, for example, hobos, tramps, and bums. The commentary by journalists and social activists began a semantic process of ordering—that is, developing terms and images (often mythic tropes) to represent the city and its residents; these representations both grew from Victorian cultural assumptions about the family and the city and subsequently codified these as social scientists took up categories and terms from the activist commentary.

In Part I, I contend that fin-de-siècle journalists and activists responded with alarm to social changes; they described urban problems as being a form of homelessness and invoked mythic tropes to represent homeless figures. I first look at how homelessness emerged. Here I argue that the term first applies to the city as a whole because it is the perceived threat to the bourgeois family and the *Gemeinschaft* ideal of small-town life. I then turn to some of the early rhetorical efforts and tropes deployed in this process of semantically ordering the city. Activists and journalists who began this discourse turned to old practices of othering found in anti-Semitic traditions. In this section, I argue that anti-Semitic tropes provide symbols for and structures of representing homelessness. Finally, I argue that the anti-Semitic tropes invoked by these urban commentators function as myth. The tropes serve a cultural and not a theological purpose and emerge in locations beyond the sphere of religion. By falling back onto myth, the language of homelessness enables the rhetoric to become a carrier of family anxieties.

Part I does not fully bring us to the sociological literature on homelessness; we shall find that after a consolidation in thinking about social displacement, which is coextensive with the rise of American urban sociology. In Part II, we discuss that consolidation. Rather, here, we analyze the early responses to metropolitan displacements by activists and journalists who turn to myth to develop ways to explain and articulate urban life. In these early responses, many of the basic traits that sociological literature later attributes to homeless individuals begin to emerge through the mythic tropes: separation from family, wandering moral and/or pathological failings, and so on. The tropes provided an argument about the characteristics of these homeless figures—valuations connected with Cain, Ishmael, or the Wandering Jew became associated with those people described as homeless. Mythic tropes were an early means for ordering a discourse that was subsequently professionalized and codified by social scientists; the sociologist's descriptions of the homeless man began to take on the characteristics of a Cain or Ishmael.

CHAPTER 1

The Fin-de-Siècle Homeless City

In the last decades of the nineteenth century, New York was thought to be a homeless city populated by unmoored (domestic and international) migrants. Anxious commentators thought the city to have overturned life as they knew it. For them, a Babelian cacophony arose from the streets, decades before towers glowered down on the mutually incomprehensible sounds. Five-story tenement walk-ups enclosed in darkness, staleness—holding light and air at bay. Journalists wrote of these throngs as spilling out from the stale, dank air of their semiprivate enclosures. Though kitchens—with roughhewn tables and stoves for warming coffee, food, and people—provided a small locus for gathering, domestic life was thought to spill forth from tenements to flow into fire escapes, streaming onto sidewalks to join among the cart peddlers and surging into the streets. These middle-class commentators' discomfort with these overcrowded cities led many to hope for Haussmann-like[1] reconstruction to run roughshod over poverty to rationalize the tenement quarters of the modern city.

Industrializing forces necessitated rational processes for production, distribution, and exchange, but in the minds of many middle-class observers, those newcomers responding to industrial demands for laborers generated anarchic urban conditions.[2] For these writers, the city's structure divided into parallel worlds of an ordered "clean, handsome, respectable quarter of the town"[3] for fashionable plutocrats and a tumult in the tenement districts thought to house three-quarters of the population in 1890.[4] The premier man of letters in this day, William Dean Howells describes the bustle and crowding of a tenement streetscape:

> The fire-escapes, with their light iron balconies and ladders of iron, decorated the lofty house fronts; the roadway and sidewalks and door-steps swarmed with

children; women's heads seemed to show at every window. In the basements, over which flights of high stone steps led to the tenements, were green-grocers' shops abounding in cabbages, and provision stores running chiefly to bacon and sausages, and cobblers' and tinners' shops, and the like, in proportion to the small needs of a poor neighborhood. Ash barrels lined the sidewalks and garbage heaps filled with gutters; teams of all trades stood idly about; a peddler of cheap fruit urged his cart through the street, and mixes his cry with the joyous screams and shouts of the children and the scolding and gossiping voices of the women; the burly blue bulk of a policeman defined itself at the corner; a drunkard zigzagged down the sidewalk toward him. It was not the abode of the extremest poverty, but of a poverty as hopeless as any in the world, transmitting itself from generation to generation, and establishing conditions of permanency to which human life adjusts itself as it does to those of some incurable disease, like leprosy.[5]

This bifurcation between plutocratic respectability and chaotic tenements was a line through the city. The line not only divided people into segregated districts of the city; this split of urban geography also divided popular images of people by class, culture, ethnicity, and language.

In the parlance of the day, it created two numerically imbalanced "halves." The everyday lives of the poor—their living quarters, work practices, social habits, and spatial arrangements—became other for middle-class commentators. Rather famously, the New York poor—their everyday lives and their urban locations in slums—were studied in Jacob Riis's *How the Other Half Lives*. In a gnostic turn against the everyday life of the poor, bourgeois commentators and reformers rejected this other and its life not merely as an unworthy banality but as an evil. For them, the other half must be redeemed or rejected. These journalists and activists dismissed the modern urban life (of the metropolitan majority), calling for a transcendence from the muck of the modern city in the hopes of a return to a nostalgic past, or at least the importation of some *Gemeinschaft*-ideal elements into the city. The critique of those unable to escape the underside of the city was simultaneously a disparagement and a call for greater urban order to minimize urban problems.

The slums—their squalor and poverty—came to be considered homeless and New York (the American city with the greatest profusion of slums) a homeless city; the city and its poverty threatened hearth and home. In these discursive arguments against mundanity, the quotidian existences of the poor were homeless; the utopic locus of home, thus, must transcend the immediacy of environs. In a bourgeois discourse on homelessness, I argue, home—in particular the "Christian home"—was a this-worldly transcendence. Home was an ideal for family that pulls this social institution out of the banalities of daily life and legitimates it. Home was not merely a social category; it had explicitly religious connotations.

This particularly Protestant articulation of home became the locus for the formation of moral citizens and pious Christians;[6] it was a sacred space forming a bulwark to insulate the Victorian family from modernizing ravages and proletarian immigrants. In the sermons, pamphlets, and popular writings extolling the virtues of the Christian home, home life not only furnished patriotic and ethical training but also "provided a means of blessing middle-class values and norms. Domestic Protestantism was not merely an individualized form of popular piety. The ideology promoted by secular and clerical writers helped to justify middle-class notions of gender, economics and taste by presenting the Victorian home as eternal and God-given."[7] With this God-given ideal for social life as the norm, commentators had a clear measuring stick against which to assess urban populations. New York Presbyterian minister and president of the Presbyterian Board of Home Missions, John Hall was commissioned by the Philadelphia-based American Sunday School Union[8] to write a book on the Christian home. Hall explicitly juxtaposes the family and its Christian home to the perils of urban life.[9] The discourse of the other half developed in juxtaposition with the Christian home ideal.

As tensions increased between the populations of these halves—the plutocrats and the urban slum dwellers—fears grew among the wealthy. The New York riots of the 1860s and 1870s[10] left the urban middle and elite classes wary of the urban poor. New York's population explosion in the final two decades of the century filled the city with an ever-increasing, teeming mass of multilingual hordes. The labor overaccumulations and subsequent housing shortages led to usurious rents, ramshackle tenements, and an overly dense population. Commentators soon began to document urban life in a call for social reforms to avert possible explosions of class antagonisms.

In 1890, this assessment of urban life (especially that of New York) took a broader outline than before—fiction looked beyond the urban elite into tenement neighborhoods, and journalism systematically documented each community of slums.[11] In this year, three famous sketches of New York appeared—Stephen Crane's *Maggie, a Girl of the Streets*, William Dean Howell's *A Hazard of New Fortunes*, and Jacob Riis's *How the Other Half Lives*. The latter two in particular emanate from a bourgeois gaze into the slums. While generally evoking sympathy, these two texts are foundational for the discourse on homelessness because they mark the starting point of establishing the modern city itself as homeless.

The concerns with the city were not mere fictive backdrops for a good story. They represented an incipient turn to bourgeois reform in the face of modernization. Activists eventually began to acknowledge that bucolic small-town life and the sense of community that was supposedly lost with its waning could never overtake the city—too many forces of capital, migration, rationalization, and technological innovation made such a return impossible.

The Christian home ideal, which fostered the family as the last remnant of a collapsed *Gemeinschaft*, would remain the measuring rod for society and that by which the city would be critiqued. Elements of the pastoral and communitarian—thought to best promote the family—would be introduced into the slums to restore order and assimilate the poor laborers overflowing in the slums. The search for order in its legal, spatial, and linguistic senses all sped forward in an often haphazard rush for reforming rationalization. The loss of community and small-town life was considered by bourgeois reformers like Jacob Riis to be a problem of homelessness; the ideal location for the family was lost to the homelessness of the city.

In this chapter, I lay out the urban problems of the late nineteenth- and early twentieth-century city and how commentators talked about these urban crises. I argue that the problems of overcrowding, cultural heterogeneity, insufficient privacy for the family, lack of green space, and general urban dirtiness were all considered aspects of homelessness. Journalists and activists considered the city to be the locus of homelessness because it brought these attributes together and because the processes of urbanization undermined older social structures of the small town, which were thought to foster the family.

I divide my analyses of the fin-de-siècle homeless city into three sections. First, I look at the emergence of the term *homeless*. I demonstrate that it was a term with no analytical meaning but a way to talk about urban problems; it arose in journalistic and activist responses to the urban boom. The term was first used to describe the city itself. The city was homeless because it embodied all that was other to the idea of the Christian home, which was itself the ideal locus for the bourgeois family. This family was ostensibly the last remnant of the *Gemeinschaft*, the rest of which the city had destroyed. After demonstrating that the concept of homelessness emerged to describe the city, I then outline how this concept of homelessness was deployed to represent threats to and the absence of order. Rural life and the Christian home—which was thought to be most easily cultivated without urban distractions—were the dual models of order, and *homeless* became an adjective juxtaposed to these ideals. Then finally, I conclude this chapter by looking at some of the processes of rationalizing the city to redress its homelessness. The family and its locus in the home provided the solution to the problems of slums. The ordering processes were not just semantic—there were institutional, spatial, and political processes as well. The discourse on homelessness was part of the semantic restructuring of the city. In the third part of the chapter, we shall see that the processes of rationalizing the city first divided the city into a series of binaries and then, as we shall see in the next chapter, turned to myth to provide the means for othering the "other half." These efforts of ordering the city emanated from bourgeois reformers who sought to avert the urban explosions that had plagued New York City and Chicago in the form of riots and had plagued Paris in revolutionary uprisings.

The fin-de-siècle homeless city bequeathed homeless individuals who were later constituted as a homeless subject. Thus I now turn to look at how this city came to be called *homeless*, what changes were thought to need redressing, and how the bourgeois reform efforts try to bring order.

The Emerging Concept of Homelessness

The year 1890 was pivotal in the formation of the discourse on homelessness. Several texts appeared that described the urban grit and grime with a new commitment to realist detail; two very important ones—Howells's New York novel *A Hazard of New Fortunes* and Riis's *How the Other Half Lives*—call the city homeless. Howells establishes the connection between the homeless city and the Christian home; Riis popularizes the term *homeless* and its connection with urban poverty. A character of Howells thinks the newness of the city demands that small vignettes should be written about the different neighborhoods, workers, and lives of the urban population; Riis's journalistic book actually does such a survey of the city. The discourse on homelessness dates to this moment when anxieties about urban social change and problems attained a new prominence. At this time, top novelists and journalists took on the city with a new urgency because they feared the potentially revolutionary unrest lurking within the city's slums.

The Christian Home and the Homeless City

In *A Hazard of New Fortunes*, Howells undertakes this new city—the post-war boom of population, building, and tensions; he shows how a family plopped into the metropolis cannot find the proper space for a Christian home and eventually comes to regard the city as homeless. The novel establishes the dichotomy of the Christian home versus the homeless city and, thus, is integral to the discourse on homelessness.

From Upper East Side parades of Sunday finery to downtown immigrant tenements, from the crassness of nouveau riche industrialists to a German socialist provocateur, Howells's panoramic cityscape newly painted the modern life of an American city. Though the portrayal of poverty problematically emanates from the bourgeois standpoint of his literary alter ego Basil March (with embellishments by the Christian socialist romanticizations of supporting characters Conrad Dryfoos and Miss Vance), Howells accomplishes one of the earliest, broad-ranging views of the modernizing American city. It was heralded at the time by Twain as "the exactest and truest portrayal of New York and New York life"[12] and lauded by Howells's Boston pals, the James brothers.

The novel traces a group of relative newcomers to New York who coalesce around a start-up literary magazine prosaically named *Every Other Week*. Basil and Isabel March—from Howells's earlier works—leave his adoptive and her native Boston (and his insurance firm) so that he can finally indulge long-latent literary interests by taking over the journal's editorial helm. Basil is brought into the project by Fulkerson, whose managerial role anticipates the subsequent rise of the profession of publicity; Fulkerson had also given the project grounding by bringing in newly minted millionaire Dryfoos, whose Indiana farm rested atop huge reserves of natural gas. Dryfoos—questing for society entrée for his daughters and distractions for his son Conrad's clerical desires—agrees to bankroll the journal and installs Conrad as publisher. The circle is rounded out by artistic editor Beaton and a small coterie of contributors—including young, aspiring artist Alma Leighton, retired Confederate colonel Woodburn who thought that slavery and agrarian gentility provided social and economic correctives to the gaucheness of industry, and Lindau, a one-handed German socialist (the other hand being lost as a Union soldier fighting for abolitionist idealism) who provided translations of works appearing in European journals.

The Marches' indecision to leave insurance and Boston for literature and New York led to a second round of irresolution, as Basil and Isabel journey through New York in an interminable housing search for the ideal space for "a Christian home."[13] They want a space, a room "where the family can all come together and feel the sweetness of being a family."[14] Their domestic ideal enwraps housing concerns into those of family and religion. The dozens of flats and houses the Marches visit are unable to furnish the necessary accoutrements to form a proper home. Isabel tells Basil, "The flat abolishes the family consciousness. It's confinement without coziness; it's cluttered without being snug. You couldn't keep a self-respecting cat in a flat; you couldn't go down cellar to get cider. No: the Anglo-Saxon home, as we know it in the Anglo-Saxon house, is simply impossible in the Franco-American flat—not because it's humble, but because it's false."[15] After failed attempts to identify a proper house—since the sine qua non's of amenities (furnishings, steam, and elevators) were beyond their means in houses, the Marches' search begrudgingly returns to flats out of economic necessity. In the March's search for the proper domicile, an admittedly banal point emerges: the primary concern of home is with family. This point is integral to the discourse on homelessness.

This popular idea of a "Christian home," which makes its way into Howells's novel, arose through the Congregational Protestantism seen with figures like the Beechers and the Stowes. This ideal requires a spatial arrangement for a family order. The *Gemeinschaft* ideal, which fin-de-siècle commentators thought to be the proper social and spatial formation to foster the Christian home, requires both kinship relations and relationship to place. In the fin-de-siècle period, new zoning laws started to limit the numbers and relations of those who could live in the same residence by foreclosing options like multiple boarders or even older extended family domestic arrangements. The spatial arrangements carved up private space to promote the formation of what, by the middle of the twentieth century, comes to be called the *nuclear family*.

The spatial necessities for forming a Christian home extend beyond the domestic space to include the balance of this private space with the appropriate uses of public space. The failure to maintain this division establishes a line that comes to distinguish the homeless population from the normative bourgeois subjectivities.

The formation of private space, which emerges through the rise of bourgeois capital,[16] contributes to the nuclearization of the family and to the religious legitimation of this new familial form. In other words, modern capital established the conditions for the transformation of the family and the need for cultural legitimation of this atomizing social structure. The legitimation took the dual form of establishing the normative ideal and othering all domestic arrangements that failed to conform.

This process appears in *A Hazard of New Fortunes*: the Marches come to find that their metropolitan life in a Manhattan flat—which could not offer a Christian home—creates a sense of homelessness. They had never had such a problem in their hometown of Boston.

After a year in the bustling multicultural metropolis of New York, Isabel and the children return briefly to their old home in Boston. They wandered through streets of puritanical orderliness and New England homogeneity but found their South End house—which they had rented out to tenants—feels alien. The encounter of urban cosmopolitanism transformed the Marches and made a return to a simpler way of life impossible—a transformation of which the Marches were aware in this return trip:

> The Boston streets seemed very queer and clean and empty to the children, and the buildings little; in the horse-cars the Boston faces seemed to arraign their mother with a down-drawn severity that made her feel very guilty. She knew that this was merely the Puritan mask, the cast of a dead civilization, which people of very amiable and tolerant minds were doomed to wear, and she sighed to think that less than a year of the heterogeneous gayety of New York should have made her afraid of it . . . she was glad to go back to him [Basil] in the immense, friendly *homelessness of New York*, and hold him answerable for the change in her heart, or her mind, which made its shapeless tumult a refuge and a consolation.[17]

The entire town made the three Marches forlorn. Somehow their rootedness was severed, and they missed the chaos and anonymity of New York.

The city's excess of gaiety and people precludes significant mooring in social relations. The relative anonymity furnished by this disconnection creates a negative freedom. The homelessness of the city—that is, the collapse of community enforcement of norms (anomie)—afforded the opportunity to get outside of such expectations. Mrs. March availed herself of the privacy afforded by shedding the panoptical presence of social life in a place of community-wide, lifelong residence. She uses this freedom to slough off such strictures as obligatory Sunday morning churchgoing.

Able to more freely assert her independence and individuality, Mrs. March appreciates the urban freedom. It arises because of the severing of ongoing contact with longstanding relations. Her close-knit circle of Manhattan acquaintances does not supplant the (now severed) bonds previously felt in her native Boston. In New York, she withdraws into her immediate family—most of her nights out are to the theater with husband Basil; the Marches rarely entertain.

In her relative immunity to the perceived metropolitan downsides of poverty, crime, and overcrowding—other than seeing a tenement neighborhood while passing through in the security of her coupe—Mrs. March finds that the city brings a refuge and a consolation. The consolation is a life withdrawn into her family; there is still some remnant of home there. Yet even this sense cannot be fully developed because of the spatial limits of a flat. The reduced sense of home available within the immediate family is juxtaposed to the homelessness of the city.

The anomic homelessness of New York only affords consolations to the comfortable. Here at the fin-de-siècle rise of modern homelessness, homelessness is not an unsheltered condition but the city's embodiment of the collapse of social structures. The term *homelessness* soon became associated with the poor slum dweller and eventually even the reject of the tenement, but homelessness here at the waning of the nineteenth century is a condition of the city.

As we go forward in this chapter, I shall demonstrate a series of shifts in the discourse on homelessness: the homeless object (1) moves from the city to people and (2) begins to become the normative term for social displacement. This emergence as the categorical term for displacement begins in the fin-de-siècle period as *homeless* starts to subsume a range of older terms like *vagrant* or *vagabond* (as well as some newer ones like *hobo* or *tramp*). This second process is not completed until the Depression (and Part II). This development rests upon the dialectical relationship between the home (and domestic sciences, which developed earlier in the mid-nineteenth century) and the emerging category of homelessness. In some way, New York, in particular, and the city, in general, threatened the Beecher-Stowe consensus of domesticity and its heir, the Christian home.

New York presented challenges to many anxious journalists, activists, and social commentators; they worried that it represented the loss of ways of life that might be coming for the rest of the country. There was a widespread sense of a need to document the city. As we have noted, Howells's *Hazard* has a dual importance for the discourse on homelessness. First, it establishes the binary of Christian home versus the homeless city. And second, it establishes the importance of documenting the city as a means to gain middle-class support for reform efforts.

In this novel of the newly homeless city, both Mr. March and Mr. Fulkerson felt that there was something unique about New York; they imagined that somehow the magnitude of the city created a qualitatively different place that would somehow pique the interest of readerships beyond Manhattan island. Before March's New York move, they already discussed the possibility of him writing a series of sketches of New York life. This idea of documenting urban life was heralded (and also sometimes independently developed) by several figures associated with the magazine. Colonel Woodburn viewed such documentation as necessary for his studies of labor and poverty to which slavery was somehow to provide a solution.[18] The publisher Conrad Dryfoos saw it as an opportunity to elicit bourgeois charity.[19] Conrad tells Mr. March, "If you can make the comfortable people understand how the uncomfortable people live, it will be a very good thing, Mr. March. Sometimes it seems to me that the only trouble is that we don't know one another well enough; and that the first thing is to do this." A documentary interest in the new city served Howells both within the narrative and as author—the booming metropolis had to be recorded and understood.

The Rise of the Term *Homeless*

These fictional ruminations on the urban poor (executed much more extensively in Crane's *Maggie, a Girl of the Streets*) were paralleled by the rise of documentary, muckraking journalism by figures like Jacob Riis (who also in 1890 published *How the Other Half Lives*), drawing upon his journalistic work for the *Tribune* and the *Evening Sun* as well as longer pieces for magazines like *Scribner's*. This work is the first in his broader normative project on home and family, which he elaborates further in other works like *The Making of an American*, *Battle with the Slum*, and *The Peril and Preservation of the Home*. The enormous popularity of this first book—11 editions in five years[20]—exceeded both Riis's expectations and that of earlier works of critique of the newly industrializing cities. He became one of the most prominent spokespeople for reform. In its nascent appearance in American social thought, the term *homeless* began as a description of the tenement; Riis popularized the term and the tenement in his "battle with the slum," through which the discourse on homelessness consolidated from urban vignettes into social science.

By carrying the then-heavy photographic equipment through tenements, beer dives, police wards, and other poverty-stricken nooks, Riis gave a face to poverty like no one had done before him. Illustrating his stories (with photographs and drawings) and showing magic lantern images (a protoslide projection) on his cross-country treks for lecture series, he sketched poverty with words and pictures that gave his pleas for reform a vitality and urgency. He trudged alongside a young police commissioner on raids of crime dens, rat-infested slums, and illegal liquor houses, and so immediately drew political attention to his efforts and elicited instantaneous municipal response. His close relationship with Commissioner Roosevelt (who later became governor, vice president, and then finally president—at the hand of one of the greatly feared anarchists who assassinated President McKinley) gave the political and popular reach of Riis's efforts a national scope. (He was offered and declined a Caribbean ambassadorship as thanks for his years of tireless reform efforts.)

Riis served on innumerable panels, commissions, and other instruments of reform, and his work moved from documentary description (à la Basil March) to normative exhortation. Because of his far reach as essayist, journalist, lecturer, and reformer, Riis's work on the homelessness of the metropolis and homelessness in the city is foundational to subsequent discourse on homelessness. Riis both documented the problems and conditions that he called *homeless* and proposed responses for social activists and policy makers. His central importance to the discourse on homelessness rests in developing a vocabulary for new urban problems, documenting the conditions to be considered as homeless, invoking mythic tropes in his analyses of the homeless city (which we shall discuss in Chapter 2), and in helping to set up the institutional responses that subsequently codified homelessness as a problem of social science and (eventually) policy.

For in his time, "homelessness" was as much (though not exclusively) a condition of the city as one of the individual. As a locus that brought together vice, poverty, greed, and unassimilated immigrants, the city, in Riis's accounts, created the conditions of homelessness. This early homelessness is quite ambiguous. The term does not correspond to the groups it will ultimately describe in the process of becoming the normative category for social displacement (e.g., tramps, bums, and vagrants). Another ambiguity arises from the term's role as a privative. At the time, the term was explicitly used as a negation of home—a connection that has been obscured by time. Riis, among others, shifts equally between the language of destroying (or preserving) home and that of homelessness; that is, homelessness describes those things that destroy home. For him, the city brought together the new threats to home and became both a homeless place and a place for the homeless. As we shall see in Part II, the former sense of homeless places fades as sociologists increasingly identify individuals as homeless.

The structure of our contemporary discourse on homelessness emerges here before homelessness is a category of science or policy. Part of responding to and documenting the homeless city included developing a language to describe it. A semantic flux between terms reveals the inability to clearly articulate the new metropolis. Activists writing about these social conditions stretched older terms and brought a flurry of new ones before the term *homeless* began to emerge in popularity, primarily through the writings and lectures of Jacob Riis.

The emerging discourse about urbanization's disruptions of society was still fluctuating between the language of place and that of relationships. A well-developed set of categories of urban social displacement was still several decades off. In the late nineteenth century, *homelessness* was merely a useful term to talk about a loose set of social practices that fell beyond the bourgeois norms without having a categorical meaning. Older terms like *vagrant* and *vagabond* were too outmoded to apply to emerging urban conditions. Newer categories (like tramps, bums, or hobos) appeared with greater frequency, even becoming nascent social science categories in the first decades of the twentieth century, before becoming subsumed by a metacategory— the homeless. Less than two decades before Riis's first book, Charles Loring Brace, the founder of the Children's Aid Society, floated the moniker "houseless";[21] Brace moves between the terms *houseless* and *homeless* in his book.

Homeless became increasingly common in the work of those like Riis whose primary concern was the preservation of family and its utopic locus home. The term *homeless* is increasingly used to represent this other in the negative discourse of familial legitimation. Riis makes moves typical of the day. As we also saw with Howells, New York City, with its overabundance of tenements, immigrants, and surplus labor, earned the designation "the homeless city" in the work of Riis. The dialectically structured title of his first book— which marks his emergence onto the national scene—posits an other to a bourgeois norm. That norm—as we learn through Riis's work—is the Christian home. The middle-class family in this utopic locus is the implicit norm against whom the other half is measured; the others are homeless.

Combating Homelessness: Bringing the Country to the City

In documenting the other half, Riis begins to conflate class tensions between the bourgeoisie and the urban working class with distinctions between the country and city. In preceding decades, popular works like the oft-cited predecessors Charles Loring Brace's *The Dangerous Classes of New York*, Josiah Strong's *Our Country*, Dickens's *American Notes*, and so on[22] had warned of urban perils. James Lane argues that most of these predecessors viewed urbanization as a locus of vice and crime that threatened the "the values of a rural society,"[23] but Riis moved the axial divisions of American society from this country-city dichotomy to distinctions between classes. We shall soon see that his ideals of social structure, housing, and life are still grounded in the country. Riis makes pragmatic concessions to repairing the city for the urban populations, unlike Brace whose career consisted of carting young urban orphans to houses and farms away from the metropolis. But his fixes are to bring elements of the country to the city; the country is still the ideal. It is the middle class who has access to the country and can bring elements of it into the city.

His motives for importing the country to the metropolis were only partially altruistic; he was very concerned about the political threats from an overcrowded urban population. Among the great achievements of reform, he cites the tearing down of Tompkins Square—the site of an 1870s urban uprising and disdained anarchist movements for "Bread or Blood"[24] by near-starving laborers—to be replaced by a park.[25] He contends that the introduction of gardens into a tenement block "does the work of a dozen police clubs. In proportion as it spreads the neighborhood takes on a more orderly character. As the green dies out of the landscape and increases in political importance, the police find more to do. Where it disappears altogether from sight, lapsing into a mere sentiment, police-beats are shortened and the force patrols double at night."[26] Riis recognizes that the city cannot be sent away; it has come so forcibly that it is to remain a feature of the modern world. Yet it must be reformed.

In his autobiography first published in 1901, Riis acknowledges that for him the slum is still contrasted not with uptown homes of plutocrats but with the countryside: "For hating the slum what credit belongs to me? Who could love it? When it comes to that, perhaps it was the open, the woods, the freedom of my Danish fields I loved, the contrast that was hateful. I hate darkness and dirt anywhere, and naturally want to let in the light. I shall have no dark corners in my own cellar; it must be whitewashed clean."[27] I argue that his ideal is closely akin to the theoretical construct of *Gemeinschaft*. [*Gemeinschaft*,] we have seen, presumed a unity of people and place where families had lived side by side for generations and developed relations in which social life functioned along the lines of family relations. While this point that Riis's description of his childhood home in Ribe, Denmark, resembles Ferdinand Tönnies's idea of community has been made elsewhere,[28] I am arguing that Riis is trying to create a space for home (as metonym for *Gemeinschaft*) in the city. Riis wants to create small havens from a heartless world into which people may retreat—he advocates more windows and parks to bring the air and countryside into urban life. The family in its Christian home becomes the last urban remnant of small-town life.

Riis's approach is quite akin to that of Brace's friend and classmate from Yale—Frederick Law Olmsted. Olmsted's Greensward Plan for the 843-acre Central Park "proposed a reformer's vision—a space designed to school both patrician and plebeian cultures by transmitting, almost subliminally, civilized values and a 'harmonizing and refining influence.'"[29] Like the later reformers, Olmsted assumed that the poor of downtown must be carefully guided in proper use of the space.[30] A space could be reclaimed from the "homeless" portions of the tenements and used as an instrument to assimilate the population into bourgeois norms; the park space could be part of the processes of urban ordering—first at the level of space and then as a tool to combat some of those social behaviors that were considered homeless.

The country brought into the city was not nature but a tool for regulating life; green space was to combat against the homelessness of the city. This homelessness was not merely a spatial problem of the city, else the parks might be able to remove the taint of urban homelessness; it also referred to the social behaviors of the other half. The parks developed bureaucracies, rules, and techniques of enforcement to abet the development of "gentlemanly behavior" among the poor; park planners also undertook processes of rationalization by increasing spatial segmentation and specialization in uses.[31] Parks were instruments to bring about an urban moral order to combat the vices of the city.[32] Chicago-based activist and reformer Jane Addams was also incredibly concerned about the role of play among youth and developed enormous plans and infrastructure to guide the direction of play to ensure that it did not go astray.[33] Green spaces, fresh air, and regulated play were instruments of socialization that could assimilate children of the poor, and often immigrant, into bourgeois norms; these elements of the country were to train metropolitan youth in the recreational practices and behaviors of the *Gemeinschaft* ideal. These elements of the country combined with the institutions of the city—schools, councils on hygiene, zoning boards, and so on—were to navigate the middle way of bourgeois reform to create the proper form of family life among the urban poor. The early discourse on homelessness was always tied to social programs—it emerged from a normative project of making the city safe for the family. ✓

Riis wants to take home (or its possibility) into the lair of its enemy—the slums—lest the masses of these tenements overwhelm its last bastions. Homes must be built for the working masses, he argues,[34] or they will soon outpace the middle class in reproduction, ending any hope for home and family.[35] I find that Riis had a three-part process for taking "home" into the slums. The first, I have mentioned, is to take the country (which is the proper place for home) into the city to create the community, or public, space for home. The second process is also spatial: to produce spaces conducive to family through laws banning certain housing structures, mandating windows, airshafts, and so on, thereby creating the domestic, or private, space for home. The third is to shape the people of the other half through schools, churches, boys clubs, and other institutions. This required not only these specific institutions but also other techniques to ensure that the poor were present in these institutions to participate in assimilating processes. These techniques included developing child labor laws, then, after the widespread flouting of these laws, developing additional regulatory mechanisms for their enforcement[36]—like creating truant officers and juvenile courts—to ensure children attended the institutions of social assimilation.

The concept of homelessness emerged in popular literature and journalism of this fin-de-siècle period. It was not an analytical category but a term that embodied anxieties that arose in response to the chaotic growth of the city. The homeless city, as Riis has shown us, harbored the radical and the criminal, afforded no privacy for the family, and provided none of the fresh air and green space of the country. In this section we saw how the homeless city was established in juxtaposition to the ideal of the Christian home in Howells's *Hazard*. We then saw in the work of Jacob Riis that the role of documenting the homeless city had two integral parts: (1) a semantic ordering that began with the rise of the term *homeless* (later to be taken up by social scientists) and (2) a normative project of shaping the space and people of the city to combat the homelessness of the city in defense of the family.

To see how the term began to become a concept, I turn to Jacob Riis's discussion of the other half, that half whose lives had to be assimilated to bourgeois norms or risk receiving the moniker of homelessness. As a description of metropolitan problems, homelessness began to describe not only the city but the people residing there. The concept emerges in juxtaposition to the unspoken assumptions of a normative family and its Christian home.

Homelessness as Other, contra Order

In this section, we shall see how the home was thought to be the locus of the proper order for a family and how that which threatened this order or embraced chaos came to be the homeless of Riis's other half. For Riis, the other half is a chaos to be tamed, a disorder to be ordered. Riis, like many other reformers of the time, is a prophet of order;[37] he clings to the venerable social watchwords, "*property, family, religion, order.*"[38] The poverty, slums, and suffering of the city follow from uncontrolled growth with its "consequent disorder and crowding."[39] Since, in Riis's account, disorder causes poverty and slums, he implies that an increase in order will eliminate social ills.

The nature of this order not only includes regulations of structures through zoning laws and housing codes (which in turn shape social interactions) but also includes discourses on behavior and provides for the institutions to regulate it. Riis argues that the loss of privacy from the crowded tenements has caused a "distinct descent in the scale of refinement among the children if one may use the term . . . the general tone has been lowered."[40] In the face of unprecedented poverty, hunger, and inadequate housing—both the amount and the quality of it—Riis is worried about the refinement of children. His project of Americanizing young immigrants calls for integrating the poor into middle-class norms—a project that required both institutional and semantic processes of ordering.

As with the Progressives soon to follow him (and the emerging social science developed as their agent), order is the order of the day; Riis calls for subordinating the chaos of the city to a rational order. The language of homelessness provides an implicit structure for this order; the semantics juxtaposition of home/homeless contains the blueprints of order. On the one side, we find home and its complementary concepts of family and community, and on the other, we find the objects of criticism in the homelessness of the city—pauperdom, haphazard urban development, and the willy-nilly social relations of the metropolis. In the fin-de-siècle period, the term *homelessness* signified the multiplicity of threats to a social order grounded in the home and family.

The nature of this order, though, is a necessary but insufficient rejoinder to the urban chaos. For Riis, rationalization was an instrument, not the goal; the ideal for space and relationships was still the country. Its ameliorative effects were to help minimize the downside of urbanization. Thus when the ideal of the country clashes with implementation of order, Riis sides with the ameliorative impact of green space and openness. The *Gemeinschaft* ideal was to create the space that could best foster the family—opening up the darkness of the slums could chase away some of the urban homelessness. The city had become homeless because there was no space for the family to flourish. The institutional, spatial, and semantic processes of ordering were tools used by Riis and other reformers to subordinate the anomic aspects of the city to enable such a flourishing.

Riis's calls for order always straddled semantic and programmatic processes—he wanted both to clearly document the problems of the city and to use the schools, police, landlords, and commissions to transform these problems to create a place where a sense of home could develop. When Riis comes across a couple of children working on their first writing lesson, they wrote "Keeb of te Grass." Forlornly, he laments, "They had it by heart, for there was not, I verily believe, a green sod within a quarter of a mile. Home to them is an empty name."[41] Maintaining coifed public spaces was less important than giving poor children a chance to romp in grass, like their more fortunate compatriots in small towns and the countryside. Also, here he explicitly equates an absence of green space with an absence of home. (No wonder the city was homeless.) Thus Riis's call for order was a middle ground between a nostalgic call for a return to the land (which we shall see in Part II as a solution proposed in the nascent Catholic Worker movement) and a full embrace of modernization. As we shall shortly see, Riis calls for business to lead the way in improving the city and seeks a full-scale restructuring of the cityscape like that which Paris saw in the middle of the nineteenth century.

Riis's sense of order slides toward the Haussmann-like modernizing of the city—bulldozing buildings, widening avenues, and creating green space that can foster a sense of home. He wants to accessorize the increasingly rationalized poor districts of the city through regulations of the number of units per block, their distribution, the number of windows and airshafts, and the numbers of tenants per unit. He sought an end to the irrational exuberance of a real estate market gone amok. Just as he worked to order urban space, his writings began to impose on the city a semantic order, which gave rise to the discourse on homelessness.

The Homelessness of the Other Half

In defining the other half, Riis begins to define homelessness. Riis's descriptions of the city segmented the population along class, race, and ethnic lines—he defined his other and its subpopulations to classify the residents of the city. "The boundary line of the Other Half lies through the tenements," Riis tells us.[42] The tenements had been developed through the bubble of real estate speculators, sweatshop owners, landlords, and others, whose quest for meteoric returns broke the backs of the overwhelmingly immigrant poor. To address the problems of the other half—in the argument of Riis and other advocates of bourgeois reform—requires tweaking capital's Gilded Age excesses to sustain the basic socioeconomic structures. Riis believes that reform is a necessary concession to maintain social order and to enervate the bellows enflaming the "volcano under the city." Thus Riis's introduction includes excerpts from a report on the 1863 Draft Riots, which concluded the following:

> "When the great riot occurred in 1863 . . . every hiding-place and nursery of crime discovered itself by immediate and active participation in the operations of the mob. Those very places and domiciles, and all that are like them, are to-day nurseries of crime, and of the vices and disorderly courses which lead to crime. By far the largest part—eighty per cent. at least—of crimes against property and against the person are perpetrated by individuals who have either lost connection with home life, or never had any, or whose *homes had ceased to be sufficiently separate, decent, and desirable to afford what are regarded as ordinary wholesome influences of home and family* . . . The younger criminals seem to come almost exclusively from the worst tenement house districts, that is, when traced back to the very places where they had their homes in the city here." Of one thing New York made sure at that early stage of the inquiry: the boundary line of the Other Half lies through the tenements.[43]

The fear of this urban explosion informs the need to know the other half; reform is a result of fear.[44] This Manichean split between darkness and light—"I hate darkness and dirt anywhere, and naturally want to let in the light"—frames Riis's analysis, his oeuvre, and even our current, early twenty-first-century views of homelessness. His concern for the other half is how to bring it into the light.

Riis's analyses of the other half distinguish where there is hope in the city—he finds those who could with some amount of reform and assimilation emerge out of urban homelessness and then those who were perhaps irredeemably lost. He identifies several places where the line is drawn between the two halves. Foremost, it runs through the tenement, as we have seen. Yet he distinguishes secondary places for delineating the two halves: (1) between pauperism and honest poverty and (2) between the flat and the tenement. Later, these distinctions will grow in importance as the city slowly succumbs to the processes of rationalization and the domain of those rendered homeless shrinks. The rhetorical distinction between populations enables the recuperation and assimilation of much of the "honest poor," "deserving poor," or whatever moniker applies to those integrated into bourgeois norms. Actually this first distinction—pauperism and honest poverty—is between two subsets of the other half; the honest poor are still within the tenement. Initially, Riis merely indicates that one can distinguish between these two with the clothesline: "With it [the clothesline] begins the effort to be clean that is the first and the best evidence of a desire to be honest."[45] (Perhaps Riis's revival-meeting conversion to Methodism inspired his adherence to Wesleyan aphorisms—"Cleanliness is next to godliness.")

The Pauper and the Honest Poor: Fostering the Christian Home in the Homeless City

A Christian home had to be clean, healthy, well ventilated, and properly decorated—these were all necessary conditions for a Christian home. The Beecher sisters, to whom we shall briefly turn, outlined criteria of domestic space, the care of it, and the behaviors necessary to foster the Christian home. For reformers, lauding the cleanliness of these honest poor is insufficient; greater interventions were thought necessary to establish conditions for the preservation of the home.

Thus the reformers' battles against everyday life extended to personal sanitation; hygiene must be instilled into children to help them improve their everyday life of filth. He recalled an example from a model school class:

> The question is asked daily from the teacher's desk: "What must I do to be healthy?" and the whole school responds: "I must keep my skin clean, / Wear clean clothes, / Breathe pure air, / And live in the sunlight." It seems little less than biting sarcasm to hear them say it, for to not a few of them all these things

are known only by name. In their everyday life there is nothing even to suggest any of them. Only the demand of religious custom has power to make their parents clean up at stated intervals, and the young naturally are no better.[46]

Riis asserts that for the slum dweller only the insertion of holy days into ordinary time warrants cleaning; the everyday practices must somehow be subordinated and tamed to ones of another order. He also cites a school that has a special school officer, a matron, whose duty is to impart "the fundamental lesson of cleanliness," by making

the round of the classes every morning with her alphabet: a cake of soap, a sponge, and a pitcher of water, and picks out those who need to be washed. One little fellow expressed his disapproval of this programme in the first English composition he wrote, as follows: "*Indians. Indians do not want to wash because they like not water. I wish I was a Indian.*" Despite this hint, the lesson is enforced upon the children, but there is no evidence that it bears fruit in their homes to any noticeable extent.[47]

In his normative project on home and family, Riis went beyond expounding on the necessities of space and hygiene; he called for public and civil society institutions to take up a part in the effort to mold the city into a family-fostering place. Institutions, like schools and the government, became instrumental in extending disciplinary order beyond the middle class where rationalized processes had already taken much greater hold. In *The Battle with the Slum*, Riis lauds the 1901 election of Columbia University President Seth Low as a reform mayor: "Decency once more moved in the City Hall and into the homes of the poor."[48] City hall was to extend the reach of public affairs into the private residences of the poor—seemingly contradicting the necessity for a wall of privacy around the family to constitute the home, which I shall discuss presently. Riis tells us that "it must be that the higher standards now set up on every hand, in the cleaner streets, in the better schools, in the parks and the clubs, in the settlements, and in the thousand and one agencies for good that touch and help the lives of the poor at as many points, will tell at no distant day, and react upon the homes and upon their builders."[49] These institutions were not only to engage in a pedagogy of class education and, eventually, assimilation but also to implement processes of "Americanizing" young immigrants.[50] Because reformers had little institutional jurisdiction over adults, they focused primarily on a longer-term project of bringing up a younger generation in their image.[51]

Enabling the home to take root in the city was a long-term project; Riis knew that it required an investment of time. In *How the Other Half Lives*, he introduces the importance of investing in the children of the poor, which he significantly expands upon in a later volume: "Nothing is now better understood than that the rescue of the children is the key to the problem of city poverty, as presented for our solution to-day; that *a character may be formed where to reform it would be a hopeless task*."[52] He takes up this theme of social formation in his second book, *Children of the Poor*, which he published two years later in 1892, and then a decade later with *Children of the Tenements* (1903).[53] His goal was not only to describe the problems of poor children but also to participate in shaping them to be "proper" members of society. Thus he published a series of volumes for child audiences—*Nibsy's Christmas, Is There a Santa Claus?, Hero Tales of the Far North, Christmas Stories* (the last two being posthumously collected)—because he felt that children's education and reading are useful tools for society to mold its younger members. He had a well-developed sense of ideology and perpetuation of hegemony.

The investment in future urban generations sometimes required breaking up the existing family to properly instill the middle-class values necessary for a Christian home. When lauding two pioneering, powerful agents "in this work of moral and physical regeneration,"[54] he cites two agencies in Five Points (whose midcentury rowdiness and prominence in the Draft Riots is portrayed in Martin Scorsese's film *Gangs of New York*)—the Five Points Mission and the Five Points House of Industry, whose programs targeted tens of thousands of children to rescue them "from homes of brutality and desolation."[55] This model of social change required interventions that removed children from their parents to place them in the care, and often residence, of the reforming agency. Here the middle-class "noble women" can effectively form the characters of these young. Jane Addams and Hull House served similar purposes in Chicago—shaping young children, especially those of immigrants, who did not know how to behave properly.[56]

It appears that the immediate family had to sometimes be forsaken for reformers' hopes of instilling their family ideals. When the honest poor were identified, they could be fostered to help them understand how to set up their urban Christian home. But paupers were often beyond help—the next generation was the only hope.

The Flat and the Tenement: The Privacy of a Christian Home

Later, Riis brings up the pauper-honest poor distinction when criticizing the large presence of alms seekers in the tenements. Alms seeking, or begging as he considers it, is for him a disease or pestilence. While the honest poor avert this ailment, the tenement hovers over the alms seeker, threatening to blot out the line dividing these two groups.[57] Nonetheless, even this distinction is still one of class—he distinguishes between those who work and those who believe "that the world owes him a living."[58] He criticizes the begging pauper, claiming with Paul, "if any man will not work neither shall he eat."[59] Essentially, this is that line between the proletariat and the lumpen; for Riis, the rabble of the city is irredeemable. The lumpen residents of the tenement were not able to be assimilated into the bourgeois family ideal.

After distinguishing between the behaviors of the pauper and the honest poor, Riis turned to the spatial distinctions between those for whom the reformers could hope and those for whom there was no hope. The second of the secondary class distinctions—which we noted previously—is the flat. While Riis acknowledges that the law does not distinguish between the tenement and the flat, observation lets one identify the flat. He wrote the following: "A locked door is a strong point in favor of the flat. It argues that the first step has been taken to secure privacy, the absence of which is the chief curse of the tenement. Behind a locked door the hoodlum is not at home . . . There may be a tenement behind a closed door; but never a 'flat' without it. The hall that is a highway for all the world by night and by day is the tenement's proper badge. The Other Half ever receives with open doors."[60] A proper assurance of privacy for a household is necessary to be on the right side of the social divide—for Riis, the family must have its own space. He wants families to be able to protect their havens from the thieves and dirt, which lurk in the dark, dank stairwells and hallways of the tenement.

In a corollary to this anxiety, household-based production comes in for a great deal of criticism.[61] As we shall see in more detail in Chapter 2, the home is to be a place for the family altar—it becomes a space for private worship set off from the concerns of the world. Riis could not want the family altar to be sullied by a tailoring or cigar-rolling workshop. Beyond the violation of domestic sanctity, the house-based sweatshop brought unmarried men and women into unfortunately close proximity.[62] Of equally great concern to Riis—and for similar moral anxieties—was the presence of lodgers. Before its time, Riis wants the family to be nuclear. Riis declares, "It is idle to speak of privacy in these 'homes' [with lodgers]. The term carries no more meaning with it than would a lecture on social ethics to an audience of Hottentots."[63] Placing "home" in scare quotes indicates the absurdity of the idea of a home without privacy. Privacy is necessary to form a family, but the hands of reform can violate it, especially when the immigrant parent does not know what is in the child's best interest.

The line between order and disorder is first and foremost that line between the tenement and the unnamed rest of the city—those sections where the quarter of the middle class and plutocratic populations reside. This division, however, must be broached to extend the reach of order ever further. Thus secondary divisions identify the populations most easily assimilated into normative expectations of order, and so a series of binaries unfold to reveal the easily recuperated and the forsaken other: honest poor-pauper, flat-tenement, clean/dirty, private/public. Riis semantically arranges and divides the city's residents into those who have preserved or imperiled the home and then further subdivides the imperilers into those who can be taught the values of home and those who cannot. In his classifications, Riis identifies the proper targets and processes for other processes of ordering—rationalization of the city targets these more assimilable groups. For the others, he proposes to target the children to make them into good Americans who know how to value cleanliness, family, and privacy—in short, to teach them the virtues of home.

Rationalizing the City

For Riis and his fellow fin-de-siècle social commentators, a home can only flourish where the family has its own space, not a space that doubles as a tailor's shop, a textile sweatshop, or a washerwoman's workplace. For them, the relegation of the other half to the homelessness of tenement life can only be reversed through creating conditions for an urban home. The home, or the family, is the solution to the slum. Riis was not the first to elevate family to its central role in social structure. Over the middle decades of the nineteenth century, home and family emerged as great concerns. The home came to represent a microcosm of social order; it was both a model of and a model for ordering the city.

The midcentury elevation of the home is most clearly seen in the work of Catharine Beecher, who wrote two books that outlined the ideal of the

Christian home. This ideal for the proper space (and behaviors) of a family came with practical suggestions of how one could cultivate such a home. As with the discourse on homelessness, the constitution of a Christian home is first a way to talk about the ideal way to order a family, and then it becomes a social project.

The Christian Home as a Model and Tool of Order

Catharine Beecher's 1841 book *A Treatise on Domestic Economy* was subtitled *for the use of Young Ladies at Home, and at School.* By the time she wrote an enlarged edition with her sister Harriet Beecher Stowe in 1869, she reversed the title sequence: *The American Woman's Home: Or, Principles of Domestic Science; Being a Guide to the Formation and Maintenance of Economical, Healthful, Beautiful, and Christian Homes*—thus the woman's home had become more important than domestic science. Domestic science is now for the purpose of forming a Christian home, whereas the home had earlier merely been the location of domestic concerns. In its new role as the end and not a means for implementing a domestic economy, home was now of central importance—it receives a double mention in the later edition, while the science of domesticity takes a secondary position. With this now greater importance placed on the idea of home in the later edition, the sisters introduce a new concept to the Beecher-Stowe consensus: homelessness. In the later 1869 edition, they replaced the chapter "On Social Duties" with a new one titled, "Care of the Homeless, the Helpless, and the Vicious." Beecher and Stowe do not define *homeless*; in fact, they do not use the term anywhere in the chapter—only in the title.

Homelessness was still at this time an ill-defined term used to discuss a range of social problems; it is not until twentieth-century social scientists start to use the term that it begins to take on a technical meaning for a clearly defined population. Addressing these social problems became integral to Catharine Beecher's brand of Calvinism. Kathryn Kish Sklar has pointed out that Catharine Beecher in her later years "recast her Calvinist heritage into a form more appropriate for the Victorian era, she removed morality from the sphere of the church and treated it purely as a social entity."[64] For the Beecher sisters, the homeless were presumably those who either did not or could not cultivate a Christian home. They do discuss some of these homeless social types—pauper and criminal classes, fallen women, and orphan children, as well as tenement dwellers. Their remedies for these "homeless" are to place them with Christian families. They cite a report from the Massachusetts Board of State Charities: "The report suggests that a better way [to help] would be to scatter these unfortunates from temporary receiving asylums into families of Christian people all over the State."[65] To end homelessness, place these homeless individuals into families with a Christian home. The dialectics of homelessness to the Christian home are made explicit here—the Christian home is the antidote to homelessness.[66]

Beyond constituting homelessness as a condition antagonistic to the Christian home, the Beecher-Stowe explanations for the "care of the homeless, the helpless, and vicious" establish many assumptions subsequently taken up in the discourse on homelessness. First, their discussion of homelessness turns specifically to urban problems, in particular those of New York City. Second, the Christian family is both that which is preserved through the proper domestic arrangements and practices and the means of ameliorating the problem of homelessness. And third, their plans include a caring space for a Christian dwelling inside the city to combat the homelessness of the city. Their solution includes the schematics for a Christian flat as well as a model for construction of a Christian neighborhood. The slum was a mission field that had to be ordered for Christian homes to be able to flourish. The parameters of the eventual discourse on homelessness are outlined in a manual on constituting the Christian home—homelessness becomes that which threatens the family. But through proper planning and structuring of the city, the Beecher sisters tell us, the metropolis could be made safe for a Christian home; it did not have to be relegated to its urban homelessness. The influence of the Christian family, according to them, was the true instrument of gospel propagation in the formation of a Christian neighborhood;[67] a properly ordered Christian home could become the foundation for ordering the rest of the community.

As we have seen, Riis makes similar diagnoses and prescriptions for the city—making the city safe for the "sacred retreat" of the Christian home is the proper way to order the metropolis. In Riis's model of the Christian home, each family member has a proper role. The family that constitutes a home is not just any family but one with a "proper" female center. As we also saw with Beecher and Stowe, a home requires a woman; the American woman is necessary for the *Formation and Maintenance of Economical, Healthful, Beautiful, and Christian Homes*. When diagnosing what he thought was wrong with one particular tenement group, Riis calls for a wider opening of the immigrant door in the Chinese community to include the wife of the "Chinaman": "Then, at least, he might not be what he now is and remains, a homeless stranger."[68] For him, a female presence as wife or mother is necessary to form the home.

And not just any woman—certain expectations of femininity, certain obeisance to familial expectations and domesticity must be fulfilled. The family cannot bring order to the city if it is not properly ordered. Riis wants women and children to know their proper place in the family, and only then can the family bring stability to the volatility in tenement social life. Before improvements by the Tenement House Commission, the old Mulberry Bend, according to Riis, "harbored the very dregs of humanity." It was "pierced by a maze of foul alleys, in the depths of which skulked the tramp and the outcast thief with loathsome wrecks that had *once laid claim to the name of a woman. Every foot of it reeked with incest and murder.*"[69] Likewise, in his discussion of stale-beer dives, Riis notes that "to the women—unutterable horror of the suggestion—the place is free,"[70] and such women who patronize these establishments do not fulfill womanly responsibilities. Stephanie Golden[71] has noted Riis's revulsion at a woman serving in an illegal stale-beer dive; he dismisses her as "a sallow, wrinkled hag, evidently the ruler of the feast, [who] dealt out the hideous stuff."[72] To be a "woman," requires certain dress, certain behavior, and certain social place. A home can only emerge with a "woman"—usually in the role of mother—as the foundation of the family. The expected female role seems to slide toward the maternal role of woman, not her conjugal one, in part because the reform efforts target children and thus necessitate a proper mother. She is, in the language of the Beecher sisters, to be the "chief minister of the family estate."[73]

A woman not imbricated in the formation of a family is suspect and, as we shall see later, is rendered homeless. To rescue the home and family, the mother must be in her proper spot: "Everywhere, consciously or unconsciously, the movement is in the air, and growing, to rescue the home from neglect, to put a stop to child-labor and to home-work that would exclude the family life; the movement to send mother and children back to the home where they are safe."[74] Beyond women observing their proper role in the family, Riis also introduces another necessary condition for constituting a Christian home.

This other necessary condition includes children fulfilling their role as child. Everyone has a proper place and must act according to their social location. "The problem of the children is the problem of the State," Riis tells us in the opening line of *The Children of the Poor*. The State must intervene to ensure that children are able to be children. The State can ensure no child labor,[75] the dissemination of lessons of cleanliness, creation of parks, zoning and building ordinances, and other social improvements to create a space in which children can be children. Yet despite the State's "interest in the child as a future citizen,"[76] the State insufficiently enforces its ordinances precluding factory labor for those under 14 years of age; an unintended consequence of these child labor laws was the production of poor perjurers.[77] The necessity of the child's contribution to family income is scarcely addressed and only tangentially so when mentioned at all. "These are the children whose backs we have been loading with the heredity of the slum, of ignorance, of homelessness."[78] Riis, Addams, and the broader bourgeois reform movement used policy, social work, and institutions besides their semantic ordering of the city to form children who understood the concepts of home and family.

The influence of a family in a proper Christian home provided the greatest reach of the gospel into society. To order the city, a proper sense of domestic space, relationships, and habits had to be instilled into the urban poor. The Christian home became an ideal of how family life was to be structured. But then this ideal became an instrument of ordering; if home life could be restored to the city, its influence might spread. This hope of fin-de-siècle reformers became the basis of many reform efforts.

Reform and Social Order

In his calls for reform, Riis sought moderation; his solutions were to be a via media to tweak a status quo in the name of self-defense. We saw that he did not call for a return to the country—he brought elements of country life into the city. He did not want to undo the economics of the industrial city to alleviate social problems; rather, he wanted to involve business interests and have them become the agents of reform. The "Bread or Blood" riots, the Draft Riot, the Haymarket Riot, and the Paris Commune had all stoked enormous fears of the violent potential of the homeless city. Fin-de-siècle activists hoped that reforming the city could avert those problems and perhaps spread the influence of the Christian home.

A first step to change the lives of the tenement dwellers was to make housing affordable. Riis wanted to change the cost of housing for the poor by reducing the income potential of landlords. Rather than addressing the underlying problem of insufficient wages, he asks for a curb to profit margins. He is suitably horrified when meeting with a "respectable, Christian" garment business owner who explains that his business plan is predicated upon a policy of alienation. The owner presents his plan for division of labor, not for purposes of efficiency but for the purpose of exploiting worker ignorance to keep wages down and to prevent worker attrition. He purposely requires that each sewer have one specialty and makes sure that his sewers do not know each other; the garment sections are sewed in homes, so the workers do not come together in a factory. Thus no one knows the entire process of assembling a garment, and he, thus, protects his interest by ensuring that the employees cannot leave him to make garments on their own.[79] While Riis is appalled by this admission (and the pride the owner takes at his ingenuity), the business practice does not mean for Riis that there is something wrong with the economic system. Business created the problem and so will furnish its own solutions; he does not entertain possibilities that might harm business:

> The business of housing the poor, if it is to amount to anything, must be business, as it was business with our fathers to put them where they are. As charity, pastime, or fad, it will miserably fail, always and everywhere. This is an inexorable rule . . . It must be a fair exchange of the man's money for what he can afford to buy at a reasonable price. Any charity scheme merely turns him into a pauper, however it may be disguised, and drowns him hopelessly in the mire out of which it proposed to pull him. And this principle must pervade the whole plan.[80]

Like some much more radical later activists (e.g., Dorothy Day), he argues against charity. It produces paupers, who are those whom we saw Riis earlier juxtaposing against the honest poor. These presumably dishonest products of alms giving are of the tribe of Ishmael[81]—in Chapter 2, we shall return to the significance of Ishmaelites in the discourse on homelessness. When he shifts to discussing "pauperdom," his rhetoric also shifts: the other half becomes the nether half.[82]

While Riis dismisses the nether half as the "wrecks and the waste,"[83] he does want to focus reform efforts on the other half. He even proposes justice as the corrective of charity,[84] much like the more radical attempts to implement Catholic social teaching a generation later.[85] However, his sense of justice remains entirely committed to business furnishing business solutions.[86] He diagnoses that the dangerous classes come not "from the poverty of the tenements, but from the ill-spent wealth that reared them, that it might earn a usurious interest from a class from which 'nothing else was expected.'"[87] His solution then ignores the workers' demands for better wages, or the later Catholic Worker's proposal for work not wages; he merely contends that business should slightly adjust earnings forecasts downward but should not give charity. For Riis, the restoration of urban order in partnership with business interests can provide a way for the middle class to assimilate the other half; the poor will be able to access a Christian home. His ideas for reform stabilize urban life, not threaten the social order. The idea of the Christian home can be a model to help dispel the city's homelessness—the home can survive among the poor as long as the urban landscape and housing can foster a family and the members of the household know how to behave as a Christian family.

Twelve years after he published *How the Other Half Lives*, Riis claims that he was right—the idea of home can survive in the poor sections of town. One must partner with business interests; he still envisions a system of justice in which the poor are not agents. The changes—housing law, land reclamation for parks, and reducing the return on investment—all happen at the discretion of bourgeois reformers.[88] He goes on to cite an example of a landlord who has undertaken such a "missionary effort" and thus "made it possible" for his tenants to have homes. The burden to enable the poor to move out of urban homelessness falls to the middle-class reformers—they have the ability to ensure the maintenance of social order.

Essentially, Riis wants to transform the poor in the *imago burgensis*. He wants a full-scale adaptation of the style of life without addressing any underlying economic conditions. This mimetic transformation, of course, cannot produce exact replicas; the poor cannot actually afford the lifestyle. Nonetheless, the reformers' hopes are that the financially underprivileged can at least comport with the air of the more genteel. The transformations necessary for this plan are twofold: a change in the physical structure of the city and a change in the consciousness of the poor. While Riis would have ideally liked a full-fledged, state-sponsored Haussmannization of New York to transform the cityscape,[89] Riis realizes that he is no longer in Europe. He will have to rely on the markets to gradually adapt the municipal infrastructure: "Business, in a wider sense, has done more than all other agencies together to wipe out the worst tenements. It has been New York's real Napoleon III, from whose decree there was no appeal."[90] Riis would have envied the public/private partnership that restructured New York City a century later to make Times Square "family friendly" by displacing the indigent to replace them with suburban megastores. For the fin-de-siècle reformers, business was to provide the necessary urban changes to ensure a well-defended public and the maintenance of social order.

The goal of Haussmann and Riis was a bourgeois self-preservation. The violent potential of the other half was the reformers' primary concern with social ills—Riis certainly acknowledged the centrality of self-preservation: "Clearly there is reason for the sharp attention given at last to the life and the doings of the other half, too long unconsidered. Philanthropy we call it sometimes with patronizing airs. Better call it self-defence."[91] For him, reform was a choice between justice or the violence of the masses.[92] He was not the only one who called for social services to avert an explosion of the "the embers of social hatred [that] have been smouldering in the vagrant class."[93] Unlike Paris's state-sponsored reworking of the city to minimize the threat of a marauding vagrant class, New York must fall back onto the market to furnish solutions.

His call for social services and businesses to help improve urban life would have been fruitless had he not defined the problems. Riis framed the issues confronting the city, defined the populations involved, identified those parties who needed to act, and outlined the actions necessary to combat the homeless city. Reformers' efforts were made possible by his outlining of the problems of the city and the tensions between the Christian home and urban homelessness. The rationalization of the city required spatial and institutional practices that arose from the discursive efforts to bring order to the city. In his central role in the discourse on homelessness, he established the problems of the city as the problem of homelessness.

This homelessness of the city emerged through a broader project of bourgeois reform, which brought spatial and institutional ordering alongside a semantic one. Jacob Riis's writings and lectures were emblematic of and did much to define what that order should be and how it could be implemented. The dialectical structure of the category *homeless* (as a negation of home) and of the most popular text in this nascent formation of the discourse on homelessness (*How the Other Half Lives*) established this homeless space and population as the other to an implicit norm. The norm was the bourgeois family and its location in a Christian home—the proper foundation for a social order. The *Gemeinschaft* ideal was thought to be the soil in which the Christian home could most easily flourish, so elements of small-town life were imported to the city to try to create the possibility of Christian neighborhoods.

At this early stage, the discourse on homelessness began to set the parameters for social reform and for social science's subsequent work on the city. Manichean splits embedded in the language of the other—between home/homeless, immigrant/native—provided a framework for the subsequent discourse on homelessness. In this fin-de-siècle era, this concept of homelessness shifted from being primarily an attribute of the city to one of people. The descriptions of those residents of the other half of the city were insufficient to other people. Thus in this fin-de-siècle development of the discourse on homelessness, urban commentators developed a new way to describe these people—they turned to myth.

CHAPTER 2

Anti-Semitic Roots of Homelessness

When fin-de-siècle journalists and activists wrote about the problems of the new metropolis, the newness of social conditions presented them with difficulties.[1] There were not standard ways to talk about the city, its new population, and the social lives emerging there. Having divided their understanding of the population into two halves—the tenement dwellers and the bourgeoisie—Riis, and many others, turned to longstanding traditions of othering to help explain characteristics of those urban residents whom they considered to be homeless. A set of binaries to other populations beyond the normative social expectations was readily available from anti-Semitic traditions and their theological antecedent of anti-Judaism. These early writers whose work gave rise to the discourse on homelessness often fell back onto such traditions. At times of great social upheaval, anti-Semitism and myth have both been frequently deployed as a means to legitimate certain social practices and exclude others. While many immigrant groups in this period were marginalized socially and politically, the discourse on homelessness relied heavily, though not exclusively, on anti-Semitic invocations. In part, there were a couple of millennia of traditions readily available to draw upon that provided clear signification of the threats imperiling the bourgeois family and the Christian home.

In this chapter, we look at the way that anti-Semitic tropes were used in writings about the city and urban life. We look at six intertwining strands of anti-Semitic images and ideas prevalent in the long fin-de-siècle period: Cain, Ishmael, the Wandering Jew, exile, the Simmelian stranger, and radicals and hobos. In the fin-de-siècle period, these traditions and characteristics are not joined together into a composite image, rather they provide a loose constellation of ideas taken up into the social science discourse on homelessness (which we shall see in Part II). The turn to anti-Semitic traditions was abetted by the large migrations of Central and Eastern European Jews to New York in the last decades of the nineteenth century.

When the American civil rights activist Jessie Jackson called New York City "Hymie Town" during his 1984 presidential campaign, he invoked a longstanding association between New York City and its Jewish populations, a tradition that has produced monikers like "Jew York." Woody Allen's paranoid cinematic alter ego in *Annie Hall* identified anti-Semitism as the reason that the rest of the country failed to support New York City in its 1970s bankruptcy. While New York City may have the largest Jewish population of any city in the world after Tel Aviv, New York is, nonetheless, not a predominately Jewish city. Nathan Glazer and Daniel Patrick Moynihan's 1960s study *Beyond the Melting Pot* recognized the limits of Anglo-conformist assimilationist ideals by describing the plurality of the city's population. (New York is equally known for its Italian, Irish, Puerto Rican, African American, and increasingly its burgeoning South Asian populations.)

This pluralism began to emerge during the large waves of immigration in the last decades of the nineteenth century. These migrations—combined with large-scale domestic movements from the country to the city—brought new populations to a city bursting to accommodate these millions thronging to fulfill the labor demands of America's urban industrialization. As we have seen, the slums—their squalor and poverty—came to be considered homeless and New York (the American city with the greatest profusion of slums) a homeless city.

In the bourgeois discourse on homelessness, I argue, home—in particular the Christian home, as we discussed in Chapter 1—was a this-worldly transcendence. It provided a model for middle-class norms, and as we have seen Colleen McDannell point out, the ideal presented the "Victorian home as eternal and God-given."[2] A Protestant middle class faced with urbanizing social upheavals crystallized its concerns about collapsing social structures on the family, which became a metonym for the organic bonds of community. The modern city was the carrier and location of this rootlessness. A dual response to legitimize the family in the face of this onslaught of modernization endorsed the Christian home ideal versus the othering of urban displacement. The other in this polarity—an emerging homeless figure—becomes a repository for anxieties about modernization.

Because "the Jew" had such a long tradition as a quintessential other in Western culture, anti-Semitic tropes furnished a series of images easily appropriated by fin-de-siècle social commentators critiquing the homelessness of the city. Anti-Semitic motifs provided symbols for and structures of representing homelessness. While taxonomies frequently distinguish religious anti-Judaism (including traditions such as Christian supersession, allegations of deicide, blood libel, and so on), from modern anti-Semitism, which is predicated upon the identification of the Jewish people as a racial group, this dichotomy is inadequate for my analysis.[3] I contend that these "ancient" tropes invoked by fin-de-siècle urban commentators are already modern; these anti-Semitic tropes were not for the purpose of disparaging the Jewish people—they were a means to criticize the modern metropolis. The old stories, tropes, and images were brought into modern settings and not left to be analyzed in themselves as a theological argument. I look at the Wandering Jew in nineteenth-century New York, the mark of Cain staining the fin-de-siècle urban tenement, and Rachel weeping for her children of the Lower East Side. These tropes are inflected by the modern anti-Semitic discourses (which may have derived from the theological tradition). In this discourse, the anti-Judaic and anti-Semitic tropes have become so intermingled that the distinctions cannot be sustained.[4]

A corollary of this claim is that the former theological tropes have become myth—they have become a mode of cultural representation rather than explicitly demanding a faith commitment. When reformers used biblical tropes in their social project, they did not elicit inspirational introspection; they used the tropes as a cultural mode of argument or representation.[5] Unmoored from religious dogma or practice, the tropes lose their premodern grounding (becoming signifiers emptied of their institutional imperatives while retaining some of their ideological function), and so writers are able to easily assimilate the tropes to new loci with a modern overlay. Older religious symbols can become anti-Semitic (rather than anti-Judaic); commentators' invocation of these tropes in discussions of the city or tramping transforms these ancient images. They become representations of modern rejections of the Jewish people.

In their study of anti-Semitism in times of crisis, Gilman and Katz have noted that anti-Semitism can be both paradigmatic and representative—both functions appear in the early discourse on homelessness.[6] By looking at six (often intertwined) strands of representation, I argue that anti-Semitic motifs were paradigmatic for the discourse on homelessness. Each of the

Jewish images is not explicitly invoked in this discourse. Rather, these Jewish representations were prevalent at the time that a rhetoric of homelessness began to emerge. They were an integral part of the milieu of the discourse; they furnished a deep, underlying structure. The paradigm of anti-Semitism furnished both symbols for and structures of representation.

Though never intertwining neatly into a unitary formation, these six strands were the initial building blocks for popular images of homelessness. Some particular tropes like Cain and the International Workers of the World (IWW) Jew appear in media accounts. The structuring role of the anti-Semitic motifs occurs, at least partially, through some binaries readily appropriated for the process of establishing an other: settled/unsettled, bourgeois/nonbourgeois, Christian/non-Christian (i.e., threats to family and social structure, the economy, and religion). Beyond these juxtapositions, the anti-Semitic motifs provide an underlying moral valuation. For example, the symbol of Cain, as a cultural form, carries traces of the theological and moral discourse from the Christian tradition; the symbol carries the moral weight without compelling a faith commitment or religious practice. The previously theological trope of Cain becomes, in the hands of Jacob Riis and other fin-de-siècle writers, a tool of social critique; Riis and other writers codified Victorian cultural assumptions about the family and the city. The differences established through these anti-Judaic and anti-Semitic images remain central to the discourse on homelessness.

The anti-Semitic images passed into relative obscurity when social science took over from journalists as the dominant institutional locus of the discourse. But later urban sociologists did take up many of the cultural attitudes distilled in these tropes. Fin-de-siècle social activists and journalists had invoked these mythic tropes to negotiate anxieties about the impact of urbanization; their responses to the city shaped much of the subsequent development of the discourse on homelessness.

But I here focus on the formation of this discourse—the symbols and structures of othering that give rise to a homeless figure. By focusing primarily on the intersections between print media and other popular forms like pulp fiction, pamphlets, and the literature of charity organizations in the long fin-de-siècle period, I demonstrate the anti-Semitic roots of the American discourse on homelessness.

Cain

The biblical figure of Cain became a popular heuristic for representing urban slums and tramps. Christian anti-Judaic traditions have associated Cain with the Jewish people or the synagogue. Jacob Riis links this Cain tradition to the problems of the modern city, since Cain established the mythical first city to negotiate his forced wandering from place and family. In the long history of the Cain tradition, he is emblematic of displacement and, through the anti-Judaic tradition, simultaneously represents a threat to Christianity.

Riis is not the only influential fin-de-siècle commentator turning to Cain to represent modern homelessness. In the country's first social welfare textbook, *American Charities*, Stanford professor Amos Warner inserts Cain in his discussion of "the Unemployed and Homeless Poor." For Warner, Cain is the precursor of "the homeless and wandering poor" who make their way through modern social service agencies.[7] Throughout the chapter, he uses a range of terms in seemingly synonymous ways—tramp, beggar, mendicant, vagrant. He always uses *homeless* adjectively to modify *poor*. It is still a term of description, not a category of analysis. Warner looks around the globe (or at least across Europe) to complaints "of the curse of vagrancy" in his inquiries into the tramp: "If, instead of extending our inquiries geographically, we had extended them historically, we should have found the same complaint of an exceptionally large number of wandering beggars made in nearly every age of which we have a record; and it has been suggested that if, just as we look for proto-martyrs, we should look for the proto-tramp, we should find him near the beginning of history in the person of Cain."[8]

The first point of interest here is that the idea of looking for a prototramp is modeled on the practice of searching for a protomartyr; with this search, Warner establishes the modernity of Cain. This quest is not a dredging to satisfy antiquarian curiosity; rather, the protomartyr inspiration refers to attempts to understand the modern world.[9] As a model for his own query, the modernity of the quest for a protomartyr points to the modernity of Warner's own problem—the tramp. Moving between the ancient mythic trope of Cain and modern homelessness, Warner acknowledges, "It cannot be asserted that even in the domain of trampery there is nothing new under the sun."[10] Changes in transportation created a modern character for the vagabond; this modern component is what makes the tramp the greatest threat to family. Because of new means of mobility, "it is increasingly easy for men to get away from their *duties to families and neighbors*, and it is getting to be easier to wander than to work."[11] As for Riis, the threat of wandering is the possible breakdown of community responsibilities. Because he juxtaposes "neighbors" to wandering, Warner connects duties to the people in a particular place. Vagrant mobility threatens community bonds; a modern Cain represents the threats of displacement that have come with modernization.

A second point of interest in the Warner passage is his methodological turn. He first does a contemporary comparative analysis, briefly looking at tramps in Germany and Russia, but trying to understand the tramp within the means of his day seems inadequate to him. Thus he turns the axis of analysis from the synchronic comparison of a spatial axis to a diachronic one of historical contextualization. Somehow the newness of the condition—the new modes of transportation and the threats to social institutions like the family—points to an insufficiency of late nineteenth-century America to account for the homeless poor. Thus Warner finds tramps transcending their present day; they are lurking in the Ur-violence at the "beginning of history." Warner's citation of Cain thus evokes multiple things: criminality (or homicide),[12] familial destruction, and wandering. These threats are many of the attributes that become associated with the homelessness of the city.

While Warner's Cain distills distinct fears or threats to society, for Riis, Cain is more. Over nearly 15 years, Riis's works continually invoke the Cain story—*How the Other Half Lives*, his contribution to *My Brother and I*, and 1903's *The Peril and the Preservation of the Home*. Riis makes recourse to Cain (and other tropes) to represent a range of threats to family norms by symbolizing anxieties about domestic arrangements, moral laxity, and laziness (especially among the urban poor). The responsibility to be a brother's keeper involves molding the poor in the image of the middle class.

Riis opens his analysis of the other half (after a brief introduction) with a discussion of the origin of the tenement: "The first tenement New York knew bore the mark of Cain from its birth, though a generation passed before the writing was deciphered. It was the 'rear house,' infamous ever after in our city's history."[13] A particular focus of Riis's harangues, the rear tenements were encircled by other buildings with little space for light or air, which marked the tenement dwellers for respiratory problems, disease, and death, as well as criminality or "a proletariat ready and able to avenge the wrongs of their crowds."[14]

Eventually eliminated by establishing municipal housing codes, the rear tenement became emblematic to Riis of the worst of urban tenement life.[15] He cites a report from the Society for the Improvement of the Condition of the Poor that concluded the inhabitability of the rear tenement. The report said, "Crazy old buildings, crowded rear tenements in filthy yards, dark, damp basements, leaking garrets, shops, outhouses and stales converted into dwellings, though scarcely fit to shelter brutes, are habitations of thousands of our fellow-beings in this wealthy, Christian city."[16] This nadir of the city bore Cain's mark, and this mark served more than mere rhetorical flourish for Riis. The Cain story is integral to both his view of the city and his response to it. Cain, for Riis, marks the tenement; the tenements compose the slums. New York is homeless because of this accumulation of slums: "The slum is the enemy of the home. Because of it the chief city of our land came long ago to be called 'The Homeless City.'"[17] He links Cain—the mythical founder of the first city—to the problems of the modern city. Yet Cain's importance emerges more profoundly elsewhere in Riis's work.

In his *The Peril and the Preservation of the Home*, the Genesis story informs both the former (peril) and latter (preservation) formulations. Riis identifies "*the* weak spot, in your campaign for the home—that home which all the influences of the modern day combine to put in peril. I mean the disappearance of the family altar."[18] Two important points emerge in this diagnosis. First, the home is under threat from modern life. He continues to elaborate on this point by delineating some of the causes of the destruction of the home.[19] But Riis's second point about the family altar invokes Cain. First, the Cain story is the first place where family devotions and an altar are established. Second, popular commentaries of the eighteenth and nineteenth centuries (e.g., *Matthew Henry's Commentary*) relate Cain's actions to the shunning of the family and the altar. Despite the "family altar" evoking a 1950s Ozzie and Harriet household with a Bible devotion around the dinner table, the altar was initially a place for the violent slaughtering of an animal (since Cain's lack of blood was an unacceptable offering).

In Riis's work, the Cain story also provides suggestions for the preservation of the home by an affirmative answer to Cain's question of God: Am I my brother's keeper?[20] Recognizing one's fellow city dweller as a member of one's family becomes Riis's proposal to save the city. The modern homelessness of the city cannot exist if the family is preserved. Riis writes,

The moral question whether I shall love my neighbor or kill him; whether I shall stand idly by and see my brother's soul stunted, smothered in the slum of my making, of my tacit consent at any rate, or put in all upon rescuing him. Brethren, we shall never rescue our city, you will never rescue yours, until we understand that that is what it all harks back to, that all these things mean one and the same thing: that I am my brother's keeper for good or for evil.[21]

He resorts to the language of neighbor, which signifies not only a relationship but also a locus of that relationship (i.e., a rooted proximity to one's brother); these relations with their language of close kinship and neighborliness are those of the *Gemeinschaft* ideal. Creating and participating in this community is the solution for social ills, but the first step is the recognition of a familial bond. Riis, like his contemporaries, feared that community structures centered on the family were collapsing in the metropolis—a threat Warner also saw as emanating from the modern tramp. Riis's own bifurcated life of urban police reporting in the Five Points tenement district and rural family life on Long Island (even requiring a move further out when development encroached on his "country" haven) provide a model for desired social relations.

If this sense of community is truly Riis's goal, his project has an inherent contradiction. The supposed organicism of community cannot be created; it is a neighborliness that arises from decades or centuries of ongoing proximity. The seeming immediacy of the relationship emerges from the immediacy of space. Producing a community in this idyllic mode is an impossibility, since production is a mode whose social form is that of civil society; produced relations are the transactional or associational ones that he decries. Riis thought that recognizing the other as brother could rectify such social ills—the mark of Cain arose from failure to recognize that "I am my brother's keeper." Because of this failure, real estate speculators set up rear tenements as "habitations of thousands of our fellow-beings." Presumably, following the logic of Riis's argument, if those residents had been regarded as brothers and not "fellow-beings," landlords would have taken better care of the housing for the poor—and the metropolis would not have the mark of Cain.

Cain's centrality in the story of the modern homeless figure moves beyond a structure of othering into a mode of representation. The figure of Cain bore the mark of urban homelessness while simultaneously evoking ancient anti-Judaic tradition. By connecting modern problems with Cain, Riis and Warner linked tramping, the city, and urban life with many long traditions of othering. The conflation of Cain and the Jews begins in the New Testament, where the gospels of Matthew and Luke forward a nascent form of equating Cain with the Jews.[22] A few centuries later, Ambrose[23] borrows the Jewish philosopher Philo's idea that Cain and Abel represent two competing views of life,[24] but he adds a particularly pernicious dual interpretation of the brothers—Cain and Abel are the prototypes of the synagogue and the church.[25] Christianity has a long tradition of anti-Judaism based on a theological assumption that the Jews rejected Jesus. In much of this tradition, there is attached to this putative rejection an additional charge of culpability for murder of Jesus; the Jewish people are considered Christ killers.[26] Cain's murder of Abel represents the Jews supposed murder of Jesus. By killing Abel, Cain attempts to kill the church and must permanently wander. With Augustine—who continues the Jewish-Christian dichotomy of the brothers[27]—Cain's wandering is forgotten. Cain's significance is settling down; he establishes a city. In *City of God*, Augustine continues a hermeneutic polarity; he juxtaposes Cain and Abel to represent the earthly city of man and the divine city of God.

The anti-Semitic Cain tradition thus straddles the dual poles of wandering and the establishment of the city as a locus of the rootless. In both incarnations (the wandering of the prototramp and the marking of the homelessness of the urban slums) Cain embodies Jewish otherness to represent a threat to the family altar of the Christian home—he embodies homelessness.

Ishmael

The anti-Semitic invocation of biblical figures in this discourse broadened the included group of Semites[28] to include another Genesis evictee— Ishmael. The terms *Ishmaelite, tribe of Ishmael*, or *street Arab* became standard in media accounts of frauds, professional beggars, and homeless children. The invocation of Ishmael evokes another rejection of familial norms—that is, illegitimacy. Like Cain, the trope of Ishmael represented urban threats to family ideals.

Conventional accounts for the rise of the term *Ishmaelite* attribute its use to a historical accident. The eugenicist Rev. Oscar C. McCulloch presented an 1888 paper titled "The Tribe of Ishmael: A Study in Social Degradation"[29] in which he outlines an argument for the hereditary tendency of certain forms of "parasitism," "unchastity," "criminality," and "pauperism."

He names the condition for one of the more than 250 nomadic families—the tribe of Ishmael—which he purports to have studied. The conventional account is that Ishmael first appears related to the homelessness in McCulloch's report, which takes its name from this historical family. However, "Ishmaelites" appear in fictional accounts of tramps at least a decade earlier.[30] Thus the relationship between the tribe of Ishmael and the historical family is rather dubious.

Even if McCulloch independently developed the category, his selection of the Ishmael family name for this group does not take place within a cultural vacuum; it has resonance with cultural traditions. Also, McCulloch uses the name Ishmael out of 250 possible family names and then places the name "tribe of Ishmael" in scare quotes; there is an allusion to Abraham's banishment of Ishmael and his mother Hagar. Ultimately, these concerns with authorial intent are irrelevant, since writers like Riis or the later University of Chicago sociologist Nels Anderson subsequently use the idea of the "tribe of Ishmael," or Ishmaelites, in contexts unconcerned with the historicity of McCulloch's family. In M. W. Law's 1903 article in *The American Journal of Sociology*,[31] he explicitly evokes the Genesis account of Ishmael being banished to the desert in the opening line, talking of "this Ishmael of the city desert." Later, Law perhaps conflates Ishmael with his half brother Isaac by calling Ishmael a scapegoat, a possible reference to the binding of Isaac. The inclusion of a negative Arab trope within the nascent discourse underlines the necessity of a turn to older cultural images to bring a semantic order to urban life. By using the shorthand of mythic tropes, Riis, Law, and others also avert any problems in explaining the connections between illegitimacy as a violation of bourgeois family norms and urban petty crimes.

The deployment of the Ishmaelite trope requires eliding distinctions between the modern nuclear family (violated in the Ishmael story) and the feudal structure of the ancient Near East (maintained in the Genesis account). While etymologically family signifies the entire household—including (especially) all the household servants, like Ishmael's mother, Hagar—the modern category of illegitimacy assumes a violation of a modern, soon-to-be nuclear family. The illegitimacy within the Genesis account results from the handmaiden Hagar failing to understand her servile role to Sarah, even though she had produced a child for Abraham. However, the modern idea of illegitimacy signified by Ishmaelites has a much more encompassing sense of pathology.[32] The trope signifies a violation of family and the production of children who can never know home. With no functioning family unit, such children are likely lost to the streets, where they become—in Riis's term—a *street Arab*. With these first two anti-Semitic strands that form the conditions giving rise to the discourse on homelessness, we see threats to the family emerging as an integral part of representing homelessness.

The Wandering Jew

Waves of immigrants moved from Europe to North America over the course of the nineteenth century. Besides their luggage bundles, they brought with them stories and legends, culture and traditions. Among these was the European legend of Ahasuerus, the Wandering Jew; interest in this figure proliferated on the North American shores. In the impressive way that legend works, Cain has long had a connection to the Wandering Jew;[33] thus these two strands are intertwined. As with all legends, the Wandering Jew has many versions; with each retelling, Ahasuerus's story accrues new adventures as he travels the globe across centuries. The basic story is that Jesus was carrying the cross through Jerusalem en route to Golgotha outside of town. He paused for a few moments rest at a doorstep, but the owner of the house—Ahasuerus—drove Jesus away, telling him to walk faster. Jesus cursed the man, telling him that he would be forced to walk until his second coming.[34] This image of Jewish wandering represents a religious threat to the Christian home.

An important narrative entrance of the Wandering Jew into America first appears across the Atlantic, in a French novel. Despite being the namesake of Eugene Sue's popular midcentury novel *Le Juif Errant* serialized in the feuilleton section of the newspaper, the Wandering Jew is a relatively minor character in the anticlerical, anti-Jesuitical work of the popular writer. Sue introduces this condemned wanderer on the Bering Straits gazing across from "the uttermost limits of the Old World" into the opening to the New.[35] His gaze to the New World probably presages subsequent claims of American sightings of the Wandering Jew. One such newspaper account saw Ahasuerus in New York:

> Quite an excitement, it is reported, was recently caused in the village of Harts Corners, a few miles from New York, by the appearance of the veritable "Wandering Jew." Now an *ordinary wandering Jew* would not be at all likely to create any surprise, seeing that they are to be met with in every quarter . . .
> The discovery was made under the following instances: On the 2nd instant, as two little boys were going a-fishing, their attention was arrested by deep groans

which seemed to emanate from an old shanty they passed on their way. The boys entered the shanty and there beheld a venerable-looking individual with a long white beard, dressed in black flowing garments, seated in one corner, apparently in pain. They manifested a desire to assist him, but were frightened off by the old fellow lifting his staff in a frightening manner. The youngsters retreated and soon returned with a number of the villagers, who, on entering the shanty, saw an individual with a large hooked nose, larger ears and finger nails about an inch long—there was no tail visible at least.[36] They asked what ailed him, and he replied that he had fallen on a stone and severely hurt his leg. In the course of conversation he also informed them he *had no home*, and that his last friend had departed this life long before the light of heaven illumined the soul of any among them, and that the voice of the only one he loved was silent in the tomb before printing was invented, or America had ever echoed the cry of liberty.

Exclamations of "cracked" escaped several of the crowd, which aroused the indignation of the Jew who asked them why they had come there if they did not believe him. They replied they came because they had heard there was a man in trouble and they wished to assist him. To this he replied, "man *can not* and Heaven *will* not." He then gave them a short account of his recent travels from Siberia to America via Behrings Straits [*sic*], through the wilds of Alaska, etc., saying that the first kind word he had heard during the whole journey was from the party he was then addressing. He then bade them adieu and departed.

In his hasty departure on this occasion as he is said to have done on many others, he left a memento by which his identity was fully proven. This time it was an old volume of extracts from the Babylonian Talmud in the Hebrew character. On a fly leaf was a short account of his birth, parentage, the sentence of the Saviour and his subsequent wanderings, all clearly proving that he was the identical *bona fide* Wandering Jew.[37]

This journalistic account of a sighting furnishes a story of the Wandering Jew's entry into the New World, which borrows from Sue's introduction of Ahasuerus in *Le Juif Errant*. Sue's prologue opens on the Bering Straits ("the land's end of two worlds")[38] with the Wandering Jew on the Siberian side looking across the expanse of sea to his sister facing him from the American shore. The fiction of the feuilleton has become journalistic fact of Ahasuerus's entry into America. Significantly, Sue's role as a backdrop to American accounts of the Wandering Jew implies a connection between the legend and political radicalism. In an epilogue that reunites Ahasuerus and his sister, *Le Juif Errant* asserts that the Wandering Jew has long championed the cause of the exploited laborer. He is finally able to be free of his curse and allowed to die when "the aurora of the day of deliverance" soon comes.[39] This conclusion to tales of imperialism and the poor of Paris seeks liberation for the workers for the world: "And so, for centuries, men without pity have said to the artisan: 'Work! work! work! without truce or rest—and your labour shall be fruitful for all others, but fruitless for yourself—and every evening, throwing yourself on the hard ground, you shall be no nearer to happiness and repose; and your wages shall only suffice to keep you alive in pain, privation, and poverty!'"[40] Thus the modern Wandering Jew seen in the United States—whose curse-lifting death has failed to come—brings in his North American wanderings a commitment to revolutionary politics.[41]

Beyond an implicit political radicalism, a second point that emerges from this newspaper account is that the Wandering Jew is both a particular figure (Ahasuerus) and a type (an ordinary Wandering Jew). While Ahasuerus may not permanently lurk through the American hinterlands, others of his type might. Thus Ahasuerus becomes a paradigm for wandering across America, and, I shall argue later, he is also a paradigm for the social form of the stranger. The Wandering Jew enters the annals of a popular imaginary as a symbol that combines Jewishness (as a rejection of Christianity) with political radicalism and wandering—all of them threats to the Christian home. The popularity of this trope of the Wandering Jew and these other strands created an environment in which social commentators could easily invoke these anti-Semitic traditions to represent a sense of otherness.

Exile

The metonymic connection between these two wanderers (Cain and the Wandering Jew) and the Jewish people relates to this next strand—the trope of exile in Judaism. Forty years of desert wandering, the Babylonian exile and the post–Bar Kokhba expulsion from Jerusalem established a connection between the Jewish people and the idea of exile. Scholar Susannah Heschel argues that "the experience of alienation is central to Judaism . . . exile itself becomes the value that is affirmed instead of an awaited redemption. Exile and redemption are central theological categories in Judaism."[42] This longstanding association between the Jewish people and alienation is central to the anti-Semitic formulations of homelessness. Heschel expands this idea of exile in Judaism: "Exile enters the first Jewish text from the earliest moment. We think immediately of the exile from the Garden of Eden, which is followed by the exile of the patriarchs and matriarchs from the land promised by God to Abraham, then the exile to Egypt which meant slavery to Israel. In historical terms, we have the exile from the Northern Kingdom as a result of the Assyrian conquest and from the South Kingdom following the Babylonian conquest."[43] After the expulsion from Eden (which is not an exile of the Jewish people per se), each exile prompted either a wandering or a captivity. Because theological tradition—in most cases, both Jewish and Christian—interprets each stage of exile as divine punishment, the Jewish people's displacement from their homeland arises from rebellion against God—the same idea that appears in the tropes of Cain and the Wandering Jew. A Christian *Weltanschauung* thus easily assimilates a sense of homelessness to Jewish metaphysical rebellion. When looking at Riis's writings about urban homelessness, we see that modern urban exile is linked to Christian anti-Judaic traditions. Riis writes the following:

> So, in all matters pertaining to their religious life that tinges all their customs, they stand, these East Side Jews, where the new day that dawned on Calvary left them standing, stubbornly refusing to see the light. A visit to a Jewish house of mourning is like bridging the gap of two thousand years. The inexpressibly sad and sorrowful wail for the dead, as it swells and rises in the hush of all sounds of life, so comes back from the ages like a mournful echo of the voice of Rachel "weeping for her children and refusing to be comforted, because they are not."[44]

The rejection of Christianity follows the immigrants into their "Jewtown" where the wailing of Rachel is to be heard. In the biblical book of Jeremiah, the matriarch Rachel weeps inconsolably for her exiled progeny; the laments and grief of "Jewtown" become connected to cries for the exile of Jewish people represented as the sundering of children from their mothers. The exile that Riis invokes thus brings dissolution in the familial home and a religious rejection of Jesus. This new exile is a condition threatening a Christian home by establishing an outside to its domain. Family dissolution and a life beyond middle-class Christian norms are precisely the two conditions forming homelessness in this nascent discourse on homelessness. The invocation of tropes like Rachel weeping for her children or Cain is an effective means to codify attributes that eventually become associated with homeless individuals; part of this efficacy is because the tropes function as myth. In Chapter 3, we shall look at how these tropes function as myth in the formation of the discourse on homelessness.

The Stranger

Anti-Semitic stereotypes have long straddled two contradictory poles: from the Shylocks of capitalist finance[45] and the Emma Goldmans of anticapitalist radicals. A slightly less dichotomous version of these two poles appears in these modern tropes that inform the discourse on homelessness. The social function of "the stranger"—made famous by Georg Simmel—takes the pure animalistic motion of Ahasuerus and attenuates the absolute detachment in a synthesis with its conceptual opposite of attachment. As this synthesis, the stranger is both near and far, both remote and close. As a part of the social group, the stranger is spatially near but brings "qualities into it that are not, and cannot be, indigenous to it."[46] Throughout economic history, Simmel tells us the stranger appears as the trader—most frequently as a Jewish trader.[47]

While I certainly agree with Simmel that the Jewish trader is a likely antecedent for the social form of the stranger, Ahasuerus himself functions as a stranger. He wanders, enters towns where he is by appearance immediately determined foreign, and is sought out for his news and objectivity—he can tell kings of their enemies, the histories of their peoples, or the happenings in distant lands. He participates in the city and moves on. This role of temporary confidant and source of objective information attached itself to the legend. Maxwell Sommerville's 1902 novel *A Wanderer's Legend* is precisely a story of Ahasuerus as the stranger. His fortuitous sixteenth-century appearance at Nuremberg's Church of St. Sebaldus on the eve of a conclave to address reformist schisms appearing within the Germanic church sets the stage for his role as informant to the assembled bishops, theologians, and other churchmen. The novel consists of his series of recitations of the peoples and faiths of other lands, disquisitions on historical events, and evaluations of the branches of Christendom. All know that he will move on, that he has seen the church's rise to power and its demise in the East; he was thus valued for his objective status and so each day is supplicated to share yet another piece of information.

His millennium and a half of wandering has made Ahasuerus a wise man. In Sommerville's novel, he is acutely aware of his function as stranger. On an ancient journey, he tells of attaching himself to a Jew trader, and, upon approaching the city, Ahasuerus encounters sentries who "recognized in me a stranger";[48] the trader's vouchsafing for him enabled his entry to the city, whereupon he decamps to the public markets to find some repose.

This modern incarnation of Ahasuerus maps his cursed wanderings onto those of the Jewish trader; the Simmelian stranger has deeper roots than the preindustrial mercantile system; it incorporates ancient anti-Judaic motifs overlain with later economic and social history.[49]

The social conditions of the modern metropolis transform the stranger from a social form of an individual into the entirety of the urban population. The problem with the urban anonymity of fin-de-siècle New York City was precisely the overabundant influx of strangers, such that all social relationships changed. Mobility had entirely undermined the seemingly organic community bonds and left only those of strangers. Thus the entire city was homeless. The denizens of the city were strangers to the nation, to the town. Without a doubt, they were by proximity a part of the urban group, but in language, custom, and appearance, they were alien; they were strangers in a strange land. The form of the stranger was perfected in defining European Jewish populations.

The longstanding idea of wandering and Jewishness took this new form with the early modern rise of trading and gave rise to this fifth strand. The ideas of mobility—relations predicated on social distance and populations with no claim upon land—are central to Simmel's analysis of the social function of the stranger. The stranger furnishes structures to the discourse on homelessness and establishes the limits to the community, which is able to participate within the ideal of the Christian home. The metropolitan stranger's migratory mobility juxtaposes to the stasis of the native, middle-class Protestant. In its new metropolitan incarnation, the immigrant as stranger embodies class, ethnic, and linguistic difference. One of the groups whose otherness extended into the realm of religion (beyond denomination-alism)[50] was precisely that group on whom the social form of the stranger was modeled—the Jewish people.

Radicals and Hobos

The formation of the final strand requires an elision between the tradition of Jewish radicalism and the radical (but mostly Gentile) hobo unions. Because the hobos wandered and had some radical elements—especially in the International Workers of the World (IWW)—magazines like *Life*, for example, collapse distinctions and attribute Jewishness to members of the IWW by discussing the Jewish Wobbly (a nickname for members of the union). Thus the image of the immigrant Jewish radical is superimposed onto that of the native migratory hobo to combine threats to economic life and the bourgeois family in an anti-Semitic representation.

In early twentieth-century media accounts, Jewish immigrants were always strangers; they were inassimilable—*Life* magazine tells us that "the Jewish mind is a totally different instrument from other minds that operate in these States. It has a different background, different racial instincts, different traditions, and with its great abilities and increasing grasp on all public concerns it is a factor of our future that deserves prayerful and attentive contemplation."[51] Jewish people—*Life* explains—operate differently than other groups; this difference is racial, and prayer is necessary to determine how to address the difference. Jewish differences marked this immigrant in a way that other (i.e., Christian) immigrants were not—by bearing the marks of both racial and religious dissimilarity. They did not come here and settle, for they were an unsettled people; as a "sojourner here"[52] or as a "restless people,"[53] the Jew was ever eager to change American life.

The tradition of Jewish sojourning was important for the formation of popular stereotypes of radicalism—the wandering is a sign of a deeper restlessness that desires change that will wreak havoc on a Protestant status quo. The Russian Jew[54] thus becomes an easy symbol for the radical threat of homelessness. To the American middle class, Russian Jews became the poster child for all radicals, so much so that native radicals came to be represented by the Russian Jew.

> We have cherished and honored in this country during the last twenty years a type of mind totally different from any of the types to which our government owes the organization, our commercial system its development, our country its growth. It is the most destructive mind in the world, the most grasping and unabashed . . . The Russian Jews . . . have no real national feeling. They are loyal to Socialism, to Internationalism, to whatever untried ideal of human welfare may be floating in their heads at a given moment, but are not bound by more than the loosest ties to any country or form of government . . . In Baruch and scores of like men we see it working for the good of the country. But . . . what of the *I. W. W. Jews*, the revolutionary Russian Jews of whom [Morris] Hillquit is one, with all breeds of bats in their noisy belfries?[55]

The cognitive processes that enable an easy collapse of a native migratory worker into a symbol of the Jewish radical by the IWW Jew or Jewish Wobbly are facilitated by the idea of the sojourning restlessness of the Jew; many traditions (e.g., Cain and the Wandering Jew) point to this restlessness.

Hobo restlessness and the social threats of mobility easily take an overlay of racial and religious difference to escalate the threat to a new register.

Beyond this more mythic connection between Jewish wandering and radicalism, there were historical reasons to associate Jewish radicals with the (primarily) native-born hobo, which furnished a seeming legitimacy to the invocation of such tropes. At a very simple level, the famed Russian-Jewish anarchist leader Emma Goldman was a longtime partner and collaborator to former hobo impresario Ben Reitman. Reitman was the sometimes director of Chicago's Hobo College,[56] a self-declared (and sometimes elected) hobo king and doctor to the hobos (as well as to prostitutes and Al Capone). Reitman was not a Wobbly; in fact his political commitments primarily extended to addressing the personal needs of individuals rather than planning for large-scale social change. While Reitman was not a member of the IWW, he was a hobo closely associated with both a hobo union and a Russian-Jewish radical. Also, he—as head of the Hobo College or as coordinator of lively debates at Chicago's Dill Pickle Club—did collaborate with some members of the IWW from time to time. Beyond the Reitman-Goldman connection, IWW actions did sometimes receive public support from prominent Jewish radicals.[57]

The connection between a few individual Jews and either individuals or actions of the IWW is hardly an important point, though. In his "avante-garde [sic] 'little magazine'"[58] The Philistine—which happened to take its name from the ancient political enemy of the Jewish people—Elbert Hubbard explicitly argues that these radicals represent a Jewish type quite similar to that described in Life.[59] "[Samuel] Gompers, [Ben] Reitman, [Emma] Goldman, Gyp the Blood, Lefty Louie, Jack Rose, all represent one common and particular type of mind."[60] Hubbard links the unsettling discontent of the Jewish radicals back to that first wandering malcontent who came to represent the synagogue—Cain. He concludes his diatribe against Louis Brandeis—whom he links to Gompers, Reitman, and Goldman—with a definition of venom: "Venom: The juice of hate. 2. The sap of reformers, moralists and socialists. . . . Venom, like everything else is subject to the law of evolution and variation. Between the venom of Cain and the venom of Tolstoy, several million instances could be quoted to prove the universality and beneficence of this breedy instinct."[61] As the most famous of modern radicals, the anarchist Tolstoy's[62] discontent has roots at the "beginning of history." By linking Russian radical discontent to Cain, Hubbard associates

Jewish radicalism with wandering and the rootless metropolis, as well as a threat to the church.

By looking at how the representation of the hobo intersects the long-standing trope of the Jewish radical, we are able to better understand the characteristics social scientists come to attribute to hobos. With the conflation between the hobo's restless mobility and the breaking of social ties, on the one hand, and the perceived Russian-Jewish propensity to be bound by only "the loosest ties to any country or form of government,"[63] on the other, we find the integration of threats to the home in its religious, familial, and nation-state senses. These journalists combine religious and political threats in the figure of the IWW Jew. Homelessness becomes a threat to an entire way of being in the modern world—to class, family, and religious structures; or conversely, home is a haven from the threats of the modern world. Those threats lurk in changes brought by immigrants—those same immigrants we saw Jacob Riis and other fin-de-siècle reformers excoriate in Chapter 1. All immigrant groups brought challenges and change to the American bourgeoisie; with the Jew, the difference was perceived as being of an entirely different order. The Jew had millennia as an other. While anxieties about the Chinese were prominent, the population was legislatively kept smaller. Catholic immigrants from Ireland, Italy, and Central Europe produced much worry, but as Riis indicated in the last chapter, they had at least heard of Jesus, unlike a young Jewish boy, whose ignorance horrified him. In the rhetorical dialectics of the discourse of homelessness, Jews became the other par excellence.

Because the hobo embraces wandering and unattachment, the Jewish radical is easily assimilated to the figure of the hobo—the early sociological category of displacement that, as we shall see in Part II, eventually cedes to the homeless man. The lack of mooring in broader social networks is precisely what recommends the hobo style of life. Thus radicalism and religious threats are represented in a figure who forsakes family life; as we saw with Riis's anxieties about urban riots, homelessness again connects to the potential for political violence. But here the anxiety is not the historical worry about bigger urban uprisings; it is codified in forms of representing homeless individuals. Hobodom provided a life, a community, and a means of support to those with no family or those uninterested in maintaining family contacts; the Jewish Wobbly represented these threats and displacement.

In this historically last strand, we see many assumptions that make their way into the early social science literature on homelessness. University of

Chicago sociologist Robert Park[64] provides an account of the role of mobility in homelessness, which contends that the hobo mind rests upon the Aristotelian idea that locomotion is the distinguishing feature between plants and animals. However, he argues, humanity has a great attachment to place, particularly the "inveterate and irrational ambition to have a home—some cave or hut or tenement—in which to live and vegetate; some secure hole or corner from which to come forth in the morning and return to at night."[65] The desire for place and stability is always connected with a family bond.[66] This overweening attachment inhibits the full realization of the contrary desire to move and roam. The wandering locomotion of the homeless figure is in itself a threat to family and its dwelling—which is merely a technological mimesis of the mother-child bond; by becoming a spatial reenactment of this bond, the idea of home becomes a utopic locus for family.

In Park's account, mobility is a basic animal instinct that is overridden by the desire for place. The locomotion of the hobo is, for him, unchecked motion; it is locomotion for its own sake: "The hobo is, to be sure, always on the move, but he has no destination, and naturally he never arrives. Wanderlust, which is the most elementary expression of the romantic temperament and the romantic interest in life, has assumed for him, as for so many others, the character of vice. He has gained his freedom, but he has lost his direction. Locomotion and change of scene have had for him no ulterior significance. It is locomotion for its own sake."[67] Park implies that the hobo is too much of an animal. The hobo fails to subordinate locomotion to a purpose or a vocation; it is only movement. By maintaining pure motion, the hobo sacrifices human needs for association. Park argues that all forms of association are predicated upon locality. Society cannot exist with the extreme individual freedom of unmitigated mobility. Presumably, cultural pressures are necessary correctives; culture, or civilization, is agonistic to locomotion. The unchecked locomotion is a purely animalistic behavior; civilization must furnish norms and social relations to tie the homeless man to place: "The hobo, who begins his career by breaking the local ties that bound him to his family and his neighborhood, has ended by breaking all other associations. He is not only a 'homeless man,' but a man without a cause and without a country."[68] The homeless man was never sufficiently bound into the family and thus neither community nor country; the ties could not bind the animalist impulses for motion.

This mobility of the hobo and radical reflects a social and political discontent that is a continual impetus to motion. Jewish radicals, like hobos, have no ties to nation or community because they are unsettled. The hobo is, according to Park, a "homeless man"; the traits of this homeless man—here is the nascent formation of the homeless figure—are those of the Russian-Jewish radical whose lineage stretches back to Cain. This final strand combines a wandering that destroys families with the bestial rejection of civilization's settling influence.

Times of Crisis

While the turn to anti-Semitism at times of social upheavals is nothing new, the figures integral to the early formation of the discourse on homelessness drew on tropes from this tradition. In doing so, they contextualized fin-de-siècle urban social crises within a broader panorama. Gilman and Katz ask the following question: "What is it about such times [of crisis] which spontaneously seem to result in the use of the Jews as the essential Other through which to define the integrity of the self?"[69] Here I sketch an admittedly incomplete answer. Christianity formed itself by distancing itself from and rejecting its parent religion. The structure of ressentiment—the structure of othering—was written into the relationship of these religions. As the political balance between the religions changed fortunes with a Constantinian edict establishing Christianity as the imperial religion, Christianity could establish the representations of rejection.

The Christian anti-Judaic heritage thus provided a ready lexicon of tropes and structures of othering. When the self—in this case, the subject of the bourgeois family—is in crisis, forming a dialectical other can quickly furnish social and discursive stability. Thus the Victorian social crises brought on by urbanization prompted a turn to traditions of anti-Semitism to legitimate the family in crisis. The positive discourse of the Christian home was bolstered through the negative formulation in the discourse of the other—an emerging homeless city and the homeless people populating it. These disparate traditions of anti-Semitism furnished a loose framework for describing the people, places, and practices of the homeless city.

Protohomelessness as a Mythic Discourse

These anti-Semitic traditions from biblical stories, legends, theological traditions, and so on function as myth; these mythic tropes codified a loose set of assumptions and ideas in the early responses to urban changes. The invocation of these images embodied bourgeois cultural attitudes and made an argument about homelessness. As part of the middle-class response to the booming metropolis, mythic tropes provided a means to draw together the attitudes we saw emerging from disparate places in the last section—attitudes about the family, politics, wandering, and stability. As we shall see in Part II (and saw in part with Robert Park), the consolidation of a constellation of cultural attitudes into a figure began a process of defining an emerging homeless man.

The social fragmentation of the modern metropolis—cognitive and spatial distinctions of ethnicity, culture, religion, language, class, and gender—established a plurality of social fields. Such heterogeneity creates the conditions in which religious narratives can be disconnected from a religious institution and become a cultural form; that is, they become myth. As myth, the new urban conditions assume a seeming naturalness; the new problem of homelessness can thus seem as if it has long been with us and has been reflected in our most ancient stories. By having a mythic overlay, the basic modernity of homelessness is elided. In naturalizing the negative form of homelessness, the discourse also implicitly naturalizes the positive formulation of home. The Christian home becomes an eternal form for social life; it is naturalized as is its pathological underside—homelessness. In the discourse on homelessness, we find that fin-de-siècle critics of the city invoked tropes like Cain as myth.

Mythic and Religious Responses to the City

The deployment of modern myth in the discourse on homelessness is quite distinct from a Sunday school lesson on Cain. In this section, I shall distinguish mythic tropes from religious responses to urban problems by different functions; the same trope can be either religious or mythic depending on its use. This difference became possible through processes of modernization, like social differentiation and fragmentation; religion, culture, arts, and so on each became distinct social fields. I define myth as deinstitutionalized religious narratives that serve a cultural function beyond the religious social field. The anti-Semitic tropes of Cain, Ishmael, the Wandering Jew, and Rachel weeping for her children, I argue, are myth because they function as such deinstitutionalized tropes.

By being grounded in myth, the discourse on homelessness becomes a problem of culture. Myth can be a latent presence within a discourse, which can be readily deployed at times of social tension. It is no coincidence that myth and anti-Semitism appeared coextensively—both here in the fin-de-siècle period and again on the European continent a few decades later. In both contexts, they arose at times of great upheaval—the chaotic boom of the American city or in the collapse of the Weimar political economy. As we saw with Gilman and Katz on anti-Semitism and will see with Cassirer on myth, these forms of language appear in times of crisis because they furnish ready-made categories and symbols for ordering indescribable situations.

Distinguishing myth from religion, however, does not mean that myth is the form of representation that appears in the discourse on homelessness. The reason I consider these primarily biblical tropes to be myth is to distinguish them from contemporary projects explicitly demanding a faith commitment. Riis's "mark of Cain" does not require the audience to somehow undertake an orthopraxy because the tenement bears this mark.

In the fin-de-siècle period, religious leaders also responded to new social problems with the invocation of biblical tropes, but their invocation was for the purpose of mobilizing audiences to act out their faith—a very different process than Riis or Warner undertook in representing the city or the tramp. A few years after *How the Other Half Lives* (in 1897 to be precise), Topeka pastor and activist in the social gospel movement Charles Sheldon wrote *In His Steps*,[70] a novel about a tramp or hobo who bursts into a Sunday morning service and indicts the congregation's lack of lived faith with a few searing questions. After his dramatic collapse and subsequent death, many of the congregants vow to ask themselves "What Would Jesus Do?" before undertaking any life decisions.[71] This church interprets the vagabond as a divine emissary; this more religious interpretation of tramping requires a faith commitment and action. Amos Warner invoked Cain as the prototramp to contextualize a new problem within a cultural and historical context for social work students. By invoking Cain, he implicitly argues that tramping (despite its historical newness) has been a part of human existence, like criminality, since human prehistory. For Warner, Cain is a form of representing social problems, not a demand to be personally transformed because of his response.

While Charles Sheldon did become involved with the settlement house movement, the appropriation of his project inspired a more personalized commitment, creating something of a Christian categorical imperative. Sheldon's book became an enormous success—still remaining in print as "the all-time best-selling inspirational novel"[72]—and was used to incite a more reflective process in daily life. His novel provides an account of the transformation of particular evangelicals; it shows a model of how a specific sphere of the population should act. However, it does not furnish a model for how American society must understand social problems. It is a call to action for the faithful, not an ordering of language and thus our collective social life.

The trope of Cain or Ishmael provides a framework to understand a modern problem rather than an exhortation to act. Sheldon's tramp could speak to evangelicals, but he could not be disseminated to a broader culture; Riis's or Warner's Cain could appear in channels inaccessible to religion. While Sheldon's project focused on transforming the audience, the reformers wrote to inspire middle-class readers to go and change those documented in their writings—the goal was to create housing in which a poor family could thrive. The invocation of Cain or Ishmael provided a means to represent a problem to a society who might undertake political action. Myth furnishes an ordering for modern society; these tropes or images function as cultural forms and not as the explicitly religious discourse of a figure like Sheldon.

Myth and Rationalization

The mythic tropes we have seen in the work of fin-de-siècle commentators were deployed in contexts of establishing a social order. As we saw in Chapter 1, the discourse on homelessness was intertwined with efforts to rationalize the city. Journalists and activists like Riis brought a semantic order to the city, as they defined problems and distinguished needs and populations. After a semantic order was established, then social services and municipal policies began to address the needs articulated by the reformers. The mythic tropes that brought together a constellation of attitudes about the city and family in images defined the parameters of the discourse; these parameters became the basis for subsequent social science and policy.

Riis's zeal for reform (e.g., calls for a complete Haussmannization of the city) often reveals inherently antidemocratic impulses. His attempt to change the habits and minds of the poor is not mere Victorian paternalism as he claims. That allegation was acknowledged by Riis, and he willingly accepted it—"Call it paternalism, crankery, any other hard name you can think of, all the same it goes down underneath the foundation of things."[73] I argue that the work of Riis, Warner, Addams, and others is more than patrician condescension. From a position perched high above the other half, and even farther over the nether half (who later become the homeless man proper), they call for statist institutions, albeit usually at a municipal level, to say that these are the type of citizens it wants, to use its techniques of social formation to form these subjects (rather than having a society in which the citizens articulate the society and state they want). The effort is to change law and social practices, using the power of the state and the press to shape how the other half is articulated and negotiated in the public sphere. These antidemocratic impulses not only manifested in their activists' processes of rooting out the homelessness of the city to establish social order. Their language (e.g., calling large populations the other half or the nether half) indicates similar impulses. In this fin-de-siècle era, before these semantic and institutional efforts produced a man constituted by his homelessness, myth provides a shortcut to forming a nascent figure shaped by the homeless city.

With the appearance of these new urban upheavals, the invoked mythic tropes quickly defined emerging spaces and, more important, populations. Marx has noted the tendency to fall back on old language at times of great transformation:

> Men make their own history, but not of their own free will; not under circumstances they themselves have chosen but under the given and inherited circumstances with which they are directly confronted. The tradition of the dead generations weighs like a nightmare on the minds of the living. And, just when they appear to be engaged in the revolutionary transformation of themselves and their material surroundings, in the creation of something which does not yet exist, precisely in such epochs of revolutionary crisis they timidly conjure up the spirits of the past to help them; they borrow their names, slogans and costumes so as to stage the new world-historical scene in this venerable disguise and borrowed language.[74]

The borrowed language—in this case, myth—is part of the process of semantic ordering; fin-de-siècle commentators' invocations of myth consolidate Victorian attitudes about the city and the family. Older valuations carried in the tropes of Cain or Ishmael were assimilated to these Victorian attitudes; responses to the nineteenth-century revolutionary remaking of the city by industrialization and mass migrations provoked writing from Riis's reporting to Elbert Hubbard's *The Philistine* to conjure up the past to represent new conditions. A borrowed language readily signifies; Cain as a prototramp is grounded in old anti-Semitic traditions, which can more quickly (and probably more clearly) represent than can a new social science term and definition.

By distilling the constellation of attitudes we saw earlier, the deployment of the tropes begins the process of connecting them not merely with the city but with individuals—Cain, Ishmael, or the Wandering Jew. This shift from the homelessness of the city to Cain as a prototramp presages the move toward what becomes the homeless man of Depression-era social science.

The mythic tropes helped bring semantic order to the urban chaos—they represented the social upheavals in readily accessible ways. To control an unwieldy population, a two-step process was undertaken. The first was establishing the norm of the bourgeois subject in the family home and trying to use institutions to assimilate as many of the poor to this norm. The second requires othering the unassimilated. Shaping them into an image of mythical pariahs abets this process. As we shall see in Chapter 3, the mythic tropes fade into dormancy as a homeless figure begins to emerge through social science, though myth later returns as the discourse confronts a contradiction between its cultural logic and policy imperatives.

The process of constituting a homeless figure is part of the very processes of ordering and rationalizing the chaotic structures of the city; this discursive process brought a semantic order to rationalizing the city. The reformers' social programs took up the rationalizing processes—they changed housing codes and zoning laws to foster the immediate family to the exclusion of boarders; they brought green spaces into the metropolis to create an environment in which families might flourish. But these grew out of the nascent discourse on homelessness, which relied heavily on the invocation of mythic tropes.

In times of basic stability, society can ground its institutions and relations within its culture. From the philosopher Ernst Cassirer, we know that in times of upheaval, myth is often turned to,[75] and from Gilman and Katz, we know that at such times in the West, anti-Semitism is also frequently invoked. As we have noted, both myth and anti-Semitism furnish easily articulated structures to establish a sense of understanding at times when social changes are so revolutionary as to be nearly unrecognizable. Myth provides a borrowed language to represent new conditions within older traditions. Cassirer argues that myth is an ever-lurking presence in the dark corners of social life that is insufficiently banished by enlightening forces of rationalization: "For myth has not been really vanquished and subjugated. It is always there, lurking in the dark and waiting for its hour and opportunity. This hour comes as soon as the other binding forces of man's social life, for one reason or another, lose their strength and are no longer able to combat the demonic mythical powers."[76] While his adverse assessment of myth is overblown, Cassirer correctly indicates that when social norms start to collapse, a turn to the past provides tools to legitimate or explain the newness of life. As Amos Warner did in *American Charities*, writers turned the axis of social understanding to ancient traditions when the pace of change thwarted any synchronic understanding.

When relationships to family, place, and society are inarticulable—when Mrs. March can no longer return to the comforts of New England provincialism, yet the metropolitan life of New York furnishes no mooring—myth can emerge. Commentators, activists, and others wanting to rein in the anomic potential of great social change can draw upon an arsenal of tropes from myth. Mythic tropes initially provide the discourse on homelessness with a way to ground an understanding of the metropolis and a tool to argue about how the city should look. Implicit within the tropes are valuations of the new spatial and personal displacements.

In the modern world, mythic tropes are assimilated into processes of rationalization; myth abets processes of ordering society. It helps provide a discursive order concomitant with broader forces of order. A myth/reason juxtaposition is an outmoded dichotomy; modern myth is an implement of rationalization and helped to discursively order the American city. Modern myth serves rational ends; it is not a form of consciousness, as Cassirer argues.[77] Before social scientists develop the means to talk about the city and to classify its populations, myth and its transcendentalizing processes elided the historicity of the homelessness of the city; its deployment helped ground the new social transformations in ancient traditions and begin to bring order to the city.

While the transcendentalization of myth that we find in the discourse on homelessness turns to ancient tradition, we do not have to turn to antiquity to transcendentally ground life. Literary critic and theorist Roland Barthes shows synchronic transcendence in cultural forms.[78] But his mythic images appeared in the (relatively) stable society of postwar France; a turn to antiquity was unnecessary to deploy a transcendental trope. Margarine or plastics have no deep history and still can communicate meaning from the perspective of a point in time. They are products placed into a stable middle-class environment; thus Barthes can synchronically analyze to understand their signification—he can contextualize a mythic image within its immediate sociohistorical context.

In the fin-de-siècle period, the social upheavals were such that commentators turned the axis of the transcendence to older traditions; the ancient tropes are used because the means available to them were inadequate to make sense of the time. The city was unrecognizable, unknown; to represent it, they turned to ancient tropes.

The antiquity of the trope has no correlation to a presumed antiquity of the condition to which the trope is applied. The Russian socialist realist author Maxim Gorky points out the inventiveness, the essential newness, of myth and its attempts to transform the world:

> Myth is invention. To invent means to extract from the sum of a given reality its cardinal idea and embody it in imagery—that is how we get realism. But if to the idea extracted from the given reality we add—completing the idea by the logic of hypothesis—the desired, the possible, and thus supplement the image, we obtain that romanticism which is at the basis of myth, and is highly beneficial in that it tends to provoke a revolutionary attitude to reality, an attitude that changes the world in a practical way.[79]

Now Gorky implies myth in a more constructive way than I find in the works of bourgeois reform. I do not attribute a political intention to the invocation of mythic tropes by fin-de-siècle reformers; the invocation was an argument to ground a problem within older traditions.

Riis and others use myth to change the world in a practical way, but it is part of the two-step process. First, the norm of a bourgeois subject and family is necessary, and then myth is used in the negative part of the project—thereby othering the social practices that need to be managed. To use Gorky for our purposes, a homeless figure might function as a realist image, while Cain or Ishmael supplement and become a mythic overlay. But because Cain historically precedes the formation of the figure within the discourse on homelessness, the image is already "supplemented." The older valuations enter into the discourse; once the mythic trope distills a constellation of assumptions—threats to the Christian home, slovenliness, violence, and so on to the image—the trope can slide away. The remaining "realist image" of the homeless figure becomes a carrier of these social anxieties and assumptions of family norms.

The image of Cain (or Ishmael) distills arguments about the city—its mire and muck are taken up into this mythic image. By forming a constellation of significations that became attached to the other (or Nether) half, the mythic tropes play a role in developing the discursive underpinnings to homelessness. Myth was integral to bring a semantic order to the city; it was part of the urban commentators' response to urban changes and codified many attitudes about the city and family. These attitudes became connected to the residents described as homeless; these assumptions of homelessness were often appropriated by social scientists who, in the first decades of the twentieth century, began to talk about homeless men.

In this chapter, I distinguish the deployment of mythic tropes in the discourse on homelessness from other religious responses to urban social problems. The discourse on homelessness became a carrier for anxieties about the family because the mythic tropes legitimated the family and othered the threats to it. Despite their biblical origin, tropes like Cain and Ishmael do not serve a religious function. Fin-de-siècle religious interventions with protohomelessness demanded a faith-based commitment and action of their audiences, whereas the deployment of mythic tropes merely proffered a cultural argument about family and social order.

Then I argue that by being deployed in contexts of semantic ordering, myth serves as an instrument of rationalization. The transcendentalization that is concomitant with myth was part of the process of ordering the city. Because of the newness of urban problems, there was inadequate language or forms of representation to articulate the conditions of the city. To explain and legitimate social life, commentators turned to ancient traditions. This new vertical axis deployed the cultural values embedded in the ancient mythic tropes. This semantic process of ordering established the parameters for subsequent spatial and institutional processes of rationalizing the city.

Finally, I finish this section, and this chapter, by looking at how the deployment of myth legitimates the bourgeois family and the Christian home besides representing the city as homeless. I look at the example of the Cain story—the importance of maintaining the family altar and being "my brother's keeper"—to argue that myth legitimates the family against the associational life of *Gesellschaft*. This fin-de-siècle clash of social structures juxtaposes the important value placed on family versus what comes to be called the associational life of social capital. This contradiction reemerges in the last decades of the twentieth century when a new family values movement (which acclimates itself to social capital) replaces the discourse on homelessness as a primary carrier for family anxieties. In the waning Victorian years, myth dually supported the family as the foundation for society—elevating it and the Christian home to a social ideal and othering people and practices that failed to meet or threatened the family ideals.

This peregrination through fin-de-siècle newspapers, magazines, feuilleton, and lectures does not bring us fully to the constitution of the social science category of the homeless man—that task fell to social scientists undertaking Depression-era urban research in Chicago, which we shall see in Chapters 3 and 4. I am here focusing on the emergence of a discourse on homelessness before analytical categories are well established and the described social conditions are still in such a state of flux that traditional cultural forms—like mythic or anti-Semitic tropes—furnish useful tools to discuss the changing circumstances. In this particular case, I am looking at how the city came to be represented as homeless. From the homelessness of the city itself, the category of "homeless" moves to apply to the poor urban tenement dweller. The term's amorphous signification then shifts from this catchall for the 75 percent of the city residing in the slums to a way of talking about a much smaller subset of this population—the residents of Skid Row. The dialectics of homelessness rest in a threat to or rejection of the Christian home. Anti-Semitic traditions of wandering and exile, radicalism and malcontents all provided tropes that embody some threat to the Christian home. In some cases, the actual anti-Semitic image became a symbol of the new homeless condition (e.g., Cain or the IWW Jew). Yet in all these, anti-Semitism provided a deep, underlying structure to the discourse on homelessness.

PART II

Consolidating Homelessness

Part II charts the rise of homelessness as the normative category of social displacement. In the fin-de-siècle period, the term began to appear in the writings of social activists and journalists. The popular term was eventually taken over by the new field of urban sociology. In the first several decades of the twentieth century, it became increasingly used in sociological studies of shelter populations and residents of Skid Row districts in the city. First used as the primary term in Alice Solenberger's 1914 study *One Thousand Homeless Men*, it did not become the normative social science category of displacement until Edwin Sutherland and Harvey Locke's 1936 *Twenty Thousand Homeless Men*. (In the interim decade, the term received a great boost in Nels Anderson's book *The Hobo*.) All three studies resulted from collaborations between academic researchers and social service providers. The rise of this category required displacing a range of other terms and subordinating entire taxonomical systems to *homelessness*. The term underwent a professionalization as it moved from the page of the journalist and activist to the scholarly journal and monograph. Many of the characteristics of the sociologists' homeless man were initially represented by the mythic tropes of Riis, Warner, and others.

The homeless man, however, was not constituted as a category until the mid-1930s. Until that time, other terms and taxonomies were also used, often representing distinct attitudes about or understandings of displacement. *Hobo* was the last term standing as a competitor to *homeless*. The stakes in the competition were far greater than vocabulary. These two terms represented two very different forms of displacement—as we shall see, the former much more embodies an agentive pure movement and freedom. The hobo embraces a detachment from bourgeois society. The latter homeless man represents the anomie, the collapse of mores and nostalgia, which we found in the fin-de-siècle commentators. The hobo seeks a life and community outside of middle-class society; the homeless man represents the loneliness of those who have lost their family. The former category is a self-definition, while the latter is imposed upon the individual in the shelter. Social service involvement was essential to the scholarly formation of the "homeless man" as the dominant social science category.

The two forms of displacement represented by these two different terms—the hobo and the homeless man—were constituted under very different circumstances. The hobo was a name adopted by one who wanted to represent his embrace of independence, individuality, and freedom. The homeless man, however, was a category formed in the social service system to describe those people whose identities were shaped through a process that Sutherland and Locke called *shelterization*. This process formed a docile population, malleable to the efforts of service providers and the proddings of social scientists.

In Part II, we see a categorical consolidation around the term *homeless*, but the moment of interpellation is deferred. Not until the 1980s (and Part III) do we find a homeless subject who acknowledges and internalizes the moniker, much like the hobo had in the early decades of the twentieth century. The category of the homeless man was consolidated in the gaze of the shelter provider and the sociologist by the mid-1930s, but the category was not accepted by the described population until decades later. Perhaps such an acknowledgement required a substantial price tag. The passage of 1987's Stewart B. McKinney Act finally tied the distribution of billions of federal dollars to homeless social services; accepting the name *homeless* became financially remunerative—thus a large number of people began to consider themselves homeless.

Part II traces the consolidation of the category of homelessness in the sociology departments of the nation's largest cities. In Chapter 3, "Discourse and Subjectivation in American Homelessness," I look at the discursive conditions necessary for the formation of *homelessness* as the normative category of social displacement. I argue that sociologists made spatial, linguistic, and institutional distinctions of particular populations to designate those who were displaced from the broader population. These individuals received the appellation "homeless man."

In Chapter 4, "The Limits of Hobosociality for Social Mooring," I argue that a consolidation of the category of homelessness required the dislodging of the competing category of the hobo from social science. We see the linguistic and taxonomic subordination of the hobo in Chapter 3, but in Chapter 4, we see the institutional difficulties presented by the hobo and his incessant movement and desire for freedom. The hobo community sees itself as an alternative form of sociality that rejects the nuclear family for a community of fellow wayfarers. The discourse on homelessness consolidates the category of the "homeless man" over that of the hobo in a rejection of both the term *hobo* and the social practices of this community. Within the discourse on homelessness, the nuclear family remained the lone form of acceptable sociality.

In the final chapter of Part II—Chapter 5, "Homelessness as Disaffiliation"—I analyze the rise of disaffiliation as the definition of homelessness. The idea of disaffiliation arose from two new midcentury trends in American sociology—studies on loneliness and the formation of the new category of the nuclear family. The term *homeless man* had just supplanted *hobo* as the dominant term for social displacement in sociological literature. Further development of the category by social scientists soon followed. An implicit assumption of the discourse had long been that the homeless person was a threat to the family (we saw this in Part I). While the idea that homelessness as disaffiliation became the dominant social science category, some activists resisted this assessment; their resistance went beyond the disaffiliation to include objections to the rationalizing impulses of modern social science and social services. Despite such activist opposition, the advocates of rationalization and the disaffiliation thesis remained the dominant voice on social displacement.

The modernizing institutions of social services, municipal governments, and urban sociology shaped a discourse and a population. Through processes of shelterization, a normative category was established, and an important foundation was laid for constituting a homeless subject. As we saw in Part I, the basic characteristics of this homeless man—threat to family, outside of society, restless, wanderer, and so on—were developed through mythic tropes. With the rise of social science in the early decades of the twentieth century, the mythic tropes fell out of common usage, but these basic attributes were taken up by the sociological definition of the homeless man.

CHAPTER 3

Discourse and Subjectivation in American Homelessness

In the early decades of the twentieth century, the extremes of urban life slowly waned.[1] The bohemianism of Greenwich Village was domesticated as social radicals found Cape Cod and the Hudson River Valley to be oases for their art production. The tsunami of immigration dwindled to a far lesser lapping onto the shores. Municipal governments claimed greater authority to regulate urban chaos; at the behest of reformers like Jacob Riis, they instituted housing and zoning laws to regulate structures and those residing within them. The federal government extended its claims over speech to render much of the activity of political radicals illegal. With the shield of the First World War, the government rounded up socialists, anarchists, and communists; it deported the immigrant and locked up the native radical. The New York that gave rise to the Draft and Tompkins Square Riots or the Chicago of the Haymarket Riot was reined in. The city became a more manageable locale.

Part of this managerial process included developing techniques to organize populations, to regulate social practices, and to assimilate those not integrated to prevalent social norms. The techniques included administrative and discursive practices that shaped the urban populations into manageable groups. The fin-de-siècle urban chaos was finally reined in through these practices to alleviate bourgeois fears of cauldrons of simmering social unrest. Processes of rationalization restored a semblance of order, though social life was irretrievably transformed. Elements of the country—green spaces, air vents for fresh air, windows for sunlight—mitigated the impacts of modernization on cityscapes.

Riisian accounts of the fin-de-siècle American metropolis pictured a homeless city. He photographed new conditions—lives newly interrupted in their exile from small-town American or European communities, which immigrants had fled in search of greater opportunity. Many of these domestic and international migrants assimilated to the new norms of metropolitan life, acclimated themselves to bourgeois modes of behavior, and became more financially secure over ensuing generations; they moved out of the ranks of the homeless. These poor laborers were acculturated into bourgeois norms, even if still economically distant from this class. The formerly rural adopted patterns of citizenship, cleanliness, and education to allay middle-class fears of urban filth and the tensions brewing in this muck. Unlike in the macadam of Paris, few of these poor were always already urban, for the American city had no medieval heritage; the American city appears with modernity through processes of modernization. From its 12,000 residents at the time of American independence to its millions just over a century later, New York outgrew its ability to accommodate populations with housing, services, work, or space.

A subset of this population was migratory laborers, professional beggars, unemployed men, and orphans. While the ranks of the homeless thinned through broader cultural assimilation, this subset stayed mired in the ranks. As the problems of tenements, poverty, and large migrations became increasingly familiar, clearer attempts at articulation and new processes of organization developed—like identifying clear social groups, in essence the ordering of all things homeless. New taxonomies of the displaced became common in early social science studies. These processes of systematically discussing social problems were the first step in managing them. Clearer distinctions of the displaced enabled new processes of management to be tailored to address unique problems. When appearing in urban discussions, the scope of the term *homeless* narrowed from nearly three-fourths of the city's slum dwellers to this much smaller group of single men, who avoided (or lost) their natal families and never developed (or abandoned) a later conjugal one. The term's amorphous signification shifted from a catchall for the city's slum dwellers to a way of talking about a much smaller subset of the population—the residents of Hobohemia, the Bowery, or Skid Row.

In a study of Chicago's homeless, the term narrowed further in the mid-1930s to become nearly coextensive with the sheltered man. Yet even in this point of seeming semantic contraction, it still implies a broader group of socially detached men—and almost always means men in particular. A prologue to the constitution of the homeless subject began with the mythic tropes of the fin-de-siècle period. The mythic tropes of the fin-de-siècle commentators created a framework for discussing urban homelessness and naturalized a set of assumptions about the city, family, and social behavior. The images of Cain and Ishmael—which intertwined with the trope of the Wandering Jew, the ideas of exile and the stranger, and the political radicalism attributed to hobos—distilled a set of implicit binaries (like settled/unsettled, bourgeois/nonbourgeois, Christian/Jew) to begin the discourse on homelessness, which culminated with the formation of the homeless man.

Before the sheltered man became fully constituted as a homeless man, several conditions arose. First, a way of delimiting this population developed—both from the "normal" population and from other groups of the detached. The delimitation took both a spatial/geographical separation and a set of distinctions in social practices. A second condition was the development of a vocabulary to demarcate the socially disaffiliated man, and a third condition contributing to the rise of a homeless figure was the proliferation of institutions to manage and form the men.

All these conditions were the products of and producers of this discourse through which the category of homelessness was eventually constituted. The discourse identified urban districts demarcated for the disaffiliated and a set of normative social practices—like marriage, heterosexuality, or sedentary work—against which the social practices of the homeless man could be juxtaposed. The semantic flux of the fin-de-siècle period settled first into a taxonomic series of distinct categories and then in the 1930s, as subcategories of the metacategory of the homeless man. While the social service agencies remained independent, municipal-level coalitions spurred the development of common practices and terminologies and extended their reach into academic and policy circles.

While most of the scholarly, policy, and social work literature of the New Deal and Eisenhower years coalesces around the category of homelessness, one prominent group from the religious left (a category hardly noticeable in twenty-first-century America) resisted the dominant disaffiliation thesis. In their recuperation of the homeless man, the Catholic Worker sanctifies poverty and homelessness, or at least the homeless man. They combined these objections with an antimodern appeal for a return to the land and a critique of the broader rationalizing and modernizing trends in social services and social science. Despite their objections, the discipline of sociology, along with social service providers, became the midcentury entity for defining social displacement.

The Space of Homelessness

Geographically circumscribing an urban space into which the homeless were separated from the broader middle-class population faced an immediate problem—mobility. Mobility and migration were significant factors in creating the urban upheavals that came to be called *homeless*; they remained integral to the discourse on homelessness. Delimiting the space of a population on the move necessitates either eliminating motion or creating a geography of spacelessness. Both processes appear in the discourse on homelessness.

An additional approach to spatial delimitation developed in the process of defining a space through which much of the wandering population passed at some time. The homeless figure became associated with the section of the city with day labor jobs, flophouses, pawnshops, cheap bars, and brothels. But only the home guard or bums remained in this location. Hobos and tramps threaten the social order with deterritorialization; they are wanderers. Their geography is one of motion—traveling on trains, walking, hitchhiking—the space of the hobo and the tramp is one of movement, not of location. Climate, however, briefly necessitates a migratory cessation—either work ends for a season or camping spots along tramping routes become wintry wastelands. And thus the hobo and tramp settle—at least for a season—in the main stem, the metropolitan stretch for the poor and, presumably, derelict.

These Boweries, Skid Rows, and Hobohemias became the locus for the homeless men. These urban districts share a dialectical relationship with the figure they help to form—they come to define a people who in turn come to define the place. Like this figure that these places come to geographically circumscribe, these spaces have their own histories of development. By looking at shifts in these place names and their dislocation from the historical locus whence they emerged, I trace the spatial delimitation as it expands from particular places to describe a section of any city demarcated for the homeless. The place names come to represent a type of space in any city rather than a particular place in a specific city.

The oldest of the space names that becomes associated with the homeless figure is the Bowery. Of the terms for spatially marking the homeless figure, the *Bowery* is the only one that did not develop specifically to describe a protohomeless subject. The Bowery was the road providing a western limit to the 340-acre section of Manhattan's Lower East Side, which became part of prominent colonial estates.[2] The road—whose name derives from a Dutch word for farm (*bouwer*)—dates to the Dutch colony of New Amsterdam. The Dutch root is related to the Old High German verb *būan*, meaning "to dwell"; considering the last century's history of the homeless in the Bowery, the term has an ironic etymology. In the mid-seventeenth century, before British occupation and the regional renaming to New York, Peter Stuyvesant had the largest estate along what was then the largest road in New Amsterdam, and his estate became popularly known as the Bowery. The region carried this name through British attempts to rechristen it and through its transformation from a sleepy, rural route to the eventual, supposed nadir of urban decadence.

Before the American Revolution, the subdividing of the region began—stores and residences began to populate the area—and by the end of the eighteenth century, the Bowery became a prominent commercial center. The southern end reached into the Five Points region of the city, which—long before the Draft Riots and Riis's work as a police reporter—was already becoming an enclave of urban poor and immigrants. As a frequent disembarkation point for new immigrants, the Bowery became a hotbed for poor, nativist resentments and resistance to new arrivals. The proliferation of gangs and the concomitant violence shooed away middle-class shoppers, stores, and residences so that by the mid-nineteenth century the Bowery had much of the vibrant street life and character excoriated in Riis's ongoing battle with the slum. The Bowery was already a tourist destination for the curious wealthy before the fin-de-siècle advent of Paresis Hall and other "resorts" for male prostitutes.[3] By the 1880s, this sightseeing practice was so common that the new term *slumming* was coined to describe the practice of curious onlookers taking titillating sojourns through the Bowery's poverty, bohemianism, and red-light districts. The population of the destitute had increased in the Bowery with an influx of Civil War veterans and others displaced by the war.[4]

Because it became so associated with the down-and-out of New York, the name *Bowery* eventually shifted from a specific place name to be used for two semantic roles. First, it became an adjective for the disaffiliated man of New York's downtown. After the "Bowery man" came to describe a particular social type, the *Bowery* was used in a second way. The term became unmoored from Manhattan and became a general term for parts of cities in which disaffiliated men congregate.

Deriving from the Old High German verb "to dwell," the spatial term *Bowery* came to signify the absence of dwelling—the Bowery man was the homeless man. This urban homelessness belied the bucolic origins of the word as it entered into English as a description of expansive Dutch farms. The Bowery came to signify a space for homelessness. It was a locus designated as distinct from those of broader urban populations to create a rhetoric of geographical separation in which a homeless figure could be constituted.

While "the Bowery" with the definite article always signifies a district of downtown Manhattan, the term comes to simultaneously be a general category for a district of derelicts and a particular place name. The Bowery is, of course, not the only name for districts of lodging houses, bars, and pawnshops. Other terms emerged later but followed similar trajectories.

The name Skid Row, however, became entirely unmoored from its locus of historical origin to become a name for a section of any city. An earlier form of the term—Skid Road—appeared in the 1880s lumber industry outside of Seattle. To move timber from forests to mills to process for the market, logs were skidded down the road. Services developed along the roads to accommodate the needs and desires of this migratory labor pool.[5] In its transformed, popular form, *Skid Row* became the most common term for spatially delimiting the homeless. Skid Row so strongly signified the locus for the homeless that many studies on the homeless were eventually named for this location, for example, Donald Bogue's *Skid Row in American Cities* or Howard Bahr's *Skid Row: An Introduction to Disaffiliation*. The Chicago School sociologist Donald Bogue alludes to the name's West Coast origins when he points out that Skid Row has become the term for where the urban homeless stay:

> The term "Skid Row" (in the West it is called "Skid Road") has come to denote a district in the city where there is a concentration of sub-standard hotels and rooming houses charging very low rates and catering primarily to men with low incomes. These hotels are intermingled with numerous taverns, employment agencies offering jobs as unskilled laborers, restaurants serving low-cost meals, pawnshops and second-hand stores, and missions that daily provide a free meal after the service. Perhaps there are also barber colleges, burlesque shows or night clubs with strip tease acts, pennyarcades, tattoo palaces, stores selling men's work clothing, bakeries selling stale bread, and unclaimed freight stores. Most frequently the Skid Row is located near the Central Business District and also near

a factory district or major heavy transportation facilities such as a waterfront, freight yards, or a trucking and storage depot.[6]

Here Bogue outlines the clearly identifiable nature of the district—its location in the metropolis and the services and entertainments available for passing the time.

The space becomes instrumental in constituting a homeless man—his activities, his morals, his interactions, and his circle of acquaintances, as well as the types of institutions involved in shaping this category. Delineating this Skid Row space provides the means to separate the homeless from those in other parts of the city. And as we shall see in Chapter 4, this spatial delineation provides the means to talk about the homeless population as distinct from the bourgeois residents elsewhere in the city.

Bogue elaborates on some of these ways of articulating differences by arguing that Skid Row men share three conditions that "distinguish them from residents of other communities in the city": the Skid Row man is homeless, poor, and has acute personal problems.[7] Here Bogue makes explicit my point that the spatial delimitation of a "district in the city" distinguishes a population of men from the remainder of the urban population. The poor, homeless man with personal problems is the other of the "normal" population; the homeless man of Skid Row is only articulable in how he is different from the people of the rest of the city. The role as other, which dates to at least Riis's *How the Other Half Lives*, continues to define homelessness. Bogue even goes so far as to use the term *normal* for the population not in Skid Row;[8] the implicit norm to which this other is compared is now made explicit.

Despite some amount of unease with this normal-abnormal juxtaposition, Bogue still finds that there is an antinomy between the Skid Row homeless man and the more affluent populations. The sociologist appropriates the fin-de-siècle binaries—settled/unsettled, bourgeois/nonbourgeois, social threat/threatened socially—and demarcates the population to which the negative formulation applies. The population is distinguished spatially, semantically, and institutionally from the broader population.

The primary distinction between the spatially circumscribed homeless man and the normal bourgeois population is the relationship to family. In Bogue's list of three conditions common to Skid Row men, two of them are markers of familial separation:

Three conditions which Skid Row men share, and which serve to distinguish them from residents of other communities in the city are:

a. They are homeless.—Most of them live outside private households and *have no family life.*

b. They are poor.—Many work only very irregularly and receive low rates of pay. For these reasons, they are at the bottom of the income scale.

c. They have acute personal problems.—With respect to society at large and in their interpersonal relations, many are poorly adjusted. This maladjustment frequently finds expression in heavy daily drinking, and in *withdrawal from conventional family living.*[9]

The spatial segregation marks an absence of family life. Skid Row became the most popular term for the urban district demarcated for the man disassociated from family life. The threats to family, which the discourse on homelessness articulated through myth in the fin-de-siècle period, now become an assumption of social science. Skid Row man was the man withdrawing from family life. As we shall see more in Chapter 5, disaffiliation becomes the defining characteristic of homelessness.

Of the three place names that become unmoored from a particular location to signify the homeless area in any city, Skid Row falls chronologically in the middle. The Bowery was a place name in seventeenth-century New Amsterdam and came to describe a social type—the Bowery man. While most common in sociological work in New York City, the Bowery became a term that signified the district of the poor and derelict. Much later in the 1880s, the term *Skid Road* appears and transforms to the more popular *Skid Row* by the 1940s. Like the Bowery, Skid Row became a name for that district of any city with pawnshops, brothels, and cheap bars. The formation of categories for urban districts distinguished from that of the "normal" population geographically focused sociologists' studies and delineated the population, which came to be designated as homeless.

The last of these names for spatial delimitation had a twentieth-century rise and demise. *Hobohemia* appears to have been coined by the fiction writer Sinclair Lewis—he titled a 1917 short story in the *Saturday Evening Post* "Hobohemia." In this story, Hobohemia is indistinguishable from Bohemia. This district in downtown New York City is populated with artists, poets, novelists, anarchists, free love advocates, and hangers-on. "Hobohemia is the place and state of being talented and free," Lewis's narrator tells us.[10] In fact, Hobohemia appears to be coextensive with Greenwich Village. When New York and Hobohemia newcomer Denis Brown is at a reception at Café Liberté (the epicenter of Hobohemia) with his would-be lover Ysetta (whom he has chased from their provincial Western hamlet Northernapolis), he faux-appreciatively looks at the crowd and declares, "'Some bunch!' said Mr. Brown weakly. 'Oh, these are just imitations—society slummers, and artists that are as disgustingly respectable as though they were merchants. The real Greenwich Villagers always go in the next room.'"[11] The Hobohemians are Greenwich Villagers. Society slummers and bourgeois artists were not only mere simulacra of Hobohemians; they failed to recognize the differences. They were content to unwittingly mill about in an antechamber with other imitators, unknowing that the supposedly real bohemians lurked in an inner sanctum.

Despite an agonistic relationship with respectability and bourgeois decorum, Lewis's Hobohemia is not a space for the homeless man.[12] Nonetheless, Lewis's Hobohemia presented lifestyles in tension with the norms of bourgeois families and homes. In the 1910s, the idea of homelessness was still broader than the narrow population of Skid Row men. When the weary Denis Brown was still trying to court Ysetta, he planned to call on her for a quiet evening. As he readied to suggest this borderline domesticity, he realized that he proposed a bohemian abomination: "He was under the impression that Ysetta was still in love with him, as she had been for all of five weeks. He was tired, one early evening. He wanted to be quiet. With a realization that the use of the expression would have got him court-martialed for espionage, in Hobohemia, he confessed to himself that he wanted to feel 'homy.' He telephoned casually to Ysetta that he was coming up."[13] The very idea of "homyness" would elicit expulsion from Hobohemia; that is, bohemianism was also a social threat to home. It was a competitor to hobodom as a social practice threatening middle-class family norms. The moniker *Hobohemia* appears to integrate these two primary threats—hobos and bohemians, though Lewis only depicts the bohemian half of this nexus. Six years later, Nels Anderson appropriates the name for the Hobo-half of the threat, where it remains until the name wanes into a historical term. The decline of the hobo brought about the irrelevancy of the Hobohemia moniker. The homeless man discursively subordinated the hobo and his place name.

Nels Anderson does much to popularize the name *Hobohemia* while simultaneously setting in motion the discourse that rendered it obsolete. His personal familiarity with this part of town is partially why he was approached to conduct and write this most exhaustive study of the hobo.

He had been a hobo before finding himself working on a master's degree at the University of Chicago and so could have a relatively easy entrée into the hobo milieu.[14] In Robert Park's preface to the book, he declares that *The Hobo* is "intended to be the first of a series of studies of the urban community and of city life."[15] The urban studies projects based at the University of Chicago, which came to be known as the Chicago School of Sociology, began with Anderson's *The Hobo*. The study of Hobohemia moved from the literary work of Lewis to the somewhat experienced-based study of a student (Anderson) to the full-fledged sociological study a decade later with Sutherland and Locke's *Twenty Thousand Homeless Men*. Because of his intimate familiarity with the hobo community and life, Anderson later wrote a handbook for hobos under the pseudonym Dean Stiff.

In part 1 of his 1923 study on the hobo—"Hobohemia, The Home of the Homeless Man"—Anderson argues that every city has a district for the homeless, which he calls Hobohemia:

> Every large city has its district into which these homeless types gravitate. In the parlance of the "road" such a section is known as the "stem" or the "main drag." To the homeless man it is home, for there, no matter how sorry his lot, he can find those who will understand. The veteran of the road finds other veterans; the old man finds the aged; the chronic grouch finds fellowship; the radical, the optimist, the crook, the inebriate, all find others here to tune in with them. The wanderer finds friends here or enemies, but, and that is at once a characteristic and pathetic feature of Hobohemia, they are friends or enemies only for the day. They meet and pass on.
>
> Hobohemia is divided into four parts—west, south, north, and east—and no part is more than five minutes from the heart of the Loop. They are all the "stem" as they are also Hobohemia. This four-part concept, Hobohemia, is Chicago to the down-and-out.[16]

Besides his claim that every city has such a district and his appropriation of Lewis's place-name, I find a couple other important points. First, Anderson says that this district is where "homeless types gravitate." Typologies shift initially from ones of different types of socially displaced persons through several permutations to become types of the homeless; we shall see this in our discussion of the vocabulary and taxonomies of homelessness in the next section. Anderson himself works through several taxonomies later in this monograph. Though he titles the section "Types of Hobos," he is already starting to talk about homeless types, as he does here.

Writing at this time of the waning of the hobo and the rise of something yet to come, Anderson's vocabulary shifts between the departing moment and creating the rhetoric for the new era—that of the homeless man. There is an almost seamless movement between "hobo" and "homeless," even though, as I shall show, his idea of homeless men is much broader than the hobo.

The second point from this passage I want to note is the transitory nature of all social relations—the homeless are "friends or enemies only for the day." Like Bogue, Anderson assumes that there is something personally wrong with the homeless man such that he is unable to sustain "normal" social relations. While Bogue found this social pathology a threat to the rest of the city—"Not only is Skid Row a physical eyesore, it is also sociologically poisonous to neighborhoods in a broad surrounding zone"[17]—Anderson finds this basic characteristic of the homeless deserving of pathos. Anderson here limits his discussion of pathology to the transitory nature of social relations. Bogue, however, implies a broader array of "social poisons," for example, heavy drinking or disease. However, these other problems follow from the maladjustment in interpersonal relations;[18] the nature of the homeless man's social interactions is (or breeds) social pathology. In both cases, the normative assumption is that social relations must have longer standing than the mere passing of exchanges. Part of the sociological anxiety around the homeless figure is this unclassifiable nature of the homeless man's interactions. In Chapter 4, we shall explore sociologists' analyses and anxieties about the social relations of the homeless man and the hobo and how these relate to broader concerns about social order, which we saw in the fin-de-siècle period.

Despite the place name's original association with the latter half of the compound, Anderson clearly distinguishes Hobohemia from Bohemia. He identifies the space (Bughouse Square) where "Bohemia and Hobohemia meet."[19] This area (even called the "Village"[20]) is the meeting spot of "vagabond poets, artists, writers, revolutionists, of various types as of the go-abouts."[21] While some political or artistic interests might overlap between the hobos and the bohemians, they still relate best as a Venn diagram—a small intersection for two primarily distinct groups. Anderson does not dwell on Bohemia; he merely appropriates the place-name for the homeless. By the time Nels Anderson published *The Hobo* in 1923, bohemianism seemed to be an enervated threat to bourgeois life.[22] Bohemia's "anti-homyness" could be disregarded, yet Hobohemia's homelessness was a thriving menace.

Anderson's study of the hobo is subtitled: *The Sociology of the Homeless Man.* The subtitle seems to imply that the threat to home (i.e., the homeless man) comes primarily from the homeless hobo. He ignores any threats from bohemianism and establishes that the homeless man is the resident of Hobohemia. Anderson lays the groundwork for establishing "the homeless man" as the metacategory for all socially displaced people. Hobohemia is the locus for the homeless; it is the threat to home.

In Anderson's text, homelessness—the very antithesis of the bourgeois home—dwelled in Hobohemia. The term *homeless* sloughed off its bohemianism and briefly became an important name for the city district demarcating the homeless. Constituting this district created a culture that shaped the people of the district:

> This segregation of tens of thousands of footloose, homeless, and not to say hopeless men is the fact fundamental to an understanding of the problem. Their concentration has created an isolated cultural area—Hobohemia. Here characteristic institutions have arisen—cheap hotels, lodging houses, flops, eating joints, outfitting shops, employment agencies, missions, radical bookstores, welfare agencies, economic and political institutions—to minister to the needs, physical and spiritual of the homeless man. This massing of detached and migratory men upon a small area has created an environment in which gamblers, dope venders, bootleggers, and pickpockets can live and thrive.[23]

By identifying a segregated area, the geography of future studies of Chicago's homeless (e.g., Sutherland and Locke's *Twenty Thousand Homeless Men*) was defined—the homeless man became the man in Hobohemia. The space only becomes Hobohemia through the discursive process of including certain spaces and institutions while excluding others—the milieu and culture of the homeless man came to be defined by the social life of the residents of this district. The category of Hobohemia arose through sociologists studying this area—the social practices of its residents, the institutions providing services, and those trying to manage or regulate them.

Hobohemia's heyday, however, was short-lived. By the time Frank Beck—Chicago minister and longtime instructor of social pathology at Chicago's Hobo College—published his reminiscences in 1956's *Hobohemia*, Hobohemia was a place of the past. The Hobo College was a continuing education program set up by hobos for hobos; classes included philosophy and politics as well as tips for life on the road. It was the brainchild of James Eads How, who also founded the hobo union called the International Brotherhood

Welfare Association (IBWA). How, who inherited money from his prominent St. Louis family, was known as the "millionaire hobo." He wanted to encourage the development of the hobo community and its alternative social life. Versions of the Hobo College were set up in several cities; Chicago's was the largest and longest lasting. How identified Ben Reitman as an early leader of the college, and he worked at the college off and on for a number of years.

When Frank Beck looked back on his years at the Hobo College, Hobohemia was no more. The chapters about people and places—Ben Reitman, Lucy Parsons (the Haymarket widow), Emma Goldman, Bughouse Square, among others—have a tone of nostalgia. Most of the people of whom he writes are long dead; the places are changed. This Hobohemia is no more. Just a few years later, Jack Kerouac laments the passing of the hobo life in his essay "The Vanishing American Hobo."[24] The hobo and his place—Hobohemia—were gone. Only the homeless man remained.

Certainly Hobohemia was instrumental in establishing a delimited geography of the homeless man. In many ways, Hobohemia was more important than the Bowery and Skid Row in delineating the space for homelessness. Anderson's analysis of Hobohemia sets the stage for the homeless man to supplant hobos, tramps, and bums; Hobohemia—despite its etymological ties to the hobo—is always already associated with the sociological category of homelessness. The advent of the term coincides with the rise of the homeless man. Beck's opening line to Hobohemia invokes Alice Solenberger's early study *One Thousand Homeless Men*[25] as a worthwhile study of the men of Hobohemia. This street—West Madison, which Beck identifies with Hobohemia and homelessness—is also central to both the locus and the new figure for Anderson; it is "a port of homeless men."[26] In an elaboration on this locus of the hobo and its connection with homelessness, Beck begins with Whitman and ends with the hobo as homeless. He writes the following:

Walt Whitman reflected the restlessness and rebellion and individualism of the hobo mind in his verse:

What do you suppose will satisfy the soul,
Except to walk free and own no superior?

The Hobohemian life begins by breaking ties. First with the family and then the community. It ends by severing all associations with static people and roving over the face of the earth. The hobo thus becomes not only a "homeless" man but a man without a cause, without a country, without, in fact, any type of responsible associations.[27]

The freedoms of the hobo become his undoing. As with Bogue and Anderson, Beck laments the unattached man. The homelessness is this disaffiliation. He saw his role as instructor at the Hobo College to counter this disaffiliation: "At the end of very course I presented at the College I stressed the idea that a romantic passion for human freedom was not enough. The highest achievement of a human life was to establish and maintain purposeful communications with other human lives. The 'bo rolls along, missing the security and the glory of an attachment to the earth, to a cause, and also the stability and satisfaction of a recognized, worthwhile position in the scheme of things."[28] The wandering of the hobo breaks ties and makes men homeless. Though giving their name to that part of town in which they alight when not on the road, the hobo is primarily a wanderer. The mobility of the hobo produces the condition of disaffiliation; this condition can be created by other practices—drinking, laziness, or begging. Disaffiliation that results from many social practices becomes the way to define social displacement; place becomes relations in a space and not a space itself.

This category of disaffiliation defines the loose anxieties of the fin-de-siècle commentators. They lamented the anonymity of the city and the decline of neighborliness. For them, the demands of modernization had so changed the pace of life that social relations were becoming transitory. The simpler ideal of a rural *Gemeinschaft* was better able to foster the family and social life. The homeless men of Chicago's Near North Side represented the fears of the early generation of social critics—men entirely without a family.

The homeless figure becomes the man of social disaffiliation. For this homeless man to emerge, a space had to be set aside, a district to rhetorically quarantine the group afflicted by social pathology. This spatial delimiting not only serves to form a coherent group but also becomes essential in defining the parameters of the figures' activities; he can frequent missions, pawn shops, thrift stores, cheap bars, and brothels but little else. Any activities elsewhere in the city are not integral to the homeless man; the locus defines the activities and specifies the institutions that have roles in constituting the homeless man. These spaces were a remainder after much of the city was assimilated to the practices of the "normal" population; these outliers kept the name homeless attached to them for they were—as Anderson told us—spaces only for men; the absence of women and children was a sign that family life did not exist here.

The terms *Bowery*, *Skid Row*, and *Hobohemia* signified those spaces set aside to study the homeless. These are areas of town in which families have no part; this space, according to Anderson, is known for its "complete absence of women and children; it is the most completely womanless and childless of all the city areas. It is quite definitely a man's street."[29] The spatial delimitation enabled social workers and sociologists to readily identify a population, identify their distinctions from populations elsewhere in the city, and laid the groundwork for developing a vocabulary for demarcating the socially disaffiliated man. The space is not distinct until it is defined as such; the space only becomes that of the homeless man when it is called the Bowery, Skid Row, or Hobohemia. With clear research laboratories demarcated in the city, sociologists began to more clearly define the populations residing in and passing through the regions; they developed new terms and taxonomies to sociologically represent this group of homeless men. Thus having looked at the process of delimiting this population of the homeless, I now turn to the emergence of this second condition for constituting a homeless figure: a new vocabulary.

The Language of Homelessness

The homeless man was not constituted as the category of social displacement until the way was clearly paved through a series of semantic and taxonomic steps. The spatial segregation of populations enabled a vocabulary to emerge around the men of this disenfranchised urban district. The homelessness of the city rhetorically came to modify the denizens of the metropolitan slums. The vague array of characteristics that came to be associated with the fin-de-siècle "homeless city"—the area of the unsettled, political and social threats, outside of family norms, nonbourgeois, and so on—began to describe people in the more dilapidated parts of the city. Certain parts of the slums—these Skid Row districts—were populated almost exclusively by men and were devoid of family life with few connections to life beyond the district. These spaces became an object of a particular type of attention—the helping professions.

Representatives of these institutions, along with journalists and academics studying the population or the institutions, developed a language to talk about these groups. The language arises through several types of intersecting institutions: the institutions in and of the Bowery (pawnshops, cheap bars, lodging houses, and brothels); the institutions in but not of the Bowery—to the extent that their raison d'être is to reform or rehabilitate the people and place (missions, shelters, and police); and institutions interested in but outside of the Bowery (universities, governments, and businesses). The third of these also mediated and developed the terms for an additional set of institutional relations—how the Bowery relates to or is articulated vis-à-vis non-Bowery institutions. Governments, academics, service providers, and journalists articulate the nature of the Bowery man, his place (or lack thereof) in the larger social structures, and how the broader society might intersect with the homeless man.

As I have noted, during the semantic flux of the fin-de-siècle period, terms arose willy-nilly. After the taxonomic chaos of the fin-de-siècle decades, the discussion of urban poverty, social outcasts, and dereliction went through years of organizing and reflection by social scientists, activists, and active hobos. Fin-de-siècle commentators' mythic tropes had represented some urban problems and so began to bring a semantic order to the city, but it was not until later that others began to codify the attributes developed through these tropes. These characteristics were to be developed into taxonomic systems.

The language for social outsiders was a broad negotiation between the argot of displaced communities and the vocabulary of those institutions managing this group. The processes of constituting the category of the homeless man were, in part, this contest for semantic supremacy, with an eventual victory for these institutions and their discourse. The category of social displacement came down to a contestation between the self-defined hobo and the service provider-defined homeless man.

In a rather self-evident way, the eventual terminological prominence of the homeless man reflects the imbalances in social locations of the interested parties. The homeless man is specifically that man who does not have a network of social relations and institutional contacts; he does not have the power by which to take on the entrenched interests of governments, businesses, churches, or social scientists. This language of outcasts emerges from this set of institutions with interests in the homeless man.

The banal point of power differentials was not always a foregone conclusion, however. The fevered pitch of fin-de-siècle rhetoric emanates from a great fear that the power imbalance favors the homeless. In 1890, three-quarters of New York City lived in the homelessness of the slums. Through efforts of reform, these ranks were significantly reduced to a more readily managed number; the homeless man is of this more easily administered population. With its eventual codification in social science, the term *homeless man* came to describe a much smaller population subordinated to social service institutions.

The language of homelessness is not merely a series of terms. Systems of classification order categories of the socially displaced. The terms, the taxonomies, and their definitions create an intellectual delimitation (much like the spatial one) with principles of inclusion and exclusion. By the time the category of the homeless man is clearly constituted in Sutherland and Locke's 1935 *Twenty Thousand Homeless Men*, several decades of social-scientific fretting had produced a framework for defining, categorizing, and delimiting this figure through many reworkings of homeless typologies. Over these first several decades of the twentieth century, the taxonomies move from types of hobos (or displaced) to become types of the homeless. Tracing these shifts, we are able to chart the consolidation of the homeless man as the category for social displacement.

In *The Hobo*, Anderson has the most extensive survey of typologies, most of which were developed by hobos primarily affiliated with the Hobo College, including three former presidents of this institution—Ben Reitman, St. John Tucker, and Nicholas Klein.[30] After his brief survey of taxonomic literature, Anderson offers his own typology: "Although we cannot draw lines closely, it seems clear that there are at least five types of *homeless men*: (a) the seasonal worker, (b) the transient or occasional worker or hobo, (c) the tramp who 'dreams and wanders' and works only when it is convenient, (d) the bum who seldom wanders and seldom works, and (e) the home guard who lives in Hobohemia and does not leave town."[31] Two important points emerge from Anderson's analyses in this section. First, he begins the shift—implied with his subtitle *The Sociology of the Homeless Man*—from the category of hobo to that of the homeless man; this transition is completed with Sutherland and Locke. The framing title of the entire section of the book is "Types of Hobos," but when he starts to delineate his taxonomy in the previous passage, he replaces the word *hobo* with *homeless man*. The newer term is becoming increasingly significant. Anderson cites Alice Solenberger's early work (1914's *One Thousand Homeless Men*) and her tendency to use "the term 'homeless man' . . . to include all types of unattached men, tramps, hobos, bums, and the other nameless varieties of the 'go-abouts.'"[32] Anderson argues that this term is the best one available to characterize the full range of inhabitants in Hobohemia.[33] Despite his title, the hobo is but one of five categories in his taxonomy. For Anderson, the homeless man subsumes all five categories. The homeless man was not yet the dominant sociological term for the unattached, but Anderson makes a strong case that it should be.

The second significant point in the passage is that Anderson's categories are malleable. In the passage, we see Anderson delineate five taxonomic categories, yet in his chapter headings—which he names after the categories—he drops one of those categories that he delineates. His chapter headings only provide for the hobo, tramp, bum, and home guard; the seasonal worker does not appear (or is perhaps subsumed under the hobo).[34] He concludes the hobo/tramp chapter with the point that distinguishing between the three (seasonal worker, hobo, and tramp) is problematic.[35]

This tendency to collapse the three migratory groups into one, I argue, is part of a dual process: the subordination of the category of the hobo and the elevation of the homeless man. The hobo was the most popular moniker for outcasts in the first several decades of the twentieth century; it was the title of Anderson's monograph, an eponymous term for the section of town where homeless men were found (Hobohemia) and the self-adopted name of migratory laborers. Such worker-wanderers established the Hobo College, published *Hobo News*, and held hotly contested elections for the hobo king. To establish *homeless man* as the term of choice for the socially displaced despite the popularity of the self-defined hobo, Anderson hearkened back to Solenberger's earlier work to provide a legitimating history to this category.

Many whose writings are integral to forming the category of the homeless man, including Anderson and Sutherland and Locke—who cite her "careful study" as an effort made "to define and secure a more adequate understanding of the problem"[36]—refer to her study as the beginning of the homeless man. By attributing to her a better understanding of unattachment, they affirm the superiority of the homeless man over other categories of displacement. They also extend their category further back into time. While it was not the dominant category at the time of Solenberger's study, she was prescient enough to understand that the urban problem was that of the homeless man and not some other form of displacement, like vagrancy.

Sutherland and Locke go on to indicate that the process of shifting the focus to homelessness—both the category and the social problem it represents—gains ground and more important institutional support in the 1920s:

> One of the earliest indications of a general shift away from concentration on the vagrancy problem to a study of the homeless man as such was the experience of the Committee on Begging and Vagrancy of the American Association for Organizing Family Social Work. This committee, organized about the time of the 1920–21 depression, soon found that it was really studying the problem of the homeless man in its larger aspects, and the name of the committee was subsequently changed to the "Committee on the Homeless." The committee emphasized that the current work done with the homeless did not have adequate organization anywhere in the country and recommended organization as the first step. They said that the policies should fall in two general classes, constructive and repressive.
>
> Thus through the decade 1920–1930 the most important development with reference to the care of the destitute homeless in America was a gradually emerging interest on the part of social work organizations, which resulted in an attempt to organize and centralize the services of the various organizations that had interested themselves in the problem.[37]

Here we see that the semantic shift from older categories like vagrant to the homeless man is later than Solenberger's 1914 study. The taxonomic and terminological consolidation took place in the sociological literature of the next two decades. As we see in this passage, in the 1920s, social work institutions serving the displaced renamed themselves after the problem of homelessness. This Committee on the Homeless was constituted at nearly the same time as the Committee on Homeless Men commissioned Anderson to write *The Hobo* as a sociology of the homeless man.[38]

While Solenberger does not signal the constitution of a homeless figure, she portends its imminent arrival. By the time Sutherland and Locke conduct their study in the mid-1930s, the homeless man is the category for social displacement. The backward nod to include her in the process is an effort to extend the reach of the homeless man further back in history. For Sutherland and Locke, it can serve to legitimate that there was a form of homelessness before the Depression of the 1930s, and for Anderson, she legitimates his semantic turn to homelessness in a study of the hobo.

Because her work is usually invoked as the Ur-study of homelessness, Solenberger's definitions and classifications become extremely important. While she erroneously argues that the homeless man has been a figure of "human society since its beginning,"[39] she does see that in the decades just before her study, new terms and greater numbers of the homeless are appearing.[40] She provides a useful point of departure for the modern homeless figure. She writes the following: "The term 'homeless man' might be applied to any man who has left one family group and not yet identified himself with another. It might include hundreds of men living in clubs, hotels, and boarding houses, and its use would not necessarily imply a forlorn or penniless condition. But for the purpose of this study the term will be used to designate those men of the homeless class who live in cheap lodging houses in the congested part of any large city."[41] Her definition of the homeless man looks very reminiscent of ones proffered by social scientists over half a century later[42] and incorporates many of the homeless characteristics that emerged in the fin-de-siècle period—urban congestion, poverty, and most importantly, being outside of family norms. Her work consolidates many of the vague ideas of homelessness floating around in the work of fin-de-siècle activists and establishes a working definition of the homeless man. This working definition was readily appropriated by both social workers providing services and sociologists like Sutherland and Locke or Bahr and Caplow. While she was not cited much at the time, her study was recuperated in later decades as her chosen category (i.e., the homeless man) became the social science category for social displacement.

The idea that homelessness is about social relations and not residential arrangements already appears in these early foundations of the homeless man. Solenberger defines the homeless man by social relations, geographically circumscribes the population to a specific urban district, and then delineates a particular set of institutions (i.e., lodging houses) by which she distinguishes the population. She actually further narrows the population by limiting the study to applicants at the Chicago Bureau of Charities;[43] that is, the population is that subset of the men without familial connections who stay in cheap lodging houses in particular sections of cities and avail themselves of the helping professions. These one thousand homeless men, who are subjected to the study because they availed themselves of services, define homelessness.

The idea of the homeless man arises in studies of the assisted; the homeless figure becomes someone subjected to a certain form of study. He is a man who has lost the near absolute freedom of the hobo. Sutherland and Locke later follow in this stead by de facto equating the homeless man with the shelter man. Homelessness becomes shaped through interactions with social services and social workers; the homeless figure is constituted through processes of managing an urban population.

Solenberger develops two distinct taxonomies for the homeless man—one for the social service administrator and another for more clearly representing the group. She posits that from the vantage point of a social worker needing to administer this population, the group includes four distinct classes of men: self-supporting, temporarily dependent, chronically dependent, and the parasitic.[44] We can see that this administrative taxonomy defines the population by the subject's reliance on bourgeois social service institutions. While these categories that assess the "degree and character of their dependence" are useful for managing the group, she proposes an alternate form of classification for clarity in discussing the pool of homeless men.[45] This latter system of classification divides "according to some common characteristic into small groups, such as insane men, aged men, boys, beggars, etc."[46] Solenberger contends that multiple taxonomic systems can fall under the rubric of the "homeless man." Here is the first move toward subordinating the varied types of social displacement under a unified category.

In 1914, the fin-de-siècle semantic chaos is still the norm; a triune division of tramps, hobos, and bums is the most common—in that taxonomy, there is no reducing beyond these three. Hobo king and sometime director of Chicago's Hobo College Ben Reitman rarely falls back onto the term *homeless*, but rather, he uses his own taxonomy. In his writings, he presents an alternate categorization of hobos, tramps, and bums based on the physical labor and motion of the homeless body. The hobo both works and moves (or wanders); the tramp wanders but does not work; the bum neither wanders nor works but remains ensconced in the city.[47] The assumption of the movement of wandering—from Cain, the Wandering Jew, exile, and the stranger—enters into these early social science taxonomies.[48]

But Nels Anderson continues with Solenberger's sociological move to have one analytic category under which the systems of classification fall—he discusses the varied taxonomies as types of hobos. However, he also starts the process of moving the typologies from that of hobos to types of homeless men. Anderson's book moves toward the mono-category in fits and starts; he cannot fully decide what the category should be. He frequently uses the then-popular term *hobo* as the category but frequently moves toward the homeless man.

The terminological shift is intertwined with Solenberger's taxonomical problem of management versus representation. The standardization of the term is integrated with the needs of the service provider. The hobo represented a population that was not easily manageable; the homeless man signified a more docile figure. To have a solitary category, the management and representation needs had to coincide or one be subordinated. The homeless man was not only more easily managed but also more easily studied—few other social scientists had Anderson's entrée into the world of the hobo. Though not for another decade (until Sutherland and Locke), this equivocation ends with the consolidation of the homeless man.

Anderson's equivocation begins with the term *hobo* itself; he seems to use it as the umbrella category quite ambivalently. We have already seen him say that the homeless man is the best way to describe the problem. He also uses the category of hobo in two different ways—a bit problematic for a single category. It is almost as if he were a timid young student unwilling to overturn conventional wisdom. After all, he was commissioned to write a report on the hobo by a group that included two of the doyens of American sociology—Robert Park and Ernest Burgess. Despite his ambivalence, he keeps the unitary category of the hobo in name only while setting the stage for a shift to the homeless man.

Because the hobo is the object of his study, he uses it as the category to frame his analysis. For Anderson, the term *hobo* has multiple levels of meaning: (1) hobo as a general term for all types of unattached men and (2) a particular subcategory of migratory laborers. The general term is evidenced by the book title; under the rubric of the "hobo," his study includes analyses of the full range of the displaced. He has a section of the book dedicated to typologies—titled "Types of Hobos." In this discussion of types of hobos, he subsumes tramps, bums, home guards, and the range of migratory workers under the single category of hobos.[49] The particular term appears in both the survey of literature and his own taxonomy, which I cited previously. However, the term is problematic for the social scientist and the service provider.

Despite writing about the hobo, Anderson already seems to be calling for a semantic shift to *homeless men*. Service providers also seem wedded to the new term; Anderson conducts his study under the auspices of the Chicago Council of Social Agencies' Committee on Homeless Men. Sutherland and Locke note the 1920s changes at the American Association for Organizing Family Social Work to establish a Committee on the Homeless. Even though the hobo was the most prominent category in the early decades of the twentieth century, the category of the homeless man was increasing in popularity.

The semantic shift marks an underlying hobophobia and a (as yet) permanent shift to the new category of homelessness; it is also inextricably intertwined with the rise of the helping professions. The three major scholarly studies—one seminal text each for the successive decades of the 1910s, 1920s, and 1930s—through which I am tracking the rise of this discourse are all collaborations with service providers.[50] For Sutherland and Locke, the homeless man is de facto synonymous with the shelter man; the same was true in Solenberger's study—she identified the homeless men as that subset of the men without familial connections who stay in cheap lodging houses in particular sections of cities and avail themselves of the helping professions.

The rise of the homeless figure as an object of knowledge is always already about managing this population; the necessity of semantic and classificatory clarity (as Solenberger showed us in her bifurcated taxonomies of management and discussion) is always connected to an explicit investigation of how best to manage the population. The shift to the homeless man rests upon the unmanageability of the hobo; this semantic shift is part of an institutional effort to rein in the wandering population.

In the decade after Sutherland and Locke's study, the term *hobo* almost completely disappears from the vocabulary of the social scientist and service provider, though it is still used within the hobo community for another couple of decades. The *hobo* is a term used, embraced, cultivated, and disseminated by the social class that these social scientists and service providers are trying to manage. The hobo's independence proves difficult for these institutions. The subordination of the category of hobo is a crucial step in consolidating the homeless man as the sole category of social displacement.

The Institutions of Homelessness

The sequestering of populations and the development of vocabulary arises through both those institutions within Skid Row and those serving and reflecting on the men of the area—they all contribute to the process of constituting the category of the homeless man. The category is developed by these institutions to describe those whose relations with society (and these institutions) is one of de facto powerlessness; that is, the category represents those men subordinated to the service and research institutions. Writing in a later era, Howard Bahr makes this powerlessness a central argument in his analysis of Skid Row: "We shall introduce one of the important themes of this work. It is that a distinguishing characteristic of the homeless is their powerlessness, and that much of the social abhorrence for Skid Row men is due to their powerlessness, itself a derivative of this disaffiliation or lack of social ties."[51] The imputed disaffiliation of the homeless man eventually becomes a broader disaffiliation than a mere lack of familial ties; the discourse expands the disaffiliation to broader voluntary and organizational relations. The hobo unions, like the International Brotherhood Welfare Association, go away with the decline of the hobo; the homeless man is left with social service agencies, Skid Row commercial interests, and social scientists who define and provide services to the disaffiliated. Social service agencies are the most conspicuous of these institutions.

While most of these are not much older than the homeless figure that they help constitute, charity, alms, and neighborliness do not appear with the modern city. The localized system of charity that reached the shores of colonial America with the Elizabethan Poor Laws[52] distinguished between supplicants from the town and outsiders.[53] Those from the local community had settlement rights to assistance from the town; one obtained these rights by being born to a family from the community or by being accepted as a town member through a vote. If a nonmember appeared likely to become dependent on the town (e.g., the disabled or widowed), they had to move on.[54] The public distribution of aid in the colonial era did not preclude private charity, which was often fulfilled as a religious obligation above the tax duties for poor relief.[55] Because this charity was so localized, the distribution of relief did not usually require an analysis of the moral character of the needy; the reputation of the individual or family receiving aid was already known. Early charitable practices functioned on principles of *Gemeinschaft*—neighbor helping neighbor. The community took care of its own, while the stranger was asked to move on.

These assessments of the supplicant, however, became commonplace over the course of the nineteenth century. The growth of the town into a metropolis often prevented the disseminator of charitable largesse from personally knowing the aid recipients and their families. Charity underwent the same sort of rationalizing transformations impacting the rest of the society. The structure of a local community taking care of itself gave way to transactional relationships in which organized charities collected funds from one group of people to distribute to a different set of people. Initially, with the burgeoning metropolis, some semblance of personal charity was maintained. In the waning decades of the nineteenth century, a protohomelessness developed, and charity changed; both were emerging from the vast urbanization taking place along the Eastern Seaboard and in other cities like Chicago: "The swift expansion of the charity organization movement represented one response of a troubled middle class to the social dislocations of the post-Civil War industrial city."[56] Organizing the bourgeois response to urban poverty was an effort to avert revolutionary upheavals; organized charity, according to late nineteenth-century commentator J. J. Cook, had "preternatural powers for fusing and moulding and tearing down and building up. Surely here, if anywhere, society will find that better thing than instantaneous revolution—gradual regeneration."[57]

The fin-de-siècle charities realized that they had no "ties of blood, sympathy or previous knowledge"[58] with the new urban populations. Yet they strove to mimic the neighborliness found in small-town life: "The charity organization ideal was to reestablish the patterns of social interaction of the small town or village, where the primary group exercised powerful social controls. The charity society was an 'artifice,' designed to restore the 'natural relations' which the city had destroyed."[59]

The *Gemeinschaft* ideals of rural life were created under the auspices of the large charity associations by establishing district offices that sent out volunteer visitors to take friendship (and not alms) to the residence of those seeking help. This paternalistic practice of the volunteer visit eventually ceded to the professional social worker, who brought training and skills to bear on the circumstances of the aid recipient. The modernizing impulses for bureaucratization, efficiency, and efficacy invaded charity, but all was in service of sustaining an ersatz *Gemeinschaft*-ideal practice in the metropolis.

While the fin-de-siècle charities still tried to model their services on *Gemeinschaft*-like neighborliness, the processes of systematizing charity led to both the formation of the profession of social work and the modern social service agency. This new agency grew out of reformers' impulses for order—they appropriated administrative systems and approaches from industry to more efficiently provide services. The social service agencies and shelters began to resemble other modern, *Gesellschaft* structures—anonymous, transactional relationships. The category of the homeless man was developed to represent people in these modern social service agencies. They emerged through the gradual demise of the neighborly visit to the needy family or individual.

These friendly visits were a form of service called outdoor relief (stipends, food, clothing, or other aid brought to the home), which began to fade, since a place of residence was, of course, necessary to receive such aid. Indoor relief (e.g., work houses, poor houses) was also available, though modeled much less on the small-town community; the Dickensian world made it across the Atlantic. Beyond this indoor relief, hobos, tramps, or bums could avail themselves of overnight shelter in police stations, at least until the advent of the municipal lodge over the 1890s.

Jacob Riis invited his friend Teddy Roosevelt, the new police commissioner, to tour the police station bunks in New York; scandalized by their squalor, Roosevelt abolished "police lodging-houses, which were simply tramp lodging-houses, and a fruitful encouragement to vagrancy."[60] After the closure of the police station bunks, the missions or municipal lodges became the major abode for tramps. The systems of indoor relief became the primary model for early homeless services, since the displaced person had no place whereby to receive aid.

The unattached went to the shelter, the mission, the labor pool, or the soup kitchen. These institutions were in a fixed location in the city; the unattached men moved to this area. The desire for efficiency prompted these agencies to locate where they could be easily accessible to the homeless. The institutions helped to consolidate a population in particular urban districts, which produced a ready-made sociological lab for academics. The process of rationalization (i.e., the desire to more efficiently locate shelters near cheap bars and pawn shops) created the districts and established the routines of those men who went to the shelters. These service agencies dotted the Bowery in New York, West Madison's Hobohemia in Chicago, and the nascent Skid Row districts of cities across the country and thus brought the forces of rationalization into these districts.

These agencies joined those other characteristic institutions of Skid Row—thrift stores, pawnshops, single-room occupancy hotels, and cheap bars—as the primary organizations with whom the nascent homeless men interacted. These primary institutions were crucial in forming the category of the homeless man. While the commercial institutions were essential in defining the spatial parameters of the homeless man, service agencies both abetted this spatial delimitation and also provided a program of evaluation, categorization, and regulation.

These service agencies established the spaces and the routines that shaped the population social scientists come to represent in the category of the homeless man. Sutherland and Locke talk about the regimented structure of the shelters and its role in shaping homeless men:

Regimentation, with its regulation and control over so many of the activities of the men and its requirement of constant waiting in line, makes the men dependent upon others for most of the things connected with their personal well-being. It lowers their morale, wastes time which might be used in looking for work, breeds a spirit of frustration and antagonism, emphasizes the men's dependency, and makes them assume less responsibility for their own welfare.

Hobohemians adjust more easily to shelter food, regimentation, and other external conditions than do non-Hobohemians. Hobohemians were habituated to a poor and coarse diet and feel at home in flophouses. The regimentation of the shelters may interfere somewhat with their freedom but it is easy to overemphasize this. For non-Hobohemians the situation is generally quite different. They were accustomed to much better food, a better bed, and a private room in a home or better class hotel. As a result, non-Hobohemians are much more disturbed by the external conditions of the shelters than are Hobohemians.[61]

The agencies gathered data, standardized the day of the shelter man, and assessed his needs and abilities while diagnosing his problems. The social science assumption was that shelters function in a continuum with the other institutions of Hobohemia to shape the men of the area into the sheltered man.[62] As Sutherland and Locke have pointed out, the twenty thousand homeless men about whom they write underwent a formative process in the slums and in the shelters. For them, the homeless man is a man who enters a shelter that forms the displaced man into a homeless man who is docile and malleable to the shelter's governance.

These primary institutions are not the sole means by which the homeless man is formed; a secondary set of institutions play an equally essential role: universities and governments, especially municipal ones. To manage the homeless, a process of reflection on services, demographics, etiologies, or habits takes place. Academic studies of social service practices and the recipients of these services begin this formation of the homeless figure. These studies define the populations, categorize them, and break down services appropriate to individual need. The second of these secondary institutions— the government—establishes policies, funds and furnishes services, and adopts certain social science data and assumptions for governance.

While these secondary institutions—universities and governments—are integral to establishing the category of the homeless man (as evidenced by the three studies we are discussing), the primary service agencies brought together the population and regulated it. The efficient running of these institutions requires a manageable population. While the fin-de-siècle need for order originated to maintain social control and avert urban violence, by the time that the category of the homeless man is established, order and efficiency are becoming ends in themselves—the fear of an imminent threat of urban violence had waned. The agencies began a process of settling a population; this process was completed by changes in labor patterns (i.e., a decrease in the demand for migratory labor).[63]

This migratory propensity of the hobos provided social service institutions with difficulties. The mobility inhibited sustained administering of social services and kept the hobo from family and other settled social relations. The relations between fellow hobos did not register as social affiliation in the assessment of shelter workers. Sutherland and Locke report that shelters "write to everyone [the homeless men] tell them about";[64] the social workers want to reach any family or settled friends. This practice frequently irritated the homeless men; those who were warned that this would happen denied having any close relatives to the shelter workers. These workers sent letters to all the family and friends mentioned by the shelter man; these were obviously people with a known address (i.e., settled friends).

The shelter workers did not pursue social relations among fellow Skid Row men as possible sources of stability for the shelter man. Fellow hobos were not easily tracked down via mail and were not stable enough to help the hobo settle down. In describing mobility's complications, Anderson focuses on the impact to those institutions within the Skid Row area:

> The mobility of the migratory worker complicates the problem of the missions, police, and welfare agencies. The mission measures its success not only in numbers of converts but in the numbers of men fed and lodged. The police department, on the contrary, alarmed by the influx of hobos and tramps in response to free meals and free flops, has adopted a policy of severity and repression for the protection of the community. Welfare agencies, opposing alike the demoralizing results of indiscriminate feeding and lodging, and the negative policy of the police, favor a program of organized effort based upon an investigation of the needs of each individual case.[65]

Investigations of each case require ongoing access to the subject being studied. Fact checking, tracking down family members, or enrolling a subject into a program adequate for a specific need all take time.[66] As we shall see in the next chapter, only a certain form of relationship is thought adequate to moor people to society—the passing relationships between fellow hobos were deemed by sociologists to be too limited for social mooring. Their wandering inhibits the shelter workers' efforts to rehabilitate the wanderer.

When clients wander from city to city, most efforts to engage them in some social service are pointless. Rehabilitation is, after all, an act of settling; a state of semisettledness (or at least an openness to this possibility) is necessary to begin the rehabilitation process. The influx of these wandering men necessitated state intervention (police) "for the protection of the community"; these early homeless men—defined by family disaffiliation—were a threat to the community. Their mobility (among other characteristics) was socially problematic.

Yet the hobo embraces wandering and unattachment. The lack of mooring in broader social networks is precisely what recommends the hobo style of life. The advent of hobos is not merely a response to capital's demands to expand transportation and industry across the country. Certainly, these migratory workers fulfilled that role. But hobodom provides a life, a community, and a means of support to those with no family or no interest in maintaining family contacts. As Amos Warner pointed out in Chapter 2, new technology like trains and steamers afforded those afflicted with wanderlust a mobility never before seen. The hundreds of miles that once had to be walked could now be crossed sitting in a boxcar. Unattachment was a desired and sought position for the hobo; they legitimated the independence that shelters tried to rein in.

The hobos embodied the threats to family life, which we saw associated with the prototramp; life had become easier for wanderers to, in Warner's words, "get away from their *duties to families and neighbor.*"[67] The homeless man was a man detached from family, but with the intervention of the shelter worker, Sutherland and Locke pointed out, he might be restored to some family, friend, or other settled person. The hobo not only withdrew from family duties; he stayed outside of most bourgeois sociality—the world of the hobo was a world unto itself. They did not need the middle-class institutions or social relations.

The hobos provided a counterorganizing schema to the shelters, missions, and soup kitchens of Hobohemia. They had their own associational life. They had unions, like the International Brotherhood Welfare Association; the more radical union, International Workers of the World, also penetrated into the hobo community to organize migratory labor. They developed their own institutions for education and services, like the Hobo Colleges. Hobo newspapers, like the *Hobo News* or the *Hobo News Review*, disseminated information about organizations, events, or recommended reading. This infrastructure of associational life itself exacerbated bourgeois anxieties. This associational life was embraced in lieu of kinship bonds. A primary goal of managing the homeless populations was to restore the homeless man to family bonds.

This restoration, however, was rarely complete. The homeless man was first and foremost the other—the one defined by a lack of home. The process of defining this population through a delimitation of space, language and institutions rendered the homeless of Skid Row as a group to be managed or contained. Assimilation consisted of molding the homeless man into a docile body who scarcely threatened the social order. After these large frameworks of space, language, and institutions established the parameters of the population, sociologists soon consolidated the category of the homeless man. The residents of Skid Row districts who availed themselves of the area's service institutions became the homeless figures—the remainder of the city was now exempt from this moniker. The population of the homeless shrank from the fin-de-siècle city to residents of the slums. As the poor families became Americanized, they raised out of the ranks of the homeless, which left primarily single men in the Skid Row districts of the city. The American city was no longer inherently a locus of displacement.

CHAPTER 4

The Limits of Hobosociality for Social Mooring

By the mid-1930s, there is a clear shift, or at least a consolidation, in thinking about social detachment. Social worker/activist, social-scientific, and nascent government policy discourses coalesce around the new category of the homeless man. Taxonomic categories and terminologies all become subsumed under the rubric of the "homeless man." This new figure supplants many categories used by earlier activists and sociologists. The homeless throngs of the city, which were a volcano imminently rising against the middle class, became a population to be managed. New infrastructures of administration and new categories of analysis formed a set of assumptions about this homeless man. Rules of shelters, routines and managerial disciplines, and intersecting factions of interests—business leaders, elected officials, clergy, social workers, police, and sociologists—all subjected this homeless man to their valuations. In the process of constituting this new category of homelessness, social workers and sociologists subordinated competing categories that could threaten the stability of this figure as the unitary category for social detachment. Spatial, discursive, and institutional distinctions demarcated that population social science identified as being the homeless men.

While, as we saw with Anderson, early decades of the twentieth century saw many terms and taxonomic categories being juxtaposed against each other (tramps, bums, the home guard, or lingering categories like vagrants), the hobo in particular maintained a position that endangered the formation of a homeless figure. The hobo was a self-defined, independent man not easily subdued by social services. Occasional encounters with service providers were too brief to enmesh him into a system of welfare. As the other categories (e.g., tramps, bums) waned, the hobo continued to be used as a category for social displacement right up until the consolidation of the emerging homeless man.

The category of the homeless man was constituted through the gaze of sociologists, service providers, municipal and business leaders, and business interests. Sutherland and Locke's *Twenty Thousand Homeless Men* correctly argues that a homeless man is clearly constituted through the intersection of these self-interested discourses. These two sociologists conducted their University of Chicago–funded study[1] and concluded that a broad range of community interests shaped shelter policies (and thus the shelter or home-less man) for their own sake:

> The social pressures which have influenced shelter policies constitute an illumi-nating chapter in the history of homeless men. These pressures have been exerted by religious, political, social work, business, and other groups in the community. While these groups were somewhat at variance with each other during the period 1901–1930, they have come into overt conflict for domination of the shelters since 1931. Both in the earlier and in the later periods most of these groups were interested primarily in their own welfare and only secondarily or not at all in the welfare of homeless men.[2]

As we also saw in the fin-de-siècle period, many of the social reforms and services provided were for the interests of the service provider, while those receiving the service were relatively incidental (e.g., Jacob Riis's reform as self-defense). By this Depression-era look back at the first several decades of the twentieth century, the self-interest of the homeless service providers is accepted as a foregone conclusion by this Chicago School study. The cat-egory of the homeless man is constituted to protect the interests of middle-class religious, business, and political leaders.

This new homeless man became a repository of anxieties—the perils of modern metropolitan life rested within this new figure. This homeless man is urban refuse; he represents those who are unable to be assimilated to the social life of the bourgeois city. The city divided against itself. It demanded labor for factory production, but when more labor appeared, the city had no answer, no provision for these poor masses. As Sutherland and Locke note, "we find that modern society has not been organized or planned for the satisfaction of the basic needs of a great mass of the population, from which the homeless men in the shelters have come as representatives."[3] These poor are the labor surplus, which the city cannot absorb. This surplus shrunk from the late nineteenth century as the schools, tenements, and economy slowly integrated more of the poor population into bourgeois social norms. The figure represents the underside of the city, that side that is necessary to produce a style of life for the top half. These are subjected to the outrageous misfortunes of poverty; they are shorn of symbols of status to a point of degradation.[4] The impoverished man entered shelters and underwent a process of "shelterization."

As we saw previously, Sutherland and Locke contend that the shelter system primarily serves the interests of a constellation of religious, political, business, and social work groups—that is, the normative group against whom the term *homeless* is implicitly juxtaposed. This process of shelterization begins long before the homeless man enters the shelter[5]—it starts with the commercial and spatial interactions in Skid Row, the Bowery, or Hobohemia.

For Sutherland and Locke, the shelterization process is the process of making a homeless man. The routines of social work bureaucracies finally shape these men into the shelter man; these agencies subjected the men to endless repetitions that produced a docility such that the service provider could cajole, manipulate, and manage. I here quote extensively from Sutherland and Locke's discussion of shelter initiation, since their accounts confirm the role of routine in shaping certain types of compliant, docile subjects—much like other large, mass institutions of regulation like the military or penal system. They write the following:

> It seems to me that the red tape of the shelters makes the men lose their sense of responsibility and initiative. Their whole life is regulated for them; they are told when and where to sleep, are awakened at the same time day in and day out, are told how much, or better how little, to eat, and when and what should be eaten. In fact, their daily routine is wholly a matter of program. Certain days and at certain periods on those prescribed days, they do certain things in a certain way. Everything is a matter of routine; and to make certain that the men do not even have to use their minds to remember these prescribed duties, they are bulletined all over the building.
>
> Day after day there is a constant repetition of the same thing: line up to dress, line up to eat, line up for fumigation, line up to take a bath, line up to work, line up to get paid. "Why in hell don't they line us up against the wall and shoot us and get it over with."[6]

And once initiated, the program takes hold of one and eliminates individual will; one becomes a subject of the shelter—it determines what the homeless man does. They continue with the following:

> The monotony of the thing at first weighs on one's mind, but with the passing of time this condition slowly changes, and only at infrequent intervals, which become more widely separated, does this monotony bother him. It is not only the monotony of shelter life but the absolute aimlessness of the things one does. There is no end to accomplish, nothing to look forward to, no reason why one should even do the things he does . . . A man's life becomes narrowed to a limited sphere of action, and after a few months his independence is broken down, his individuality disappears, his identity is lost, his personality becomes reorganized, and he becomes shelterized.[7]

This shelterized man is the homeless man; the moment of interpellation is deferred until the 1980s, but the subject is de facto formed at this stage. The disciplines of shelter life panoptically shape him into a homeless man. This man is defined by his social disaffiliation—he is the man without a family.

In Chapter 5, we look at the social life of the homeless man and how the rise of the disaffiliation thesis relates to the formation of the category of the nuclear family. In the discourse on homelessness, the family is the presumed foundation for social life; other forms of sociality, like that of the hobo community, were inadequate to moor one in society. Because of this centrality of the family, sociologists and social workers reject the alternative hobosociality.

The importance of family is evident in the category of homelessness itself. To be homeless is to be without a family. At least since Alice Solenberger's study, homelessness is always about leaving a family. The centrality of family to this discourse reflects broader theoretical frameworks shaping the homeless man. Earlier I noted Jacob Riis's fear that the rise of the associational life of civil society (groups like Robert Putnam's venerated bowling teams) would destroy the family. The social work profession assumed that being with one's family is a necessary good—so much so that the social workers, according to Sutherland and Locke, sent letters to the families of all the new shelter men. The hobos certainly had a vibrant associational life, but these types of social relations were irrelevant to the helping professions. In fact, we have seen that the intersecting bourgeois interest groups wanted to settle the hobo community into sheltered life (the hobo life was a threat to bourgeois family norms). Reestablishing the man's relationship to a family (natal or conjugal would do), they presumably hoped to settle him down and tie him into social life.

The 1936 Hollywood screwball comedy *My Man Godfrey* (directed by Gregory L Cava) affirmed the necessity for a family and the inadequacy of the hobosocial community. The film denies Godfrey his retreat to the hobosocial world of his fellow homeless men, despite establishing a profitable club in which the men work and building permanent flats in lieu of shanties. This early social entrepreneurship affords a world in which Godfrey may work and live with his fellow forgotten men. But both the generic imperatives of Hollywood romantic comedies and the cultural assumptions shaped by the discourse on homelessness inhibit this denouement. The movie closes with him quickly marrying to settle him into a family and not the community of men.

This hyperbolic concern with the family highlights a rift that is still a central debate in the contemporary American public sphere—that is, the family values and social capital movements. I shall return to these debates in Part IV, when we encounter the attempts to decouple family anxieties from the homeless figure to join them with broader movements concerned with social capital. The family values movement laments threats to community, which is based on kinship and place. The putative *Gemeinschaft* has dwindled to the nuclear family; as the last bastion of this type of social relations, it is vehemently clung to. The thesis of declining social capital laments the loss of voluntary life; the associations were networks of transactional reciprocity in which the social relations have an exchange value. Both factions look at the presumed precipice of unmitigated individualism and fear its nihilistic propensities. However, they offer contradictory proposals to redress supposed social ills: one an embrace of modernity and the other a critique of it.

These tensions are evident in the discourse on homelessness. Large-scale debate about the best form of social structures in the United States, I contend, is basically coterminous (and often coextensive) with the rise of the discourse on homelessness. These debates arose as Americans attempted to negotiate the ravages of modernization and the havoc it wrought on social life; these are the very same debates from which the discourse on homelessness emerged. For instance, Jacob Riis and Jane Addams were integral to early talk about proper social relations in a modernizing America. Fin-de-siècle commentators responded to social changes with calls to do whatever was necessary to protect the family. The homeless man is constituted through an atavistic desire for a return to a supposedly lost social form—that community life thought to foster family. The contemporary family values movement is the intellectual progeny of these reformers' efforts to make the city safe for the family.

In the Depression era, the fields of social work and sociology were still identifying the family as the proper form of sociality and actively sought to destroy the alternative hobosocial community. Even though there was a vibrant social life in the hobo jungle, it was excoriated as a locus of vice and pathology. The elaborate range of associations—like the International Brotherhood Welfare Association, Hoboes of America, the Hobo College, and even the International Workers of the World—were not hallmarks of the social connectedness of the hobo. The discourse on homelessness was at this time primarily blind to such institutions, and when they were acknowledged (e.g., in Anderson's *The Hobo*), it is not as a viable alternative to other social services.

Hobosociality was insufficient for social mooring because of two interrelated reasons. The first relates to my argument about family. An implicit Hegelian model of concentric relations grounds civil society in the family; on this read, the family must be the root institution of society. The interconnected social structures are the Hegelian series of concentric relations between the family, civil society, and the state. In this model, the broader social structures are predicated on the preceding ones—each structure is the building block for next one. Thus presumably, without family relations, one is not interconnected to civil society and the state. However, most associational life is not mediated through the family (excepting, probably religion); one usually joins voluntary clubs as an individual. These two social forms enter into tension because their structures are predicated on different expectations about the nature of social relations. Figures like Riis or the more recent Focus on the Family or Family Research Council presume that families provide primary relations that are not self-interested. While not necessarily altruistic, these relations are supposedly organic ones of binding sentiment; they are not instrumental but ends in themselves, whereas the associational life of social capital is still ultimately about productivity. We need not turn back to Marx[8] for this point; Robert Putnam's analogy between social capital and other forms of capital makes this explicit: "By analogy with notions of physical capital and human capital—tools and training that enhance individual productivity—the core idea of social capital theory is that social networks have value. Just as a screwdriver (physical capital) or a college education (human capital) can increase productivity (both individual and collective), so too social contacts affect the productivity of individuals and groups."[9] Social capital increases individual productivity. While the means-ends distinctions of these social relations are more idealistic than empirical, the assumption that organic familial relations—rather than those of voluntary association—will solve presumed social ills underlies the contradictions that we shall confront as we later look at efforts to assimilate concerns for the family with those of social capital.

This assumption that familial relations are the panacea for presumed social ills is taken up in the discourse on homelessness and the social work/sociological institutions producing this discourse. The helping professions dismiss the associations of the hobos and homeless for a second reason. These associations create a locus beyond the reach of bourgeois institutions. By being under constant observation, the shelter man posed relatively little social or political threat, while the hobo institutions were beyond this vigilant eye; surveillance does not fully extend to the hobo jungle or unions—though a quick study of the FBI's investigative files on James Eads How (the so-called hobo millionaire) or Ben Reitman, among others, shows that this surveillance actually did reach into these associations. Even if some clandestine monitoring of the hobo associations could happen, the surveillance was not as effective as techniques of management for averting social upheaval. The associations did not usually subject themselves to the tools for assimilating the homeless "into more profitable uses," as Bahr phrases it. The IBWA was created to establish a modicum of hobo self-sufficiency by supporting the independence of the hobo community from broader social institutions.

Early research on social services, like that of Sutherland and Locke, has argued that the services primarily maintain the interests of service providers. If the interests of the individual hobos were central, such agencies would try to integrate them into the thriving hobo social networks. Instead, as we saw previously, shelter workers attempt to contact any family or settled relatives of those whom they serve. However, the discourse on homelessness grew out of fear; these fears rose in response to the uprisings of the Draft Riots, the Haymarket Riot, the Tompkins Square Riot, and the "Bread or Blood" demonstrations. Here I must distinguish between a particular objection to the hobo associations for mooring individuals and a more general problem of associational life. Service provider objections could be to the class of the association and not to associations per se. But the social workers in shelters did not try to plug the homeless men into bourgeois associations; they sent letters to family members. In Part I, we saw Jacob Riis object to bourgeois associations for undermining family life. The family was the institution of choice for mooring people, to reattach the disaffiliated. In part, the discourse on homelessness arose through efforts to preserve the family; it was taken as the foundational institution for social life. Other institutions or social relationships were inadequate.

This discourse on homelessness excludes the hobo, who eludes the shelters and other institutions of homelessness; this exclusion marginalizes him. The exclusions happened through processes of defining and describing the new homeless man as well as through institutional distinctions—the hobo did not frequent the shelters but did go to his own organizations. By the mid-1930s, sociological and social work discourses focused on the homeless man; the hobo became a nonentity. A small, aging hobo population with few remaining institutions lingered in obscurity as social disaffiliation and the homeless man take center stage in studies and social services. The labor demands of the Second World War eliminated the hobo life.

To carve a niche for the homeless man, sociologists dismissed the hobo as the normative category for social displacement. More than the institutional resistance, more than his wandering, the hobo carried a lore that legitimated him and his decisions. From Frank Beck's Whitman quote in the last chapter, we have seen a propensity to both valorize the wandering spirit and wrap it up in an American lore. Anderson writes about this lore: "Hobos have a romantic place in our history. From the beginning they have been numbered among the pioneers. They have played an important role in reclaiming the desert and in subduing the trackless forests. They have contributed more to the open, frank, and adventurous spirit of the Old West than we are always willing to admit. They are, as it were, belated frontiersmen. Their presence in the migrant group has been the chief factor in making the American vagabond class different from that of any other country."[10] This unique status of the hobo made him less docile and less malleable. While mobility presented logistical difficulties to assimilationist efforts, the romance legitimated the hobos' refusal to settle and integrate into a life thought to be unthreatening to an anxious middle class.

Years later, in a reflection on the relationship of Skid Row homeless men to the broader society, Howard Bahr opined that efforts of assimilation were part of a civilizing mission:

> The Skid Row men are of interest because in many respects their ideas and customs are the antithesis of much that the "civilized" American sees as valuable and

sacred. Yet every year many outsiders join the tribe, and after a short time they cannot be distinguished from the natives. Further, they and several related tribes located on reservations in other areas of the country have been recognized as problems and objects of social action for many years. In general, the basic question has been: "Is it better to leave the tribesmen [the homeless men] alone on their reservation [Skid Row] or shall we disperse them and try to socialize them into the dominant population?" As with other minority populations, the public has been concerned with the problem of assimilating the tribesmen, often against their will, into more profitable uses.[11]

The interventions that formed model citizens of those receiving assistance from the helping professions not only could not reach the hobo; there was insufficient demand to reform this rugged pioneer who represented a certain form of Americana. While the hobo was in tension with these normative assumptions of proper social relations, he was not to be integrated into the civilized America. The fears of hobosociality did morph into, include, and overlay anxieties of homosexuality—we shall return to this point in the next chapter. Thus the romantic lore of this American ideal was problematic on many grounds. The hobo was another ideal—the Western pioneer—which could not be a model for everyone but could be trusted to disappear with the foreclosure of the frontier. The homeless man was not a mere resister to the bourgeois norms for family life; he was their antithesis.

While a sense of community may have existed among the hobos, social scientists found it an inadequate mooring into social life. The alternate form of social life exacerbated middle-class fears—the hobos were under government surveillance and, as we shall see in the next chapter, represented threats to normative heterosexual mores. The fracturing of sociality into any number of forms could undercut the hegemonic position of the emerging nuclear family as the basis for social life. By establishing the homeless man as the unitary category of social displacement, sociologists working in Chicago ensured that this framework for social life would continue—any threat to family and home was othered. With the demise of the hobo, all the socially displaced were now subsumed by the home-homeless juxtaposition. The hobo community and its alternative institutions, unions, associations, and social practices carved niches not subsumed by this dialectic. Social science had no room for the hobo or hobosociality; the threats to the social order all collapsed into the figure of the homeless man. Everyone either participated in family life (or did not challenge its dominance in the social order) or was rendered homeless.

CHAPTER 5

Homelessness as Disaffiliation

Hobosociality was an alternate form of social life; it integrated freedom with a wandering spirit.[1] The hobo community was a group still governed by its own norms and thus remained outside of the urban structures of governmentality, while the homeless figure was also displaced but subordinated to these structures. The marginalization of hobos and their community brought displacement under the purview of a rationalizing city and its structures of governmentality—through this process the homeless man was formed.

The sociological consolidation of homelessness as the normative category of social displacement required spatial, linguistic, and institutional segregation of the displaced from broader populations and the marginalization of the competing category of the hobo. *Homelessness* became ascendant first as an analytic category and only later as a popular term. After the homeless man was established as the category of social displacement, much sociological work shifted to fleshing out this category. In the next few decades following the Depression-era marginalization of the hobo, the category of homelessness became a more extensive sociological term. Many core attributes were carried over from the early fin-de-siècle responses to urban problems, which were formulated with mythic tropes: separation from and threat to family and an odd combination of settled and unsettled (from the Cain tradition), a sense of being in but not of a place (from the Wandering Jew and the stranger), and an imputation of pathology (from the Cain and Ishmael traditions). Social scientists began to systematically codify these loose assumptions in the development of the category of the homeless man.

Loneliness and the Nuclear Family

The consolidation of the categories of social displacement into the homeless man is coextensive with broader shifts in the bourgeois family. The family does not go nuclear until after the bomb, but the movement toward this category is already under way in broader sociological work. The homeless figure comes to be defined as the disaffiliated man; the formation of this definition is closely intertwined with two important developments in the social sciences: the advent of the concept of the nuclear family and the near simultaneous rise in sociological studies on loneliness.

These two developments in social science provided a dual framework for developing the category of disaffiliation. At this midcentury point, American sociologists regarded the nuclear family as the last bastion of sentiment relations and a bulwark against the increasing threats of modernity. For them, either loneliness threatened the family or the family was to be a panacea against the emerging problem of isolation. The 1949 coining of the "nuclear family" in the work of anthropologist George Peter Murdock and the early 1950s proliferation of studies on loneliness—for example, David Riesman's *The Lonely Crowd*, Paul Halmos's *Solitude and Privacy*, and Margaret Mary Wood's *Paths of Loneliness*—are major steps on the way to clearly demarcating the homeless figure as the disaffiliated man. While in Sutherland and Locke the homeless man was the sheltered man, this emerging homeless man becomes mediated through the problem of loneliness and its relation to the nuclear family. The new figure becomes the disaffiliated man.

Sentiment and Interest Relations

The paths of isolation taken to form this figure go through Mary Margaret Wood's 1953 study on loneliness; she expands the trendy topic to include the unemployed, the hobo, and the homeless. Wood makes explicit the discursive connections between *Gemeinschaft*, family, and the problem of homelessness. Her analysis relies on Theodore Abel's two categories of social relations: sentiment relations and interest relations.[2] Abel points out that in his *Gemeinschaft und Gesellschaft*, Tönnies was "the first to recognize the difference between what we have termed interest and sentiment relations."[3] By invoking the sentiment/interest (or *Gemeinschaft/Gesellschaft*) distinctions in relations, Wood defines this homeless figure as the disaffiliated man.

Commentators and social scientists felt that the expansion of the field of interest relations in the United States in the first half of the twentieth century coincided with the contraction in that of sentiment relations. These, Wood argues, are narrowed nearly to the point of the nuclear family. She writes, "The field of the sentiment relationships has, on the contrary, been narrowed. The concept of the family, which is the great fountainhead of the sentiment relationships, has become more exclusive. Generally, only the more immediate kin are now included within the family circle. The obligations of kinship which formerly held the larger inclusive family structure together have ceased to function except among near kin, and even here they tend to be replaced by bonds of a different nature."[4] The immediate family becomes the last bastion of sentiment and emotion. It is the last haven against a modern world of pure instrumentality. However problematic this vision of the family might be, it enables the inevitable relation between home and family; this relation renders those disconnected from a family as homeless. The bonds of a different nature (i.e., transactional relationships) are those whose rise Jacob Riis lamented; these outside demands drew people away from the family altar. This separation from family, and thus any form of sentimental ties, is an unnatural aberration;[5] Wood and the 1950s loneliness literature cannot imagine meaningful relations in the modern world unless mediated through the nuclear family. The man—and here Wood is more interesting than most commentators on homelessness, for she looks fleetingly at single women in boarding houses— disconnected from a family is homeless. In her analysis of poor or working class men who are unmarried and have little education, she contends that they are "largely deprived of the good times more fortunately placed young men and women have together. When they are older, the tragedy of homelessness is borne upon them."[6] Without the stability afforded by the family and its close personal relationships, those homeless men are lonely and restless; Wood argues that their mobility is an effort to escape their loneliness.[7]

As we saw in our discussion of hobos and radicals in Chapter 2, sociologist Robert Park has a different account of the role of mobility in homelessness—mobility is a basic animal instinct that is overridden by the desire for place. The hobo's pure motion indicates animalistic impulses unchecked by civilization. Wood finds the mobility of the lonely homeless to follow the familial disconnection—wandering is a fleeing from loneliness in search of some more adequate relations. In Park's account, the locomotion of the hobo is movement for its own sake, not Wood's purposeful flight from isolation to a quest for new fulfillment. For Park, "restlessness and the impulse to escape from the routine of ordinary life, which in the case of others frequently marks the beginning of some new enterprise, spends itself for him [the hobo] in movements that are expressive merely. The hobo seeks change solely for the sake of change; it is a habit, and like the drug habit, moves in a vicious circle. The more he wanders, the more he must."[8] The unfettered animalistic impulses of the hobos set this community outside of the civilizing roles of metropolitan institutions, and somehow their own institutions served no civilizing role.[9]

Park's argument implies that the ever-new, ever-changing hobo life prevents the civilizing roles of stability. The social relations of modern associational life—that is, interest relations or *Gesellschaft*—require reining in unfettered mobility.[10] Society cannot exist with the extreme individual freedom of unmitigated mobility. The city brought rules and order to govern itself when the multiculturalism of the metropolis undermined the possibility of an informal set of norms of a homogeneous community. Mobility resists the strictures of society. As I noted earlier, cultural pressures, or civilization, are necessary to correct hobo locomotion. Park even finds that the meager cultural products of the hobos—a few poems—are primarily produced at times of enforced stability (i.e., prison). Civilization must furnish norms and social relations to check locomotion and tie the homeless man to place.

While Wood and Park differ on mobility as a means or an end, while Anderson thinks it is both, they all find family to be the appropriate palliative—this common ground is the important point. Being without wife and child, according to Anderson, increases the hobo's mobility and instability.[11] For Wood, the figure's integration into family averts the loneliness that gives rise to wandering. For Park, a similar process takes place: "The hobo, who begins his career by breaking the local ties that bound him to his family and his neighborhood, has ended by breaking all other associations. He is not only a 'homeless man,' but a man without a cause and without a country."[12] But the locomotion is not a condition that arises only after ties with family are severed. For Park, locomotion is the rejection of civilization; for Woods, it is a search for it. In both cases, there is an inadequate family.

The Nuclear Family

The disaffiliated man appears in this literature on homelessness after the idea of *Gemeinschaft* and its sentiment relations contract to the nuclear family. At this point, anyone outside the orbit of a nuclear family is represented as being unable to have strong, meaningful, and emotional bonds. Social affiliation means affiliation with a family; the word *affiliation* here fulfills its gendered etymology—adopting as a son. The disaffiliated man has broken the bonds with his natal family and does not have (or has also broken) any with a conjugal one. Because he is not linked to a family and its locus, he is homeless. Disaffiliated man became the normative definition of the homeless figure through these 1950s developments and continued as a prominent analytical category into the early 1970s. In this period, many explanations developed for the homelessness of this figure, but they all maintained that the problem of social disaffiliation was at the root of homelessness.

While this consolidation of social sciences around this univocal account of homelessness has not sustained to the present (a decline to be explored in Part III), for a couple of decades, the problem of homelessness was the problem of the disaffiliated man. Columbia University sociologist Theodore Caplow described this state of sociology as a consensus about the origins of homelessness, despite being a proliferation of terms for displacement. He wrote the following:

> If we compare the various explanations that have been offered, taking account of divergent terminologies, we discover that there is not really much disagreement nowadays about the etiology of homelessness. Whether the homeless man is described as under-socialized, sociopathic, anomic, nonaffiliated, kin-isolated, attitudinally passive, non-addictively alcoholic, having a negative ego-image, or economically marginal, the diagnosis reflects substantial agreement about his condition and its origins. The typical homeless man has had a long history of social undernourishment which has discouraged him from seeking satisfaction in family relationships, self-improvement, voluntary associations, or work.[13]

By the time of this 1970 essay, this consensus was on the brink of fracturing. Much like Anderson before him, Caplow wrote of a culture about to be entirely transformed by broader social changes—an overseas war, deinstitutionalization of the mentally ill, industrial flight from urban centers, and dramatic increases in unattached females. But in this moment of reflection, Caplow describes the homeless man as being without any social attachments. Elsewhere, he makes it clear that homelessness is a condition in which affiliative bonds are absent or attenuated. In this definition of homelessness, he contends that homelessness is best understood through studies in the difference between the homeless and settled persons.[14] In such studies, we would presumably find the links that tie settled persons, links

like family or voluntary associations. Caplow opens the possibility of relationships more broadly than the nuclear family to include the associational
life of civil society.

This seeming shift in juxtaposing the homeless man to the family to a
newer contrast between the homeless man and any social bonds is not as
stark as it first appears. Caplow's definition is the "absence or attenuation
of the affiliative bonds that links settled persons to a network of interconnected social structures."[15] These interconnected social structures are the
series of concentric relations between the family, civil society, and the state
of which I spoke in the last section. As I pointed out, this model erroneously posits that the family is the institution that facilitates one's access to
these other relations. While Caplow wants to integrate homeless men into
multiple social structures, the family is still fundamental to his analysis.
Though he might seem to legitimate a broader social engagement for the
homeless (e.g., their own associations), he does not move the disaffiliation
thesis beyond its connections to the nuclear family.

Elsewhere, research that came out of Caplow's collaboration with Howard Bahr seems to undermine the connections between homelessness and
the family. Bahr's paper "Family Size and Stability as Antecedents of Homelessness and Excessive Drinking"[16]—which came from a multiyear research
project on which Caplow was the principal investigator[17]—at first appears
to belie my thesis that the homeless figure is constructed as the other of the
bourgeois family. He argues that survey data cannot establish that either size
or stability of the natal family can be considered significant indicators in
the etiology of homelessness (or excessive drinking). However, this study by
Bahr and Caplow does not claim that homeless men lack this disconnection
with family. They are analyzing the family in which the homeless men grew
up; that is, this study is a sociological analysis of the historical background
of the homeless man, not a survey of his present state. In fact, they actually reaffirm that home signifies family and thus maintain the dialectical
negation of family in the discourse on homelessness. Bahr here analyzes
some of the literature on "broken homes," which he defines as "a family in
which at least one of the parents is permanently absent."[18] Here he makes a
direct correspondence between home and family; the only modification he
provides from the term *family* corresponds to the modification of "home"
by "broken."

The sociological thesis that homelessness is a state of disaffiliation maintains the fin-de-siècle-era assumption that homelessness is a condition of

being outside of or threatening to family norms. Even when social science starts to talk about integrating homeless men into a broader range of social structures, the centrality of the nuclear family sustains.

Deviance as Threat to the Family

This practice of locating an etiology of homelessness in family background became commonplace. It not only affirms the home-homeless dichotomy but also precipitates the propensity to define threats to the family. We saw Bahr identify family break up and excessive drinking as common problems or pathologies contributing to homelessness. Homelessness continues into the 1970s to be a state of violation of family norms. Initially in the fin-de-siècle period, homelessness threatened to entirely displace the bourgeois family. Eventually, the category of homeless was reduced from an overarching threat to family to a mere violation of family norms. These violations, nonetheless, elicited much anxiety.

Donald Bogue dedicates a chapter to this line of inquiry into the pathology in the family of origin. While he finds that a poor home environment is conducive to marital strife, adult nonmarriage, or alcohol problems,[19] he concludes that coming from a good home[20] is no guarantee against ending up on Skid Row. He likewise dedicates a chapter to the family life of men on Skid Row. Throughout the 1950s and 1960s, studies of homelessness frequently analyzed their subjects' natal and conjugal backgrounds; the homeless man could not be understood apart from a relationship (or lack thereof) with family. When family background proves insufficient to account for the figure's homelessness, studies follow Bogue's pattern to determine why the man remained single; that is, the normative expectation is conjugality. The single adult male deviates from this norm, and so the deviance must be accounted for. Other forms of deviance are tested to assess their role in abetting deviation from family norms; drinking habits, infidelity, and sex lives of the homeless man are subjected to scrutiny.

The sexuality of the homeless man was a source of anxiety before Bogue's 1960s story. From the older days of the hobo, the possibility of homosexuality receives passing (or sometimes oblique) mention but is rarely dwelt upon. These communities of men with few, if any, social ties were thought to provide a forum for this supposed sexual deviance. Nels Anderson—who, with an air of discomfort, most extensively explores the role of homosexuality in hobo culture—explains the "perversion" of homosexuality as the result of sex isolation.[21] Bogue, however, looks at homosexuality as a prior condition to possibly account for a lack of desire for marriage. He concludes that most of the single men in Skid Row are not "active homosexuals" but merely undersexed men with a low level of interest in women, though there is a "small but significant proportion of active homosexuals."[22]

Whether homosexuality is considered an effect of isolation from women (Anderson) or a possible cause of this isolation (Bogue), the implicit question (or perhaps, not so implicit)[23] remains: *why is this man not married?* or *why is he not in a family?* The homeless man remains at odds with the more common familial expectations of "civilized Americans." Obviously, more is at stake in these sexual anxieties than a lack of marriage. However, I am focusing on the anxieties about the family.

The anxieties about family are more than sexual threats to heteronormativity, but this homophobia does exacerbate the perceived threats of the homeless man. Anderson's account of homosexual activity arising from sexual isolation from women reveals an alarming fear of the inevitable result of those who do not have proper relations with the family. Margaret Mary Wood reaches a similar conclusion: men who have no outlet for their emotional needs other than other men will establish these seemingly abnormal relationships.[24] In the Anderson/Wood interpretation, the failure to integrate the homeless man into family life can lead to familial destruction—no new families will emerge from the same-sex relationships. This unfounded fear of the family's demise through a lack of conjugality is rarely played out fully; Anderson stops short of unwinding the implications.

The unease about sexuality is related to a broader concern about gender roles and the proper form of domesticity. In the hobo jungle (camps along train routes), the hobo "can become domesticated without the aid of women . . . The hobo learns here the housewife's art of keeping pots clean and the camp in order."[25] Beecher and Stowe showed us that the housewife's art—or her domestic science—is the female role, for the home is her domain. Hobosociality upends these norms; bending gender and sexuality norms exacerbates the perceived threats to family life. The anxieties about threats to the bourgeois family are not always fully articulated—angst rarely is.

While the assumption of gender roles (and their relationship to family norms) is central to the discourse on homelessness, our concern with these articulations of "deviance" is broader than the sum of pathologies. These sociologists assess each deviance—alcoholism, infidelity, homosexuality, violation of gender norms, and so on—in terms of its relation to the nuclear family. They ask questions like the following: Does the pathology arise from the family of origin? Does the deviance inhibit the man from starting a family? Did the deviance lead to the breakup of his family? In the sociological work on homelessness through the 1960s, etiology and pathology are articulated only with respect to the category of the nuclear family.

Testing the Disaffiliation Thesis

Toward the end of this period, the necessary relation between family and homelessness appears to be brought into question. Sociologists using the disaffiliation thesis had until this time defined disaffiliation as the separation from family relationships. Thus the research into the pathology and deviance of the homeless man always focused on their relationship to family. This concern oriented to questions of either etiology—*what in the natal family contributed to the pathology and/or disaffiliation?*—or pathology to explain the man's inability to establish a family. But over the course of the Bowery Project, the definition of disaffiliation was called into question; the researchers wondered if disaffiliation was only connected with the family.

In another publication from their multiyear Bowery Project, Caplow and Bahr point out that they shifted their definitions of homelessness over the course of their study. They began with one that included the traits of family relations, age, amount of rent paid, and employment status.[26] They later shift to a seemingly broader sense of general disaffiliation: "We moved in time to the position that homelessness is a condition of general disaffiliation from social organizations. Traditionally, the homeless man has been viewed as 'unattached,' and to describe homelessness in terms of disaffiliation is not an extreme departure from earlier definitions, but it does extend the phenomenon from the skid-row population to all persons characterized by the absence or attenuation of affiliative ties."[27] Here Caplow and Bahr are writing at the time of the demise of the category of the disaffiliated man; they both document and abet the demise. The near indexical relationship between homelessness and the lack of family relations collapses within their work, but they sustain the framework of disaffiliation for homelessness. While they shift their definition, it does not expand the pool of the homeless to include people with familial ties. The absence of family is still a necessary condition; it is just no longer sufficient. Their seemingly broader definition narrows the pools of the homeless to only include those disconnected from family who also do not have extensive connections to voluntary associations or other communities.

This late 1960s shift takes place long after the collapse of hobo communities; Bahr and Caplow are in effect excluding the single adult who still has extensive social connections. Thus individuals like the single, young urban professional or the hippie in a communal living situation are not homeless. The disaffiliation thesis sustains despite a tweak in the social science term. Bahr and Caplow continue to write about the disaffiliated man into the 1970s, when the consensus that the homeless man is the disaffiliated man fractures (a process we shall explore in Part III).

The framework of disaffiliation also rests upon a semantics of family. We have already seen the unreflective shifting between the terms *home* and *family*, both in the work of Bahr and Caplow and in those whose works they cite.[28] The language of the categories of affiliation, and its negation, also assumes familial relations. Their colleague James Rooney in his contribution to Bahr's *Disaffiliated Man* volume—which grew out of the Bowery Project—establishes that the Skid Row, unattached male[29] has to be understood in his distinction from the stable, family-oriented community: "The continuous development of a distinctive single man's culture was associated with increasing differentiation, isolation, and opposition from the stable, family-oriented community. The unattached men could not be included in the status groups of the resident community because of the differences of values stemming from the former's lack of structured responsibility, particularly as expressed in the lack of restraint in recreation, pursuit of immediate pleasure, and lack of concern for the future."[30] The disaffiliated man embodies a set of values antagonistic to the bourgeois family and so can only by understood through this opposition. The demise of the hobos eliminated the familial threats from a population prone to wandering, but the underlying framework of the homeless man as a figure without a family remains within the discourse on homelessness.

Bahr argues that an inevitable consequence of this disaffiliation is powerlessness. The negative freedom resulting from the attenuation of affiliative ties comes along with a loss of control over one's social (and nonsocial) environment.[31] Because power develops or manifests in relations, because it is always wielded through institutions, the lack of social relations and absence of organizational ties renders the homeless man powerless. Robert Park made a similar point in "The Mind of the Hobo." The only form of social relations legitimated by this discourse on homelessness, though, is the family. Hobosociality was first dismissed as inadequate to moor individuals to society, and then, as the hobo community slowly disappeared, the alternate form of sociality became irrelevant. The homeless man is that individual who is literally subjected to those who have institutional authority over him—like the police, missions, or social service agencies. With no other social moorings, the homeless man comes to be defined by institutions of power.

In this social science framework, the family is the foundation of social life; it is that which settles and moors individuals. But the homeless man of Skid Row is the antithesis of the settled—"their ideas and customs are the antithesis of much that the 'civilized' American sees as valuable and sacred."[32] The disaffiliation thesis continues to be the way to define the problem of homelessness through the 1960s.

The Catholic Worker: Resisting Disaffiliation

The sacredness of bourgeois life was critiqued by (at least) one group who resisted the otherness of the homeless.[33] Their personalist embrace of the homeless and sacred duties to extend mercy to them shaped a response to the rise of the homeless man quite at odds with the broader society. The Catholic Worker grasped at models of charity discarded through the rationalization of alms; they were a reaction to social service practices that developed through the modernizing of older charity.

With the ever-increasing organization of charities, the fin-de-siècle personalist practices of volunteer visitation gave way to the emerging professional class of social workers. Demands of education, applied training, and professional affiliations changed the face from whom the poor or sick received services—detached professionalism became the increasing norm. By the time of the Depression's exponentially increased demand on social services, the rise of social workers was fairly complete. This new profession and the new transactional interactions that came with managerial duties were not lauded in all quarters—even among those who had significant roles in the development of social work practices. In an earlier era, these nascent tensions arose between the settlement movements and charities, who increasingly undertook a thorough vetting of a family before delivery of any service. Jane Addams expressed the outrage of those receiving charitable assistance delayed by these calculations: "When they see the delay and caution with which relief is given, these do not appear to them conscientious scruples, but the cold and calculating action of the selfish man."[34]

These fin-de-siècle shifts in charity marked the infusion of the instrumental practices of *Gesellschaft* into the previously personalist practices of almsgiving. The person and the relationship were subordinated to a world of seemingly objective calculations to determine if the impoverished person (or family) was a good investment; the practices of capital became those of charity. Charity is a sign of power imbalance. The impetus for autonomous associations to furnish necessities declines with the hobo; charity and its social service heir subject the homeless to its ministrations. The inability of social settlements to meet the Depression's increased demands gave greater opportunities for the expansion of the large-scale bureaucratization of social services.

As I have already discussed, the formation of the homeless figure comes through the processes of the modernizing of charity; the homeless man is the anonymous product of anonymous services. The mid-1930s consolidation of the categories of social displacement in the figure of the homeless man was a semantic consolidation that paralleled the institutional ones in the rise of large-scale social service bureaucracies.

With this rise of professional social work, the lines of the late twentieth-century debates about faith-based organizations were already being drawn—calculating efficiency versus the personalist approach of a religious charity. The personalist camp has devolved primarily to the realm of the religious right, whose critiques of bureaucratic services have more to do with opposition to government-sponsored social services than to the particular practices of service administration or management.

An early resistance to this institutionalization of poverty and its remedies emerged from the ashes of the Greenwich Village left group that had formed around *The Masses* and its postsuppression heir *Liberator*. The radical journalist Dorothy Day, who had a brief early start at these magazines, cofounded the Catholic Worker movement with Peter Maurin and began publishing its newspaper in 1933. Maurin developed much of the intellectual framework for the movement, which rested on the insistence that charity is personal. In her 1950s autobiography *The Long Loneliness*,[35] Day recollects an early exchange between Maurin and herself about the nature of charity in the modern world. She wrote the following of Maurin:

> If he had no money he went without food. He always advised people to beg if they were in need. But I know he did not like to beg himself. He preferred to go without. I used to taunt him gently with this.

"That is why people prefer going on relief, getting aid from the state," I told him. "They prefer that to taking aid from their family. It isn't any too easy, you know, to be chided by your family for being a failure. People who are out of work are always considered failures. They prefer the large bounty of the great, impersonal mother, the state."

But the fact remained, he always reminded me, no matter what people's preferences, that we are our brother's keeper, and the unit of society is the family; that we must have a sense of personal responsibility to take care of our own, and our neighbor, at a personal sacrifice. "That is a first principle," he always said. "It is not the function of the state to enter into these realms. Only in times of great crisis, like floods, hurricane, earthquake or drought, does public authority come in. Charity is personal. Charity is love."[36]

This personalist approach to charity uses the same principle that Jacob Riis used to ground philanthropy—I am my brother's keeper. The Catholic Worker movement formed lay religious communities in which they tried to live out this principle. They combined this communitarian impulse with a desire for the locales in which such communities could best flourish, where people could work for subsistence and not a wage, and where they could resist the proletarianization that came from urban life.

Like Riis who also called upon people to be their brother's keeper, the Catholic Worker calls for a return to the community lost with urban upheavals. The atavistic turn of the Catholic Worker extends Riis's efforts to instill elements of rural community into urban society beyond Riis's via media accommodation of modernity. Riis bemoans the ills of the modern city but accepts that it cannot be sent away. He calls for a greening of the city while also availing himself of its institutions—the schools, the police, the churches. He wants to bring the country into the city to temper the extremes of modernization and the city.

The impetus of the Catholic Worker movement is a rejection of modernity. For them, charity comes from the *Gemeinschaft* ideal of taking care of one's own; kinship-like obligations (being a brother's keeper) make demands upon one up to a point of personal sacrifice. The sectarian movement created a lay religious community within the city linked to farms—"agronomic universities" in Maurin's phrase—away from the metropolis that afforded opportunities to fulfill their mantra of work not labor. For Peter Maurin, any future social order required a return to the land, which could furnish a home through community. Day wrote of his attachment to land: "Every talk of Peter's about the social order led to the land. He spoke always as a peasant, but as a practical one. He knew the craving of the human heart for a toehold on the land, for a home of one's own, but he also knew how impossible it was to attain it except through community, through men banding together in farming communes to live to a certain extent in common, work together, own machinery together, start schools together."[37] He wanted a communal return to land, which rejected the organizing of industrial labor by rejecting industry; his vision was a premodern paradise with a community of brothers (and sisters). This *Gemeinschaft* ideal required "personalism and communitarianism."[38]

Similar to Riis, Maurin uses the Cain story to frame his critique of modern social ills and a dependence on organized relief. Maurin felt that relying on anonymous government relief is a failure to recognize one's obligations to one's brother. The Catholic Worker neighborliness, not bureaucracy, should be the tool for relief. In an article for *Commonweal,* Day makes the centrality of the Cain story explicit: "When Peter Maurin talked about the necessity of practicing the Works of Mercy, he meant all of them. He envisioned Houses of Hospitality in poor parishes in every city of the country, where these precepts of Our Lord could be put into effect. He pointed out that we have turned to state responsibility through home relief, social legislation, and social security, that we no longer practice personal responsibility, but are repeating the words of the first murderer, 'Am I my brother's keeper?'"[39] As I demonstrated with Riis, the Cain story is far more than merely a question of being a brother's keeper. Cain was a tiller of the soil and thus tied to the land. The insufficiency or inadequacy of his devotion to God precipitates the violent rending of his family. This follows the murder of his brother; he is expelled from his family and cut off from the soil—the kinship and spatial groundings on which *Gemeinschaft* are based. Losing ties to soil and breaking up the family are coextensive. Cain establishes the first city as a place to settle after he loses the ability to till. The city arises from the two violent punishments of expulsion from family and land no longer yielding to him. Cain's urban progeny gave rise to technological innovation—all bronze and iron tools were developed by them.

With Cain, we have a small précis of that supposed later shift from *Gemeinschaft* to *Gesellschaft.* A small community of kinships bonds—which relies on the land for harvesting and grazing—breaks, and new, reputedly less fulfilling, spatial and social relationships take over. The severance of these more intimate bonds also necessitates severance with the land; the city then arises with all its technology. Dorothy Day and Peter Maurin read the Cain story as a cautionary tale of modernization.

The Catholic Worker's personalism, however, was no match for the rationalizing forces ordering the city. They remained a dissenting voice of retreat from the modern world that failed to sway the direction of the discourse on homelessness. They set up houses of hospitality in cities around the country, but they did not stave off the rise of social service agencies—they merely provided an idiosyncratic alternative to social services. In part, the invocation of the Cain story ran counter to the trends toward scientific efficiency in constituting a homeless man. Myth (or, in this case, perhaps religion) was an unnecessary cultural form at a time when order was being restored to the city. Even the problems of the Depression could not replicate the fin-de-siècle urban chaos; the city now had a language by which to be structured. Thus the Catholic Worker movement's resistance to modernization only furnished a unique outlier to the discourse that constituted a homeless figure through social science literature. They have continued to exist on their own without significantly impacting the institutional or discursive responses to homelessness.

This homeless figure became the normative category for social displacement as the twin concepts of the nuclear family and social isolation became prominent in American sociology and anthropology. In these new trends, the homeless man became that individual who found himself outside of family structure—the disaffiliated man. The language of homelessness, which had developed in the earlier era to describe threats to the Christian home ideal, had now become the mere absence of such a home. The absence of such family relationships was a working assumption of sociological literature throughout the New Deal era through the 1960s—therefore, all etiologies, pathologies, or deviances are analyzed in terms of their relationship to the nuclear family. Though questioned and resisted, the disaffiliation thesis of homelessness continued to be the dominant way of defining homelessness through the 1960s.

In the New Deal era, the discourse on homelessness incorporated a new stability. Political change in the city and the sociologists' consolidation of disparate categories of social displacement changed the landscape of the city and social science. Sociologists settled on the category of the homeless man to represent the urban displaced on Skid Row. The need for myth subsided; it had served its purpose in bringing some meaning-making mechanism to bear on the chaos of the new metropolis. But its turn to latency does not mean that it entirely went away. Social science became the dominant mode to discuss the family and the displaced through the Depression and Eisenhower years. The categorical stability held through the 1960s—the homeless figure was the disaffiliated man; a basic consensus was reached. Quibbling about etiologies and the relationships to particular pathologies dominated social science at this time. But the attributes that had emerged through the fin-de-siècle invocation of mythic tropes—unsettled males that were a threat to family, and pathology as a medicalized form of sin— remained untouched. They became the characteristics of the homeless man.

The rise of the homeless figure as the disaffiliated man is the underside of the rise of the nuclear family. These two were intertwined in midcentury sociological work, much like the homeless city was intertwined with the Christian home a half century earlier; the homeless city or man did not exist without the family norm. Commentators and sociologists developed the homeless category in juxtaposition to the family norm. But this consensus that the category of homelessness represents threats to or the absence of family norms began to be threatened in the latter part of the twentieth century. For the fracturing of the disaffiliation thesis, we now turn to Part III.

PART III

Fragmenting Homelessness

Disaffiliation remained the definition of homelessness as long as the category of the nuclear family continued to be fairly stable. The consolidation of the category of the homeless man in the 1930s and the 1950s further elaboration of this figure as the disaffiliated man continued through the conclusion of Bahr and Caplow's late 1960s Bowery Project. The publications that continued coming out from this project into the 1970s (e.g., Howard Bahr's *Skid Row: An Introduction to Disaffiliation*) continued with the same basic discourse on homelessness. The early discourse that emerged through mythic tropes defined the parameters for constituting a homeless figure—separation from or threat to the family, pathology, and an unsettled nature. As we saw in Part II, these attributes were taken up by sociologists studying the urban displaced of Skid Row. This broad framework of disaffiliation and pathology continued until we start to see fractures in this consensus in the 1970s. As in the fin-de-siècle period, journalists first documented conditions that challenged the basic understandings of urban life, and then later sociologists take the issues up in earnest. For instance, the term *bag lady* is coined in popular parlance in 1972, predating the first full-length study of homeless women by four years.[1] In the 1960s, several changes in urban, family, and social life began to change some of the conditions that inform the discourse on homelessness.

As any conventional view of American history would tell us, the 1960s began to see breaks in the Pollyannaish accounts of American culture. Urban tensions, antiwar sentiments, the nascent appearance of a counterculture, the appearance of a new left, pathologization of the African American family, the rise of second-wave feminism—all these (and more) are thought to contribute to the breakdown of the idyllic America of the 1950s. No matter how problematic such narratives are, there were indeed social and cultural shifts beginning in the 1960s and continuing for the ensuing decades. The upheavals were not as violently visible as those at the waning of the previous century, despite explosions like Watts in 1965 or Chicago in 1968. But underlying structural changes over the late 1960s and early 1970s created new conditions for the collapse of urban manufacturing, the rise of inner-city poverty, a revanchist backlash against the postmodern metropolis, and the emergence of a globalized economy. These changes in the economy and the city brought further change to social life, and the nuclear family was not beyond these impacts. Such shifts began to fracture the consensus within the discourse on homelessness.

In the face of such social changes, the discourse on homeless began to shift. In Part III, I show that the changes in family and social life that begin in the 1960s established the conditions for the greatest challenge to the discourse on homelessness: the homeless family. The logic of the discourse—homelessness as disaffiliation—assumes separation from a family. Thus the idea of being homeless when with one's family was structurally impossible. But before this contradiction comes to the fore, several steps were taken from the disaffiliation of the homeless man.

In Chapter 6, "Fracturing Consensus: Women and Minorities," we look at two historical shifts that prompt adapting changes in the discourse. First, we see the appearance of women on the streets and in the sociological literature. There were always a small minority of women who appeared in the discourse on homelessness. For instance, in the early hobo days, Boxcar Bertha gained popularity for her autobiography, which she told to Ben Reitman. But women were always a small minority and thought of as incidental to the discourse. When women began to appear on the streets and then in newspapers, social scientists had to acknowledge the gendered assumptions of their research. In this discussion we focus primarily on Howard Bahr's chapter on women in *Skid Row* because it is the first sociological acknowledgement that women have been effaced in the literature on homelessness.

A second, similar assumption fell to the wayside for similar reasons—the almost exclusive whiteness of the homeless man. The assumptions of the discourse were integrated with particular spaces of the city where social science research took place—the Skid Row, Bowery, and Hobohemia sections of town. These sections where sociologists studied the homeless man were in the "white" sections of town. As we shall see in this chapter, basic discursive assumptions were reinforced by the ways that definitions of *homeless* were operationalized. The introduction of the categories of both homeless women and African American homeless followed shifts in the social roles of single women and the African American family. Opening up the gender and race assumptions of the discourse enabled the next major step in the discourse on homelessness—the rise of the homeless family.

In Chapter 7, we look at the early discursive attempts to negotiate the homeless family. The homeless family appeared—in the streets and in literature—in the 1980s. Already having to acknowledge cognitive blind spots to homeless women, the literature on the homeless faced an even larger blind spot with the homeless family. It required judicial action before social service providers and sociologists (belatedly) would recognize that one could both be with one's family and be homeless. This moment of the lawsuit—1982's *McCain v. Koch*—is also when the constitution of the homeless subject is complete. A subject expresses frustration that its family is not being recognized as homeless—the family declares that I am homeless and that you, the state (or the city of New York), must recognize my homelessness, and in so doing, I shall receive services. The greatest test to the discourse on homelessness is also the culmination of the subjectivation process. When a group of families in New York sued the city for its failure to recognize their homelessness, they both accepted the moniker and challenged the cultural logic of the discourse.

Negotiating this contradiction between court rulings and the discursive logic became a great challenge. As with each major shift in the discourse, the initial work was undertaken by journalists and activists. Because he wrote one of the first, very influential books on homeless families, we focus on the work of popular Pulitzer Prize–winning writer Jonathan Kozol in this chapter. As with the fin-de-siècle commentators, he relies extensively on myth to ground his discussions of homeless families. This return to myth brackets the homeless family from the homeless figure. As prominent sociologists, like Peter Rossi or Christopher Jencks, move forward from this point, they continue Kozol's practice of de facto bracketing the family from broader analyses of homelessness. Myth again provides a framework for thinking about homelessness and the family. It then recedes as the discursive order was reestablished and the family was segregated from the negative valuations associated with the pathologized, disaffiliated homeless figure.

This atomized homeless figure moves from a category of social science to a legal category codified in the federal law—the Stewart B. McKinney Act, later updated in the shorthand of McKinney-Vento. The legal recognition of the homeless arose from the seeming explosion of homelessness in the urban streets of America. Certainly, the numbers of homeless people appear to dramatically increase over the course of the 1980s. Part of this increase relates to economic changes in the cities, which had begun in the early 1970s—the demise of urban manufacturing, gentrification, and the collapse of the cheap lodging houses and single-room occupancy motels (SROs) found in old Skid Row sections of town. This combination of job loss, loss of housing for the poor, and the reentry of the middle class into urban areas set the stage for tensions surrounding the newly displaced. Those losing housing and jobs no longer had SROs, and so the bottom of the housing market hit the sidewalk as young urban professionals started to reclaim urban space.

In Part III, we find that the fracturing of a discursive consensus leads to shifts in the gender and racial assumptions of the discourse. No longer was the homeless figure exclusively the (white) man of Skid Row. This opening of the discourse created the possibility for a further opening—the constitution of the homeless family. The rise of the homeless family prompted several changes in the discourse. First, the homeless man was relieved of his role as the primary carrier of family anxieties about the impact of modernization. Second, as we shall see in Part IV, the family anxieties found another cultural locus—the family-value debates. The homeless figure, fully distinguished from the homeless family, became increasingly policed to create family-friendly urban spaces. These shifts in the city and the family grew from the 1960s urban changes that transformed cityscapes and fractured the discursive consensus that homelessness was disaffiliation.

CHAPTER 6

Fracturing Consensus
Women and Minorities

The univocal definition of the homeless figure as the disaffiliated man could not sustain. Even the most insensitive of social scientists had to ground their arguments with reference to some form of empirical research. The assumptions of age, sex, and race upon which this literature rested had always faced challenges, but, eventually, the limits of the disaffiliation model became evident in the streets. Though a cognitive blindness had hidden populations from the sociologist's gaze, eventually journalists and activists identified new trends and new terms (e.g., bag lady) to make sociologists have to acknowledge their blind spots on gender and race. And so the social science literature on homelessness had continued to reaffirm its basic assumptions. The spatial, linguistic, and institutional delimitations—which established the conditions necessary for the consolidation of the category of homelessness—created this framework for the subsequent study of homelessness.

In this chapter, we see this framework begin to fray. By the middle of the 1970s, women and African Americans were increasingly documented as homeless. Before either of these groups had the adjective *homeless* attached to them, there were a series of changes in the structure of the American metropolis combined with other social and political changes. The collapse of urban Fordist manufacturing, technological changes that enabled ever-greater distances between production and distribution, changes in middle-class marriage, and pathologization of the poor, urban African American family all set the stage for the fracturing of the consensus of the homeless figure as the disaffiliated man. The mutual interactions between this constellation of social, economic, and political changes create the conditions for changes in the discourse on homelessness, changes that include the appearance of women on the streets.

Women Alone: Bag Ladies on the Streets

Before monographs on homeless women appeared to establish the existence of this group (beyond the usual passing nod in studies on homelessness), the term *bag lady* gained sway in popular parlance. The homeless woman was on the streets and in the newspaper before social science recognized the limits of its spatial delimitation. The intersection of institutions, taxonomies, and urban geography created the conditions to render the homeless woman invisible to the social scientist. The overwhelming maleness of Skid Row and its primacy as the social-scientific laboratory effectively excluded women from the ranks of the homeless. The turn to some form of inclusion of these socially excluded women was rather ham-handed; the social science literature did not know how to integrate these women. The social science disaffiliation thesis always posited a male homeless figure—it is the "filius" (son) who is disconnected. Because of these, and other, difficulties, the efforts to study homeless women qua women (not just as some outlier to the studies of men) used existing sociological paradigms under which to subsume homeless women. Extant studies of alcoholism provided an easy entrée.

Sociologist Howard Bahr makes an early effort to establish homeless women as a legitimate category of analysis. In his 1973 *Skid Row*, he gives them a chapter unto themselves and a few years later cowrites the final volume to come out of the Bowery Project exclusively on homeless women; these studies do, however, use exceedingly small samples. Years later, Peter Rossi notes the paucity of women studied by Donald Bogue in the 1960s (3 percent of Chicago's Skid Row residents) and Howard Bahr in the 1970s (64 women over the course of a year) compared to his mid-1980s study, which found women constituting 25 percent of Chicago's homeless population.[2] Despite the small samples, Bahr realizes the limits of applying the same assumptions of homeless men to women. Yet when Bahr proposes to establish this new line of inquiry, he takes the popular, and to a lesser extent professional, view that there must be some pathological behavior among the Skid Row residents. This assumption of pathology, as we saw in Part II, was often used as an explanation for disaffiliation—if one were "normal," one

Strand Book Store

828 Broadway
New York, New York 10003
212.473.1452
strandbooks.com
strand@strandbooks.com

	Date:	03-25-2019
Sale: 7599906	Time:	06:18 PM

$2 Dollar Book

3	Item Price:	$2.00	
	% Discount:	50.000%	$1.00

1 items	Subtotal:	$1.00
	Sales Tax (8.875%):	$0.09
1296954	Total:	$1.09

	Cash Payment:	$2.00
	Amount Tendered:	$2.00
	Change Due:	$0.91

Thank you for shopping with us.
Customer: Brett Bates

Printed by: walker   Register: BASE2-Shift1

March 25, 2019 06:18 PM

Hardcovers/ Merchandise in original packaging are
eligible for a full refund if returned within
3 days of purchase. These items may be returned
for store credit/exchange within two weeks.

Paperbacks, excluding clearance items, may be returned
within two weeks of purchase for store credit or exchange.

All clearance items are final sale.

Receipts must accompany all returns and exchanges.

Follow @strandbookstore
Show us your #STRANDHAUL
Happy Reading!

would presumably be with one's family.[3] The pathology of alcoholism is the point of entry to Bahr's study on homeless women. The category of women alcoholics, he acknowledges, is broader than that of homeless women; the latter are a subset. While his own evidence belies this assumption,[4] he takes it as his starting point, primarily because there is an extant body of literature with which he can work rather than start with a tabula rasa.[5] Of his turn to the literature on alcoholic women, he writes the following:

> Homeless men have been widely studied, but there is no comparable body of literature on homeless women. Occasional studies on the female drunkenness offender point to the fact that some women alcoholics are homeless, but few follow-up investigations focusing on the life histories of these women have yet been undertaken. Explicit discussions of homeless women alcoholics almost always are singular accounts of their unsavory character and bizarre way of life . . . Accounts of this type constitute tangible evidence that homeless women exist, but, provocative as they are, such case histories have failed to stimulate much social research.[6]

This introduction to his chapter on homeless women hardly paints an accurate view of his study—only two of the four case histories he explores cite women with alcohol problems, yet he uses studies of female alcoholics as a means to frame his analysis. A third case history is of a woman who talks about using pills.[7] Bahr's argument rests on an a priori assumption that something is most definitely not right if women are homeless—the location of this "not rightness" he finds in the homeless figure.

The few women who appeared in the fin-de-siècle literature had this same imputation of pathology. We saw Riis appalled by "a sallow, wrinkled hag" working in a stale beer dive, and Jane Addams's brief foray into women's homelessness was in an article that implied connections between the sheltered woman and prostitutes.[8] Even the majority of the mythic tropes—like Cain, Ishmael, or the Wandering Jew—cannot provide for ways to articulate women's homelessness. The gendered connection between woman and home was so great that a homeless woman was inconceivable. A female was the foundation of a Christian home; the foundation cannot lose its hominess. Pathology could be the only explanation; it explained the abnormality of a nonfamilial female.

Bahr's account of the disaffiliation of females is different than that of males. Alcohol abuse accounts for the woman's disaffiliation, though Bahr finds that familial discord presages drinking problems. He writes, "The family background of almost all female alcoholics can be seen in terms of a disorganization syndrome, which may include inadequate parental rearing practices, conflict in the home, maternal domination coupled with submission and instability of the father, and parental alcoholism."[9] The female is able to be homeless because she is from a home with conflict—that is, a home that is not truly a home. Even though Bahr rejects the widespread thesis that alcoholic women embody a greater pathology than do alcoholic men,[10] he, nonetheless, establishes different standards in the evaluation of men and women. When he discusses the role of personal problems with men on Skid Row, he undertakes the trio of disabilities, disease, and drinking,[11] yet the collapse of this list to the final problem in his analysis of homeless women can only partially be accounted for by the limits of the literature. His shelter sample is small; therefore he can only summarize the rates of disability and disease.[12]

Bahr argues that the relationship between alcohol and isolation (the necessary condition for homelessness, as we saw in Part II) is not, however, a simple cause-and-effect connection; "social isolation appears to be both an antecedent and concomitant factor in a vicious circle: Deviant drinking occurs as a response to social isolation; excessive drinking increases social isolation, which in turn leads to heavier drinking."[13] Distinguishing the two forms of drinking—deviant and excessive—enables him to explain a dialectic of alcohol abuse and homelessness for women. Isolation leads to drinking, which increases isolation and then more drinking; thus isolation and deviance/excess become the two root causes for women to be homeless. The homeless women were disaffiliated because they never had a stable home without conflict—substance abuse was used to negotiate this discord. The discord is a necessary condition for considering a woman homeless. The dialectics of the language of homelessness are here instrumental in the advent of the women in the literature; the home has to be somehow denigrated for a female to become homeless—conflict and pathology thus appear as culprits of this denigration.

While this turn to alcoholic women arises in part because Bahr recognizes the limits of the literature on homeless women, he further marginalizes women already at the margins of both society and scholarly literature by subsuming them under categories of deviance. As the bedrock of home, there is no way to articulate the problem of homeless women beyond an assumption of deviance. Even more important, Bahr also ends up replicating the spatial and semantic problems that he identifies as erecting the social-scientific blinders around homeless women. He writes,

The scarcity of studies of homelessness among females may be attributed to a number of factors. In the first place, Skid Row women are rare . . . Since women are rarely present in the places where social scientists have studied homeless people, it is understandable that they have been overlooked. Furthermore, because homeless women are not ecologically concentrated in areas such as Skid Row, they have not been perceived as threatening the social order or as neighborhood problems. Politicians and neighborhood organizations have not been concerned with "cleaning up" areas where "unattached" women live, and as a result there has been little interest or financial support for the study of these women.

Finally, the definitions of homelessness used by sociologists have usually been operationalized in such a way that women are, for all intents and purposes excluded. For example, if homeless people are defined as those who participate in facilities and institutions of Skid Row, the probability of encountering a woman is exceedingly low.

Nevertheless, there are compelling reasons why careful attention should be given to this population. For one thing, unlike the "conventional" female alcoholic, the homeless woman may find it difficult to remain a "hidden alcoholic." Moreover, investigations of the drinking behavior and misbehavior of homeless women may greatly increase the value of present findings about the homeless men.[14]

His admission of oversight triangulates the three types of segregation (as we saw in Chapter 3), which were instrumental for constituting the homeless man: spatial, linguistic, and institutional. In this study, the three do not cohere, and so there was no female homeless figure. Bahr's definition (language) of homelessness is those who participate in facilities (institutions) of Skid Row (space). Women were not in the space and thus not intersecting the institutions of Skid Row. Therefore, they were not considered under the definition of homeless. Women are a priori excluded because they are not brought under the gaze of the social scientists studying homelessness.

Equally important to the inability to identify women as homeless is the issue of social threat or, as Bahr refers to it in the previous passage, "threatening the social order" or "neighborhood problems." Because a seeming diffusion of homeless women mitigates the possibility of being perceived as threats or problems, politicians and neighborhoods do not worry about "cleaning up" areas where they are found. While the discourse on homelessness has always been intertwined with fears of a social threat, the nature of the supposed threat has shifted. In Volunteer Special's *The Volcano under the City* and Riis's fears of "Bread or Blood" riots, the problems arose from over-accumulations of labor—the demands of production for low wages created a city with too many poor. But the improved urban economies assimilated much of this labor. In Bahr's concern with neighborhood problems, we infer a move that becomes explicit with 1990s gentrification efforts—the threats shift to consumption. "Neighborhood problems" are a euphemism for activities (e.g., panhandling, urban camping) thought to drive down property values or chase away customers.[15]

The reasons, which Bahr cites previously for overlooking homeless women (place, institutions, lack of threat, and definitions), are interrelated. He tells us that he undertakes his research in the place where homeless men are ecologically concentrated; the institutions of Skid Row set a parameter for those of the displaced being constituted as homeless. He tells us that the definition arose from this place and its institutions. The concentration of this unattached population in this place (primarily affected by the institutions) constitutes a threat to the social order, or at least a problem to the neighborhood. The social threat arises through the constitution of the homeless as a group; the social services were to "clean up" areas around this group to diminish the possibility of threat. In the fin-de-siècle period, there was a great sense of political threat and danger signified by the term *homeless*—an urban mass might riot or revolt. The Cain tradition invokes the first homicide; the collapse of radicals and hobos—before the constitution of a homeless figure—indicated political fears. Despite a seeming lack of danger, Bahr thinks that homeless women ought to be studied. The primary reason he cites relates to drinking behavior (and secondarily, it will provide insight into homeless men); somehow he assumes alcohol problems are the norm for homeless women and that they will provide an interesting comparison with women of other class and status backgrounds.

The problem of the homeless woman, however, goes far beyond the spatial limitations of studies, or the classificatory system of a social scientist. The problem of the homeless woman is the problem of "woman." The privative of homelessness is a life deprived of hearth and home, warmth and comfort. The underlying role of gender constructs long rendered the idea of a homeless woman unthinkable. Home is constituted by and through the female presence. As we saw with Catharine Beecher and Harriet Beecher Stowe, the woman is the sine qua non of the home and family. The assumption of conjugality and natality is a male begotten by or joining to a woman. As we shall see in Chapter 7, before a homeless family can be constituted in the Reagan years, a homeless woman must first become possible.

The possibility of a homeless female necessitated several shifts in the idea of "woman." Never entirely monolithic—the middle-class homemaker was the heir of Catharine Beecher's treatises on domestic science—the woman (as wife and mother) was to make the home. For the agent of homemaking to be rendered homeless, cracks had to first appear in the edifice of the dominant conceptions of homelessness. The univocity of the disaffiliated man as a middle-age or older white male had to weaken in its position as the sole category of homelessness. Social and economic conditions, likewise, had to give rise to the discourse of unattached women. The discourse emerges with the advent of the unattached bourgeois female. Such conditions of detachment had already existed among the poor without giving rise to the category of the homeless woman. Once the unattached female appears in bourgeois discourses, she was then more readily identified in analyses of the poor.

The category of the homeless woman, however, doubly marks a loss of her womanhood. To be homeless means that she is void of maternal abilities—the nurturing qualities around which home is purportedly constituted. But in this category, she also loses her sexuality; she is denied even the agency of the whore half of the popular feminine dichotomy. Her homelessness is represented as a state of mind (void of the ability to nurture) and a state of body (void of sexuality). She might be constituted as a woman in a technical, biological sense, but she has no womanliness.[16] To be described as homeless, a woman is stripped of her femininity, which is foundational for the home. This homeless woman is not even a Magdalene; she—in her early incarnation as a bag lady—is a parody of the Upper East Side bourgeois woman. The shopping bag lady was constructed as the underside of this urban stereotype; the clutch on bags from Saks, Bergdorf Goodman, and upscale boutiques is supplanted by more humble, wrinkled cast-off bags hoarding found treasures discarded from the consumer culture of the metropolitan environs.

Shopping-bag ladies were even more of urban outsiders than the disaffiliated man of Skid Row; in part, this marginalization is because the daily life and practices of bag ladies derive from traditional female roles of the white, middle (and upper) classes:

> In a society in which women have little power, their lives are considered unimportant compared to the lives of men. Indeed, there may also be certain differences in the life-styles of homeless women and homeless men that tend to reinforce women's invisibility. According to sociologist Jennifer Hand, shopping

bag ladies are urban economic outsiders who "live in nooks, crannies and niches," using public or semi-public places "for their own practical purposes," and differ from homeless men by using ploys derived from specifically female roles, like shopping, sorting, selecting, collecting, to gain access to urban facilities.[17]

But the image of the bag lady[18] is shorn of the respectability, panache, and femininity of the urban bourgeois practitioners of these roles. Those latter women might carry bags with their consumables and even with supplies for many occasions; the toted parcel or purse is not the sum of one's possessions. The bag lady takes her "home" with her through the streets—the home enters into the public, while her bourgeois counterpart ventures forth for public life but returns to privacy to unload or stow away the newly bought commodity. The construction of the bag lady maintained the racialized structure of the discourse on homelessness; the image was of a white woman parodying that of an Upper East Side matron. The widespread racializing of the homeless as African American enters the discourse over the 1970s–1980s period through popular pathologization of the African American family and not through the portrayal of bag ladies.

The source of bag ladies' possessions is also quite different; the woman who returns to her home purchases the products in her bags and her purse—she is part of the urban economy. Those possessions of the bag lady are literally the refuse of the city's economic life. Alix Kates Shulman describes the differences between the bag lady and her bourgeois counterpart; she points out how the bag is a locus for both connecting and differentiating between the bag lady and bourgeois women:

> In our culture, the ubiquitous bag—women's indispensable gear, whether purse, tote, or shopping bag—remains an almost universal female sign, connecting "us" with "them." It is not always easy to tell homeless women from other women. Even women with comfortable homes commonly carry around in their bags supplies for every occasion, from papers and pills to folding umbrellas and food. Nor is it only the homeless in this commodity-obsessed society who spend much of their time collecting, shopping around, squirreling things away. Nevertheless, there is a great difference between those who carry shopping bags for convenience and those who must—the difference of extreme poverty and isolation. While most of us have cupboards drawers, closets, and some even have attics, cellars, and safes in which to store our worldly goods, the homeless have only their shopping bags. Everything they own must travel with them.[19]

Seemingly, the bag lady carries her home with her, but this is a home reduced to consumption—the affect and the family, which are discursively central to home, are absent. Her home in the streets lacks a private sphere, and so she has only the consumables for a home and none of those sentiment relations about which Mary Margaret Wood wrote in Part II. The complete lack of privacy for the homeless woman makes her condition quite problematic, since the private sphere is where modernity had relegated women. As we saw with Jacob Riis's argument for the importance of a locked door, homelessness is constituted through an insufficiently delineated public/private divide. Disaffiliation arises from the lack of a private space in which to retreat with a family.

In fact, the homeless woman takes the isolation of the disaffiliated man to another register, since he might at least have interactions with fellow Skid Row residents or become an habitué of its institutions. Because the homeless woman is not "ecologically concentrated," because she is so dispersed throughout the city, she does not—according to the literature—have any social interactions. The "appearance" of the homeless woman is, in part, possible because homeless men began to disperse across the city and no longer concentrated in ghettoized Skid Row areas. This dispersal was just beginning in the late 1960s and early 1970s as Skid Row areas began to be torn down. As we saw in Chapters 4 and 5, the disaffiliated man in Skid Row has some interactions, just not the ones to properly moor him to society. The male-male bond of fellow Skid Row frequenters does not ensure that a man will not pick up and move along with the coming of spring. Land and its agricultural cycle rooted men to their families and communities in earlier eras; now the institution of the family was the last mooring to keep people from wandering away and pursuing self-interest over social obligation. We have seen commentators like Riis, Warner, Park, and Beck lamenting the propensity to break these weakening social relations for a wandering life. With Simmel, we saw that the social relations of the wandering stranger leave this figure outside society, and thus the trader or stranger always moves on. The ability to sell labor affords a mobility and a luxury to disaffiliate—the physical ties to land had previously inhibited such motion.

The discourse on homelessness arose through the collapsing of clearly ordered spatial arrangements. When land defined relations, space was the predominant component in constituting social life. But the discourse on homelessness arose through the devaluation of space. It arose to describe a city overflowing with a population that had forsaken the spaces of their ancestors for the opportunity of more money. The problems of homelessness arose through urbanizing transformations of spatial arrangements and the inability of these transformations to reconcile with a modern public/private split. Homeless women completely upend the public/private split.

With the figure of the homeless woman, contradictions of modernity are brought to the fore; with the discourse of the homeless woman, any discursive ties posited between modern homelessness and older forms of social displacement collapse.[20] I have already argued that claims of the antiquity of homelessness are spurious for they fail to recognize the different socioeconomic conditions giving rise to the particular forms of social displacement. With the homeless woman, any such claims melt into air. Premodern forms of social displacement (the mendicant, the knight-errant, and the trader) or early modern ones (like the vagrant or vagabond) are, as a class, exclusively male. The lone class of socially displaced females was prostitutes, but they required a certain form of social integration combined with distance. The client base came from within a particular society; the prostitute could not be so ostracized as to fail to draw from this pool. In the case of high-class courtesans, like *hetaera*, they moved freely among social elites; other low-class prostitutes slunk about the social margins. The prostitute had to have regular, ongoing interactions with her clients. The discourse of the homeless female is one of isolation; this discourse severs the possibility of a vestigial relationship with any form of premodern social displacement. The economic processes that created home as a space protected from the vagaries of the public life of politics and production also created the homeless. The dialectics of home and homelessness arise through these same processes of modernization. Homelessness negates the privacy, the nurturing, the security, and the emotional bonds of home; it negates the discursive world of feminine space and the relations inhabited there.

Though the category *homeless woman* begins to appear in the 1970s, it is not until the latter part of the decade and even more so in the 1980s that it becomes an extensive one warranting focused research beyond being an also-ran in the broader studies of homeless men. While Howard Bahr's analysis belies his move to subsume homeless women under the alcoholic, he does so because of the very gendered idea of home, so gendered that Freud, as we saw earlier, argues that the desire for home or dwelling is a desire for the womb. The gender problems come to the fore as the concept of home contracts under the sway of modernization. As each layer of meaning of "home" was penetrated by migrations and the city, a tighter rhetoric clung to the diminishing layers. The final foundation of home clung to the personalized realm of the nuclear family. The home-homeless dialectic proffered no space for women or families not subsumed under the home half of the binary. The dichotomy was gendered; homelessness negates the feminine realm of hearth and family. Before the family could be rendered homeless, women first made their appearance in the discourse on homelessness, and then, after the dialectic broke open, the longstanding tensions between family ideals and homelessness eventually exploded. The homeless woman presented a problem of sexuality, a problem of public life, and an affront to the very idea of family. While the sexual threat of men alone had been great, it did not have the layers of valence residing in the body of the homeless woman. Fear of homosexual practices in the hobo jungle or Skid Row SROs simmered, but still, it was an anxiety redressed with approbation. The gendered idea of home problematizes homeless women in ways that homeless men do not.

By dwelling briefly on this point, we see that at the first and most rudimentary level, the homeless woman prepares the way for the homeless family. Until a woman alone can be homeless, homelessness cannot define a mother and her children. The category of the homeless woman combines with the pathologization of the African American family to fracture the discursive assumptions that homelessness was the problem of the middle-age white man on Skid Row. Beyond this important transitional role, the homeless woman and the idea of the gendered haven of home point to a fundamental anxiety of American modernity. As we have seen with Berman and Lukács, modernity is a fear of homelessness; it is—as Novalis said in another context—the urge to be at home everywhere. The metaphysical grounding upon which society had long rested gave way; the social became the basis for grounding, and the family was the tool for this. Woman has a unique role in this grounding. She is mother; she is wife. The public/private split reinscribes the neoplatonic metaphysics of processing forth from ground (from home), to a journey, and then a return; the home is the point of emanation and return. Men leave for work and return. Trials and tribulations face him in this sojourn. The metaphysical journey became a social one with the separation of production from the household. Woman was the anchor of the locus of sentiment, roots, and family. Woman was the familial glue that held the last bastion of meaning against the slings and arrows of modernity's outrageous fortune. As one sees with Tönnies, woman was integral to the primary relations of *Gemeinschaft*, while a father was incidental.

Within the discursive logic, woman could not be homeless or else modernity wins against community and family, roots, and emotions; it overwhelms meaning and purpose in the world. By breaking free of her domestic chains, she decentered the male point of social origin and return. While the widespread entrance of bourgeois women into the marketplace effected a modicum of this social displacement, it pales when compared to that of the homeless woman. The bourgeois woman undertook the same pattern of procession/return, but she left the form of home as the emanation point; there was a spatial signifier still marking this place. With this bourgeois woman, a public/private division still exists, but the language of public and private has no space for the homeless woman—the homeless woman is not a public being, for she does not have access to modes of production. The homeless woman is now outside but still has no access to production; she remains invisible because she does not fit into discussions of public life. The homeless woman becomes a problematizing cite for the gender and family ideals, which shape the discourse on homelessness. Her appearance, however, is a necessary condition for the appearance of the categorical contradiction of the homeless family.

Pathology and the African American Community

The fracturing of the consensus that the homeless figure was a white, middle-age resident of Skid Row extended beyond the question of gender to race. Women only appeared in the literature on homelessness after women began to appear as pathological objects in loci antagonistic to the family in a range of other discourses (e.g., critiques of feminism, literature on alcoholism). One of these discourses of pathology was the means for opening the discourse of homeless women, and thus she was from her inception a pathological category. At the time of this fracturing consensus in the 1960s and 1970s, African American men also begin to appear with increasing regularity, until the popular image of homelessness eventually became that of a poor black man. African American males only begin to appear in the discourse after the 1960s' studies of the crisis in the Negro family—for example, the Moynihan Report, a mid-1960s study that, as part of the War on Poverty, popularized social pathology in the African American community. This pathologization of African American families in general, and males in particular, emerges as the political gains of the Civil Rights movement were being codified as legislative ones with the Voting Rights Act of 1965 and the Civil Rights Act of 1964. The demise of legal sanctions for racial prerogatives gave rise to ideological means of sustaining the racial status quo. The appearance of literature on the African American homeless also coincides with an increase in the attribution of personal pathology to the homeless figure; this coterminous relationship between the African American homeless man and an increased assumption of pathology is not coincidence.

The problems of American cities in the 1970s arose from lingering issues of gender and race. Looking back from a 1990s vantage point, urban geographer Neil Smith points out how the shifting relationships between the metropolis and capital reached a crisis in the 1970s as the city's role as the locus of social reproduction was undermined by its inability to sustain the modes of patriarchy and racism upon which the reproduction was based. He writes the following:

> The new urban revanchism is in many ways tied to the shifting niche of cities in the global economy. There is a lot of truth to the contention that whatever other myriad functions and activities it housed, the late-nineteenth- and twentieth-century capitalist city is geographically defined as the locus of social reproduction. Keynesian urban policy, from the 1930s to the 1970s, was devoted to the broad-based subsidy of local social reproduction that underscored capital accumulation in economic, political, and ideological terms. And from Lefebvre to Castells to Harvey, the so-called urban crisis of the 1970s was understood as emanating from a crisis of social reproduction having to do with the dysfunctionality of racism and patriarchy, and from the contradictions between an urban form constructed according to strict criteria of profitability but which was called into service as a means of reproducing a labor force. The reproduction of class and the accumulation of capital were in stark contradiction. Nearly a quarter century later, amidst the white heat of "globalization," these diagnoses seem almost quaint, and the urban scale has been significantly unhinged from such definitive responsibility for social reproduction.[21]

The 1970s economic crises, which marked a turning point in the delinking of production from social reproduction, established urban conditions whereby inner-city populations were left in enclaves of little economic activity. Smith continues, "Amidst the restructuring of production beginning in the 1970s and with class- and race-based struggles broadly receding until the late 1990s, city governments had an increased incentive to abandon that sector of the population surplused by both the restructuring of the economy and the gutting of social services."[22] De facto abandoned by both the global economy and municipal governments, these inner-city residents formed a population that within the ensuing decades would swell the burgeoning ranks of the homeless. These abandoned urban poor were easily overlooked—as Smith points out—because of racist and patriarchal dysfunctionality. The vilification of the inner-city African American had taken on a new tenor in the mid-1960s.

In his justifiably infamous assessment of the mid-1960s African American family,[23] Daniel Patrick Moynihan argues that African Americans as a group urbanized relatively late, but this process of urbanization exacerbated social problems already present in the African American community. He wrote,

> Country life and city life are profoundly different. The gradual shift of American society from a rural to an urban basis over the past century and a half has caused abundant strains, many of which are still much in evidence. When this shift occurs suddenly, drastically, in one or two generations, the effect is immensely disruptive of traditional social patterns.
>
> It was this abrupt transition that produced the wild Irish slums of the 19th Century northeast. Drunkenness, crime, corruption, discrimination, family disorganization, juvenile delinquency were the routine of that era. In our own time, the same sudden transition has produced the Negro slum—different from, but hardly better than its predecessors and fundamentally the result of the same process.
>
> Negroes are now more urbanized than whites . . .
>
> The promise of the city has so far been denied the majority of the Negro migrants, and most particularly the Negro family.[24]

While in the last decades of the nineteenth century, violent urban upheavals gave rise to the discourse on homelessness, they were—according to Moynihan—now in the 1960s wreaking havoc on the African American community. In his argument, the African American community came belatedly to urbanization, and this accelerated encounter destroyed traditional life without proffering the "promises of the city" (e.g., jobs, opportunities, education). The historicizing problem of the idea of belatedness has been well criticized in other quarters and other contexts, so I need not dwell long on such arguments against Moynihan. Writing on the idea of historical development in European colonizing and colonized segments of the world, historian Dipesh Chakrabarty critiques a common stagiest theory of history that emerges. In this theory, the colonized are relegated to the waiting room of history from which they will belatedly emerge into political modernity.[25] Arguing in a similar stagiest fashion, Moynihan argues that the late-coming of the African American population to the modern metropolis places this community in the position of only just now in the 1960s confronting modernization and its social havoc. The African American community was late coming to the city, late coming to modernity, and thus late to adapting to the demands of this social life. But my concern here is not with the validity of the Moynihan Report but the cultural conditions it created for the American city; thus I need not dwell here on the problematic theory of history informing his report.

The report brought together the dual dysfunctionalities of racism and patriarchy by pathologizing most African American households for being headed by women. Moynihan writes the following: "In essence, the Negro community has been forced into a matriarchal structure which, because it is so out of line with the rest of the American society, seriously retards the progress of the group as a whole, and imposes a crushing burden on the Negro male and, in consequence, on a great many Negro women as well."[26] While Moynihan concedes that there is no necessity to patriarchal structure, he argues that since "ours is a society which presumes male leadership in private and public affairs,"[27] a minority group should conform or face a significant disadvantage. He bolsters his claim by pointing out that the small group of middle-class African American families exempt from "the tangle of pathology"[28] were ones following a strict patriarchy. The African American community was crumbling, and he identifies the absence of a patriarch as a large part of the problem.

Moynihan's analysis fell back on the commonplace assumptions of the family's central role in social reproduction. He wrote the following:

> The role of the family in shaping character and ability is so pervasive as to be easily overlooked. The family is the basic social unit of American life; it is the basic socializing unit. By and large, adult conduct in society is learned as a child . . .
>
> But there is one truly great discontinuity in family structure in the United States at the present time: that between the white world in general and that of the Negro American.
>
> The white family has achieved a high degree of stability and is maintaining that stability.
>
> By contrast, the family structure of lower class Negroes is highly unstable, and in many urban centers is approaching complete breakdown.[29]

The sense of belatedness lingers in Moynihan's argument here that the Negro family has been unable to stabilize, as has the white family. Through its late encounter with modernization, the African American community was only just confronting the anomic propensities of the city. The very urbanizing problems that created homelessness in the fin-de-siècle tenement were now bringing homelessness to the African American community. It is not until the large-scale urbanization of the African American community that African Americans come to be considered homeless. The bag lady's pathology discursively emerges because she fails to fulfill the feminine role of homemaking; here the African American community is charged with pathology because women make and lead the home; furthermore, the stereotype of the absent male falls outside this home and so soon appears as homeless in sociological literature. The racial and gender dynamics combine to render African American males homeless.

The centrality of a traditional family structure for social life has been an undergirding presence of the discourse on homelessness. Normative expectations of a two-parent household informed the Christian home ideal and the rise of the nuclear family. In the earlier family ideal, any domestic arrangement that strayed from the norm was rendered homeless—extended families residing together, boarders sharing a family flat, or poor families doubled or tripled up in a small flat. By the postwar rise of the nuclear family, economic growth and zoning laws had eliminated many of these alternative living arrangements. Thus homelessness became the marker of the single male who failed to remain within the confines of a nuclear family.

As we have seen in this chapter, these disaffiliated men did not long remain the lone homeless; the consensus began to fracture in the late 1960s through early 1970s. Women began to appear in the streets, and the African American community became a locus of imputed pathology, just as the urban economy began to remove manufacturing and jobs from the city. The assumptions of the discourse had created enormous blind spots for urban sociologists—the spatial and institutional parameters, which shaped the language of homelessness operationally, excluded women and minorities. With the former, the gendered idea of home abetted this exclusion; with the latter, a "belated" encounter with the modern city delayed their inclusion in the ranks of the homeless.

Once these groups began to appear in journalistic and social science accounts of homelessness, a time of flux entered the discourse on homelessness over the decades of the 1960s and 1970s. African American men were newly (and increasingly) noted in the sociological literature on homelessness. Not fulfilling their expected roles as family patriarch, they embodied pathology and so did the matriarchal family structure in the African American community. The family with an absent patriarch was not the nuclear family and so was easily othered. A woman alone was not fulfilling proper gender roles. As we have seen, a female was a sine qua non of the home. These two groups were the first to begin undoing the basic assumptions of the discourse, but the greatest challenge to this framework appeared a decade later in the early 1980s. Unfolding an internal logic, the discourse on homelessness began trundling toward this new problem—the contradiction of the homeless family.

CHAPTER 7

The Homeless Family
and the Return of Myth

The homeless family did not become a focus of social science literature until the mid- to late 1980s. It did not immediately arise after the fracturing of the consensus that the homeless figure was a disaffiliated man. This fracturing was part of a constellation of urban and discursive changes over the 1960s–1970s period. The urban crises of the 1970s intertwined with issues of race and gender to inflect the dominant modes of social reproduction; this group of social and rhetorical changes established the conditions for an even larger urban problem in the Reagan years. In the early 1980s, the internal tensions between family ideals and homelessness exploded with the emergence of the homeless family. Social scientists and service providers had failed to identify the homeless family, even though John Steinbeck and Dorothea Lange had seemingly documented them in an earlier era. The disaffiliation thesis of the discourse rendered the homeless family invisible in ways similar to Bahr's analysis of the obscurity of homeless women. Because of their definitions and the operationalization of their research, sociologists could not find families who were homeless.

The appearance of the homeless woman was a first step toward this contradictory formation of the homeless family. As a constitutive component of the concept of home, woman had to be able to be rendered homeless for a family to subsequently be so. As we saw with the Moynihan Report, the family with an absent father figure was pathologized—the family norms assume a patriarchal family structure. The increase in female-headed, single-parent households enabled certain families to eventually be marginalized by the moniker *homeless*. This process of establishing the homeless family appears to be a discursive decoupling of the philosophical critique of modernity—which had coalesced around the family—from the homeless figure. It set the stage for an ill-fitting reconciliation between the discourse and empirical and policy changes. Policy fiats changed the definition of homelessness, but the discourse on homelessness was unable to fully assimilate these changes. The homeless subject remains a locus of anxieties about urbanization and its impacts on social reproduction.

In this chapter, we trace the rise of the homeless family from its emergence in a court ruling, through an important early, popular account of homeless families, and finally into the sociological appropriation of this new category. The court ruling established a cognitive contradiction and thus precipitated a shift in the means of defining homelessness. This new figure was no longer primarily a disaffiliated individual but soon became someone without a fixed place to stay (though disaffiliation continued as a leitmotif). This continuation of disaffiliation in any form could exist alongside the homeless family only if this homeless family was bracketed from the broader discursive framework. In Kozol's early, popular account of families, we find that mythic tropes bracket the homeless family—it is a distinct set of concerns and issues and so need not be subsumed under the broader discourse on homelessness. This bracketing is implicitly taken up by the social science literature of the late 1980s and early 1990s; sociology has one set of analyses for the homeless figures—individuals without a place to stay—and another for families. The logic of the discursive framework of the homeless figure as the other of family norms thus sustains.

The cultural logic of homelessness so connected this discourse of family displacement and disaffiliation with a critique of modernity that only judicial (*McCain v. Koch*) and legislative (Stewart B. McKinney Act) fiats could forcibly sever the structure of homelessness. This rending of the family (and the implicit critique of modernity) from the category of homelessness required that a new legal definition overlay the long history of the concept—homelessness became a material condition and not about social relations through an imposition from above. But the logic could never be entirely suppressed. Even despite the legal-judico intervention in the redefining of homelessness, the basic discursive structure of disaffiliation continued in social science. The structure of homelessness still negates a term that has broader connotations than the legally defined absence of a fixed shelter. Legalism cannot deny the cultural logic of homelessness.

But why then does a critique of modernity need the family? Why is it the locus of this critique? And why, after a century and a half of anxiety about the family, do these concerns linger? The American family has transformed from its mid-nineteenth-century incarnation. Domestic space, the generations residing in a dwelling, distribution of labor, and gender politics have all altered in such detail that they would be incomprehensible from the nineteenth-century vantage point.

The problem of the homeless family tests the discourse—it stretches when faced with empirical conditions that contradict the basic premises of the philosophical critique of modernity. A partial conciliation to the new empirical conditions could easily sustain the basic discursive framework of disaffiliation. The homeless families could be pathologized—like Moynihan's Negro family—and themselves become an other to bourgeois norms; a new dialectic of homeless family/"normal" family could emerge without disturbing the logic of the discourse. But the literature on homelessness does not seem to take this response. Rather, the early interventions on the homeless family tend to bracket it; the earliest monographs set the homeless family aside and exclude it from the rules and norms governing the discourse on homelessness. This practice of discursive segregation of the homeless family is first seen most extensively in Jonathan Kozol's *Rachel and Her Children*.[1] The Pulitzer Prize–winning author's study of homeless families in New York City established this pattern, which became commonplace in subsequent sociological literature. The homeless family was not subsumed under the same rules as the homeless figure. The homeless family came to stand outside the discourse on homelessness, and thus the discourse could sustain in its critique of modern American life. This position on the outside was not codified in law but remained an implicit cultural logic unconsciously underlying the discourse on homelessness.

In a pattern, which we first saw in the fin-de-siècle period, the first significant writing on a new trend in the discourse on homelessness emanates from activists or journalists. From Jacob Riis to the journalistic popularizing of the term *bag lady*, social scientists have lagged behind these activists and journalists engaged in documenting and addressing homelessness. Jonathan Kozol continues this trend. He is an activist awarded with fellowships from top foundations (Guggenheim, Ford, and Rockefeller, among others) for his work with and writing on children and education. As with the earlier activist work on homelessness, Kozol's interventions may not have a direct causal impact on subsequent sociological work, but his book *Rachel and Her*

Children establishes a framework for understanding the homeless family; this framework continues in most of the important works on homelessness that appeared after him.

In Kozol's work, the entire structure of the homeless family is wrapped within the mythic overlay of "Rachel weeping for her children"—the same trope we saw in Jacob Riis's discussion of Jewish slums. This biblical narrative haunts the text beyond its obvious titular role and the eponymous pseudonym for a homeless family residing in New York's Martinique Hotel. Unlike McCulloch's nineteenth-century choice of Ishmaelites as the eponymous family for his study of professional beggars, Kozol changes identifiers; that is, he has named each character populating the text and selected Rachel and her children for the work's title. His name-giving for all the families reveals a penchant for biblical monikers—he uses names like Lazarus, Benjamin, and Rachel, and he also demonstrates a proclivity for biblical reference beyond this act of name-giving. These three biblical names that I here mention frame how Kozol wants us to read his homeless characters. First, Lazarus evokes the tale of the rich man and Lazarus, who was a poor, sore-covered man daily waiting at a gate and longing "to satisfy his hunger with what fell from the rich man's table" (Luke 16:19–31). Likewise, the name Lazarus evokes Jesus's friend in Bethany, whom Jesus raised from the dead (John 11). The same moniker connotes the poor, ill, and down-and-out of Kozol's character and a possibility of restoration.

Far more important than the brief Lazarus connection is the overarching framework of exile and wandering that comes from the figure of Rachel. As we saw earlier, Rachel was already mythologized within the biblical text to have a metonymic relationship with the Jewish people. The narrative frames his analysis in much the same way that Cain shapes Riis's—themes, motifs, and structure conjure the story of Rachel and the Babylonian exile. Kozol opens the book with a carpenter.[2] He—whom we learn is Peter (another biblical name)—is married to a homemaker named Megan. This family serves as a good introduction to Kozol's recuperation of the homeless family. Much of his time, I argue, is spent bracketing the homeless family from the anxieties that connect to the homeless figure. Peter and Megan were an intact family with a father who worked in construction and a stay-at-home mother taking care of the children. Their idyllic life was interrupted by a house fire that destroyed Peter's work tools and, thus, his means of livelihood. Through this destructive process we are told that "the children have been scattered—placed in various foster homes."[3] Violence and fire sundered the family and destroyed the home—scattering the children. These are the precise conditions giving rise to the matriarch Rachel's tears for her children. The violence of war destroyed the Jewish homes and scattered her children. Her progeny are carted away, and the nation destroyed.[4] Kozol closes his brief three-page introduction with the lament—"Why are so many people homeless in our nation?"[5] The idea of the (Jewish) nation implicit in the title is again invoked. The Jewishness of homelessness again percolates when the entire family becomes homeless.

As we saw in the trope's brief appearance in Riis's *How the Other Half Lives*, "Rachel weeping for her children" reinforced the connection between urban living conditions and the idea of exile in Judaism. The trope, which a century earlier invoked anti-Judaic traditions as a way to other the proto-homeless subject, now appears in a move to disconnect the homeless family from the homeless figure per se. Partially, this versatility attests to the malleability of myth—Cain can be a Gnostic or Byronic hero, as well as a Christ-killing, diabolic presence. But more than this plastic nature of myth, the inversion relates more to Kozol's particular storytelling.

In Jeremiah, the matriarch Rachel weeps for her progeny who are being carted off into Babylonian exile—the family is sundered. Kozol's story begins at an earlier stage—before the family dissolution. The families in his study are intact but have an ever-looming possibility of state-sponsored breakup—a threat that the children will be carted off into the foster care system. Rachel is still with her children, and the invocation of the trope shows what may befall those families if American society does not intervene. The exile that comes with familial dissolution is the imminent threat, but there is the possibility for hope. By juxtaposing the homeless family to what he calls the lifestyle homeless (i.e., the street homeless or the homeless subject), he is able to imply that without our intervention, this is the future of these children[6] and their parents. Rachel weeping for her children is here a cautionary tale; in Riis, it invoked extant urban life.

After framing the narrative within the story of Jewish exile and a rent family, tropes function as topoi to evoke the story throughout the narrative. Kozol calls a newborn—the youngest of all the children in the book—Benjamin, which is the name of the youngest of Jacob's 12 sons who were each the namesake for one of the 12 tribes of Israel; Benjamin was also one of Rachel's' only two sons. In the Genesis account, Benjamin is the innocent "baby of the family" who is wrongly framed for stealing from Pharaoh's palace. In Kozol, Benjamin becomes a symbol for the innocent homeless to whom things are done. For instance, Kozol states, "Homelessness is not an act of God. It is an act of man. It is done to people like ourselves. It is done to people such as Benjamin."[7] Or when he relates the perils of homeless families to a friend, he connects Benjamin with Rachel: "I tell her about Benjamin and Holly. I tell her about Rachel and her kids."[8] Having only daughters, Rachel's child could not carry the name Benjamin, but here Kozol narratively connects the two. Holly (Benjamin's mother) is sent into a state of wandering and can find nowhere to alight with Benjamin.[9]

Myth and the Politics of Culture

Now of course, one can easily discuss these topoi as coincidence. Biblical names are common in American culture. Yet the particular names connect to tell an overarching story of homelessness; while biblical themes abound,[10] Kozol tells us one story of homeless families, and through these tropes, he evokes or implies another one. As we saw with Riis and Warner, biblical tropes have become myth. Unmoored from institutions, practices, or a faith commitment, they provide a deep cultural basis for communication and legitimation of his story. A discursive turn to myth at the moment of the rise of the homeless family is not coincidence. First, as we have seen, myth is always latent within the discourse; it does not go away. Myth is a part of culture; it is a form of argument.[11] It is unnecessary when society furnishes the means to legitimate itself from within. When the ability for this legitimation is called into question, the axis of justification turns from the horizontal one of the contemporary day (a synchronic axis) to the vertical one of a "long cultural" justification (a diachronic axis). The potential for such a turn is always available to a culture so long as it is never forcibly severed from its cultural traditions.

Second, the connections of homelessness to Jewishness have also remained implicit. The exilic notions that were connected in part with the trope of Rachel resurface, albeit now in a seemingly recuperative mode. The shift in the function of the trope from an anti-Semitic othering to this recuperative role marks broader changes in American culture. First, mid-century geopolitical events contributed significantly to the amelioration of Jewish status in the United States—a combination of Holocaust guilt and the formation of an unquestioned political support for the newly formed state of Israel (consolidated through Cold War politics and evangelical theology) improved the domestic lot of American Jews. Second, a sense of

Jewishness has been assimilated into the deep cultural formation of American identity—best evidenced in the commonplace idea of a Judeo-Christian ethic as the basis for American law and culture. Even Anglo-American biblical scholarship is marked by this last shift; it has cast aside the paradigms of classicizing Germanic biblical scholarship (most famously seen with Rudolf Bultmann), which considered Christianity primarily derived from Greek philosophical thought. More recently, Anglo-American biblical scholarship searches for Jewish roots of Christianity in works by W. D. Davies, E. P. Sanders, and Mark Chancey, among others. Thus the Jewish connections with exile remain dormant within the discourse, but the signification of this has changed. Kozol's assimilation of the Jewish roots of homelessness with Christian ideas—names, stories, and quotes—ensures an integration with Judeo-Christianity and not a return to an anti-Semitic othering.

The third and most important reason for the reappearance of myth has to do with the relationships between different forms of argument—culture functions when socioeconomic explanations are insufficient or unable to address the situation. And closely related to this claim—culture functions as a form of argument against policy. When empirical or statistical evidence is cited on behalf of policies, then a turn to deep culture can still posit an argument that can stand up against empirical data. (Judicial "founders intent" arguments function much in this way—they rest on a denial of the existence of intervening history and contemporary society, which furnish contexts, in favor of a deep historical argument.) Myth is the cultural form that appears when contemporary social and political arguments are unable to make sense of a situation or when the empirical evidence contradicts a cultural tradition.

I have already started moving from the question *why myth?* to the underlying one—*why culture?* Beyond the latency of myth, what created the necessity for the turn to a cultural argument? Why is there an insufficiency in a social argument? Why at the particular historical moment of the Reagan era does the discourse need a cultural as opposed to social-class-economic critique? At this moment, we can see a broader movement in political life—the culturalization of politics. This trend has continued to our present moment. Culture wars have become (in part) a surrogate for social conflict; the rise of the culture wars corresponds to globalization's spatial separation of the process of production both from those who own the means of it and from the locus of consumption. Critiques of privilege, power, and, in short, capital have in North America (and, to a lesser extent, in Western Europe) become sublimated into a range of culture debates. Changes in the city and its relationship to capital have precipitated a new language of social and policy debates. International political and economic changes have given rise to a new domestic politics, one more intertwined with cultural arguments. Neoliberal dismantling of welfare states and capital's globalized reach has created conditions whereby flows of information and finance no longer need spatial proximity to loci of production, distribution, or consumption. The necessary spatial centralization that gave rise to the urbanization of capital has broken through to deterritorializing capital arrangements. Thus over the last couple of decades, the mass of industrial workers have increasingly had oceans and layers of subcontractors disconnecting them from their bourgeois bosses. Webs of interconnection leave the Filipino seamstress or the mechanized Indonesian cobbler far more than six degrees apart from the Wall Street firms from whom their labor is ultimately demanded. The geographical ghettoization of the proletariat creates spatial arrangements conducive to capital's consolidation without major concern from labor. The enervation of North American labor is abetted by the implicit threat of relocation of jobs elsewhere in the globe, if too great demands are made on wages, benefits, or other concessions.

The potential for large-scale North American social protest decreases with the ever-increasing spatial separation of an actual industrial proletariat. First, those workers most explicitly experiencing exploitation and an alienation on an even larger scale—their products are not even for consumption in their own hemisphere—are separated from the state and the space whence the exploitation arises. Second, with the demise of a domestic manufacturing base, a general sense of economic well-being is evoked in the United States (despite a loss of real wages). The fin-de-siècle conditions of poverty, which arose from the urbanized overaccumulation of labor to meet the demands of the rise of industrial production, are a historical moment. Not to say that American urban poverty does not exist in the waning decades of the twentieth century or in the first decade of the twenty-first, but this poverty has more to do with industrial flight and capital's deterritorialization rather than the fixes of it in urban centers; the contemporary poverty formed by industrial capital is ensconced in the global south. Technological fixes enabled the reversal of the spatial arrangements we encountered in Chapter 2—the shipping of industry rather than the migrations of labor. This spatial fix averts the social threats from labor overaccumulations. Thus globalization creates conditions to minimize social unrest within North

America (Seattle World Trade Organization protests or the Occupy Wall Street movement, notwithstanding). In the absence of any widespread labor movement or consolidated class antagonisms, culture has become the venue in which political disputes are primarily worked out—thus the phantom issues of family values take center stage, while social inequities remain marginal. The Victorian era origin of many of these culture wars saw them quite explicitly tied to class interests; for example, Riis's making of an American was the formation of an assimilated bourgeois citizen-subject. As the class threats subside into the realization that a Paris Commune will not establish itself in Manhattan's Five Points, these culture wars still reflect class interests, though at more subtle levels.

The demise of organized labor, the hiddenness of rampant industrial poverty (which has been replaced with the individual homeless easily dismissed on the grounds of individual pathology), and an assumption of (or entitlement to) affluence has—in older terms—undermined the subjective conditions for social change. New means become necessary to create a sense of a need for change or to articulate problems; the surrogate for these social/class wars of the past has often been culture.

The discourse on homelessness is imbricated in these broader trends in American society—like economic changes, the rise of the postindustrial city, and the culturalization of politics. The homeless are not people with access to the means of production, and they are visible at the given moment. It is precisely at the moment when they were gaining in visibility and thought to be spilling out from the ghettos of the Bowery that the turn to myth happened.

It was precisely the adequacy of the empirical explanations for the homeless figure that necessitated the turn to myth. The empirical explanations seemed sufficient to account for the 1980s burgeoning problem of homelessness—people had no place to stay at night because the bottom of the housing market (i.e., the Skid Row SROs) was eliminated. But these accounts worked against the deep cultural assumptions of the discourse on homelessness; homelessness as a purely material condition would strip the discourse of its links to the family and the critique of modernity. As I have already argued, the turn to myth arises in response to two different forms of crisis. The first—which we saw in the fin-de-siècle era—was the inability of a society to legitimate itself from the means of the day; thus social explanations turn to deep culture. The second of these primary forms of crisis—which we find here with the Reagan-era reappearance of myth—is similar in that it is a breakdown in social explanation. But this crisis arises from a contradiction between deep culture and the contemporary social or policy accounts. The discourse on homelessness had from its inception been intertwined with the mythic tropes of deep culture. They become unnecessary for social legitimation when the discourse and the social science and policy literatures are coextensive with the deep cultural assumptions. But when the empirical data and policy explanations contradict the deep cultural assumptions of the discourse, myth no longer remains latent; it reappears as a tool of discursive legitimation.

The policy move to an empirically verifiable definition of homelessness—not having a fixed place to stay at night—combines with the seemingly adequate etiological explanations of mental illness, substance abuse, laziness, and pathology to define a homeless subject. The sufficiency of these created the conditions by which all homeless—including the homeless family—might be quickly accounted for by such explanations. To break the homeless family out from this explanation—and thus preserve the discursive formulation of the homeless figure as other of family—it became necessary to turn the axis of explanation for this particular group of people. The homeless family was rendered distinct; it had a different account—a different explanation, a different problem—and presumably needed a different response. While the mythic tropes are not the primary way of discussing the homeless family, myth did its job of discursively bracketing the homeless family. Once done, the explicit use of myth was no longer necessary—it could return to a state of discursive disuse.

With the 1980s rise of the homeless family, a series of tensions within the discourse on homelessness and in the social life of the urban poor emerged. The need to bracket the homeless family follows not only from the discursive logic that intertwines the homeless figure with anxieties about modernization's impact on the family. The Moynihan Report already demonstrated the discursive practice of setting apart the poor urban African American family in the process of buoying the white bourgeois family. The bracketing of the homeless family does not take the easy route and sever the poor family to preserve a rhetorical protection of the middle class. But to undertake this recuperative move, the homeless family has to be distinguished from other elements of the homeless population. This distinction was not between the poor urban family and the middle class but rather between the homeless family and the homeless subject. Jonathan Kozol certainly makes this latter distinction:

It is worth adding also that this book is not about the "lifestyle homeless"—young people, for example, who leave home out of the wish to drift and wander for a time, much as children of the counterculture might have done in the late 1960s. Such people, if they are in danger, need protection. They are not the subject of this work.

Finally, the emphasis is not on those who were confined in mental hospitals and were deinstitutionalized ten years ago. The emphasis, if anything, is the reverse: It is the creation of an institution that makes healthy people ill, normal people clinically depressed, and those who may already be unwell a great deal worse . . . And it is this institution, one of our own invention, which will mass-produce pathologies, addictions, violence, dependencies, perhaps even a longing for retaliation, for self-vindication, on a scale that will transcend, by far, whatever deviant behaviors we may try to write into their pasts.[12]

Here we see him mapping his recuperating project onto a series of tensions, ones that we find embedded within the discourse on homelessness. The homeless family is not to be articulated through a dialectical distinction with the middle-class family but by othering the rest of the homeless population. Kozol cements this bracketing with his use of mythic tropes, which legitimate the families. The efficacy of this bracketing requires, on the one hand, longstanding distinctions between the lumpen and the proletariat and, on the other, the absence of any organized structures for the poor—whether laborers, unemployed, or others—that could redress social issues that impact the homeless.

These two distinctions are intertwined. The homeless fall into that class of people often considered unproductive. While many may labor—in the early twentieth century, the wanderings of the hobo were to meet the demands of temporary or seasonal labor—as a class, they are constituted as unproductive. Since at least Marx's distinction of the lumpenproletariat (the rabble) from the proletariat (industrial laboring class), some form of distinction has been maintained between those populations from which come the individuals subsequently constituted as homeless figures—whether in a Bowery or Skid Row motel, a shelter or on the sidewalk—and the "working poor."[13] We have seen Riis distinguish between the honest poor and paupers and identified the clothesline as the division. The wage earners of the working poor do not need a mythologization because their status is not as controversial—they are participating within a bourgeois work ethic. Their status is easily accounted for through the supply and demand of labor economics. The manufacturing proletariat had through unions and labor policy improved their lot; the service sector wage earners were not as great, but still their status did not threaten any major political narratives. But the homeless individual living in the streets and parks of American cities—the 1980s homeless figure who was no longer contained within ghettoized enclaves—does not integrate into narratives of prosperity or hard work. Some cultural explanations appear to elide the contradictions between the 1980s explosion of homelessness and political claims like Reagan's that no one went hungry in America. The dissonance between this popular rhetoric and the street-dwelling realities contributed to the need for myth—but the homeless individual was still easily dismissed for substance abuse or mental health problems. Explanation for the existence of this underclass was necessary yet does not fully account for Kozol's turn to myth.

The urban lumpen as a class exists outside the boundaries of bourgeois civil society—they are not integrated into the structures of capital or society; they thus have little infrastructure for self-provision. When the hobo was still a viably distinct figure, this marginal group had infrastructures like the Hobo College, the International Brotherhood Welfare Association, and the International Workers of the World. But part of the formation of the category of homelessness was Sutherland and Locke's process of shelterization—a process that has many parallels in the social service institutions Kozol analyzes.[14] And if not entirely subjecting the population to the space of the shelter, the figure—as we saw in Part II—is constituted by the institutions of Skid Row, but these were not institutions made by the efforts of the disaffiliated men populating the area. Without any associations, institutions, and so on, the homeless as a class did not organize themselves. But in this institutional disarray, the boundaries of the population remain ambiguous—who is included and who is excluded? Why? In the fin-de-siècle era, we saw a continuing contraction of the term *homeless* from the city, to its residents, to the residents of the slums, to the residents of Skid Row. In the last couple of decades of the twentieth century, the moniker began to expand and include larger populations—larger in numbers, larger in geographic dispersal, and larger in the social formations (i.e., families).

The need to somehow separate this last group from the pathologies and assumptions plaguing homeless individuals became necessary to ensure the discursive disconnection of the homeless figure from the homeless family. In several different ways, Kozol distinguishes the homeless families whom he studies from the population of homeless individuals or "lifestyle homeless" by including habits of work, hygiene, honesty, and so on—that is, many of the pathological characteristics that have been connected with the concept of homelessness since it applied to the fin-de-siècle metropolis.[15] In the 1980s, the two groups—homeless individuals and homeless families— were beginning to have strong rhetorical connections—most importantly the new application of the common term *homeless* to both groups after long being semantically distinct. Categorically distinguishing between these groups required a mode of explanation beyond the sociological and economic accounts by which all homelessness was being defined. The bracketing of the homeless family was necessary to sustain the philosophical critique of modernity, which forms part of the discourse on homelessness. The discourse was built around the premise that the family was the last remnant of *Gemeinschaft*. The homeless family threatened to undercut the disaffiliation thesis; it threatened to undermine the very semantic structure of the category as the other of family and its utopic locus of home. The new empirical conditions were culturally incoherent and thus necessitated discursive negotiations if the cultural logic was to sustain.

The gender and race fractures in the disaffiliation thesis had already started the sociological shift toward the McKinney Act-policy definition of homelessness as a material condition. With that change, the conditions whereby the homeless family could be formed and thus assume the broader assumptions of the problems of homelessness began. Columbia University urban economist Brendan O'Flaherty's look back to the 1980's rise of the homeless family from the vantage point of a decade later argues that there were two reasons for the slow rise of this group:

> Before roughly 1982 in North America, families were not thought of as homeless for two main reasons. The first was linguistic: homelessness meant disaffiliation, and if you were part of a family you couldn't be disaffiliated. The second reason arose from the centrality of street homelessness: since very few families were seen on the street, it was difficult to think of shelters or hotels as keeping their inhabitants off the street. But given the unprincipled way the term "homeless" is applied to single adults, invoking some sort of principle to exclude families doesn't seem warranted.
>
> In North America during the 1960s and 1970s, the families that would come to be called homeless were usually referred to as "families in emergency housing" or "families in disaster centers" or "families of battered women."[16]

The dominance of street homelessness (e.g., people living on the sidewalk or alleyways) as the normative model of the homeless figure only precedes

the homeless family by little more than a decade. The disaffiliation definition seen with Bahr and Caplow kept the "homeless" as men in Skid Row
motels, not street dwellers. The dramatic rise of this latter population took
place primarily over the course of the 1970s. So O'Flaherty's first reason
(linguistics) also significantly delayed homelessness as being considered a
condition of people living on the street (his second reason for a failure to
recognize a family as homeless). He is taking a very brief transitional period
in the formation of homelessness and reifying it—the processes that led
to the homeless figure as a street dweller were the same processes that
enabled the formation of the homeless family. The processes involved
the seeming decline of the disaffiliation thesis in response to changing accounts of street populations, changing demographics, and shifting
geographies.

This supposed decline was resisted, although primarily for institutional rather than discursive reasons. Brendan O'Flaherty writes that the
constitution of the "homeless family" met with great resistance and only
judicial intervention enabled this process: "The year 1983 and the first use
of the term 'homeless families' also coincides with the filing of *McCain v.
Koch*, designed to establish judicial oversight over the family-shelter system.
The city opposed this suit more vigorously than it opposed the companion
suits (*Callahan v. Carey* and *Eldred v. Koch*) for single adults, and the case
was not finally decided until 1986, but it may have hastened the linguistic
change and may also have been responsible indirectly for some improvement in the quality of shelters."[17]

While some institutional services were available to families and not to
homeless individuals, and vice versa, the impetus behind the *McCain v.
Koch* court case was that the municipal institutions established to provide
homeless services were inadequately meeting the needs of families—that
is, the institutions needed to treat both populations the same. Homeless
families—because of fears of children being taken away from them—do not
tend to congregate in public spaces but much more frequently try to remain
relatively hidden. The political implications of the public life of a homeless individual are not as dire. However, since the 1980s, many cities have
adopted legislation establishing much of homelessness as a status crime; for
example, laws against loitering or urban camping make the state of having
nowhere to live other than a sidewalk illegal. After this judicial intervention,
the term *homeless family* could enter into both everyday and social science
parlance.

Once the linguistic line was crossed and a family could be homeless, the history of the term—its pathologies and nuances, its association with the city, and its relationships to Victorian family ideals—became signified within a family. The discursive logic entered into a contradiction: Homelessness was a condition of separation from or disaffiliation from family, but the discourse also had the awkward formulation of a "nonfamily" family. I identify a multistep process that facilitated the discursive negotiation to undo this conundrum. First, after the interventions of Kozol, the family was rendered distinct from those homeless individuals who were on the street. But since the same term *homeless* applied to both groups, the term then had to be redefined. The codification of the redefinition came later with 1987's Stewart B. McKinney Act.[18] The segregation of the family through practices like Kozol's distinguishing between the homeless family, on the one hand, and the lifestyle homeless, the deinstitutionalized, or bag ladies, on the other, established that the homeless figure and the homeless family were not the same, even though they were subjected to similar processes of subjectivation. A subsequent step required that this distinction had to in some way be legitimated. The language (homelessness) and the institutions (shelters) were in part the same for both the family and the homeless individual; only the spatial structures—locations of congregation, the publicness of their lives, and so on—remained distinct. This legitimation (as we have seen with Kozol) initially took the form of myth. Once the distinction had become well established, the particular tropes, like Rachel and her children, were no longer invoked; rather, the distinctions were replaced with language of "deserving" and "undeserving" for families with minimal concern for the children who were "innocent" in the process—as if someone is guilty of being without shelter. As with the New Deal–era rise of the homeless man, the language of myth recedes at moments of discursive stability. With the waning of the mythic tropes, a cultural bifurcation remained even though the two groups were no longer legally distinct. The cultural bifurcation created a bit of a discursive versus a legal/service schizophrenia. The one umbrella term subsumes both the homeless family and the lifestyle homeless, deinstitutionalized, and others, but the structure of services is where these are most evident. Programs serving homeless families are usually quite distinct from those serving homeless individuals.[19] For example, see the breakdown in service categories in the United Way 211 help information systems for most metropolitan areas.

The discursive bracketing continued in the field of sociology and in part in the field of social services.

Part of this bracketing was first to distinguish the family from the homeless individual. An additional step was also crucial—on the one hand, ensuring that no other pathology attached to the homeless family and, on the other, positing that these very families inhabited the crucial bourgeois virtues of hard work, thrift, and faith. Kozol explains the homelessness of his families from fire, job loss, lead paint dangers, and family illness. In this last case (family illness), which is his first full narrative and interview with a family, a woman and her children became homeless precisely because of her attentiveness to family. Her father was at sea, and her mother became quite sick. She left school to take care of her mother, lost work, and when her mother died, soon found herself without a place to live.[20] He has a clear standard of the proper way to be homeless. He juxtaposes a woman whom he calls Kim to Rachel: "No two people in the Martinique are quite alike; but no two people could be less alike than Rachel and a woman I call Kim. Kim stands out from almost every other person I have met here. Her energy may be a helpful and instructive counterpoint to much of the hopelessness and panic we have seen."[21] It is not a coincidence that Kim is the most "bourgeois" of his homeless parents—hardworking, thrifty, well adjusted.[22] She was a preschool teacher living in a fixer-upper house that had a complete breakdown of the heating system in midwinter—"In a matter of weeks she was reduced from working woman and householder to a client of the welfare system."[23] To ensure that the cognitive wedge between the homeless family and individual remains in force, he splinters the categories—he makes an argument for difference to undermine claims of pathology. His argument implies that as long as there are families headed by women like Kim, we cannot impute pathology to the homeless family. These families are not exceptions; rather, these nonpathological families without substance abuse, prostitution, and other stereotypes of the "undeserving" displaced demonstrate that there can be no categorical connection between the homeless family and pathology. He writes that "The use of the unrestrictive term, 'the homeless,' is in certain ways misleading. It suggests a uniform set of problems and a single category of poor people. The miseries that many of these people undergo are somewhat uniform. The squalor is uniform. The density of living space is uniform. The fear of guards, of drugs, and of irrational bureaucracy is uniform. The uniformity is in their mode of suffering, not in themselves."[24] The causes of homelessness are so varied, he argues, that we can make no blanket statements about the homeless; however, his argument continues, the effects of homelessness are common—it is shelterization, which creates a de facto uniformity (at least in parts of the experience).

I agree with Kozol that the monolithic category is problematic; a taxonomic system that acknowledges distinctions between populations is desirable. It need not be the fin-de-siècle dual criteria of motion and labor, but a new system of evaluating is necessary—some form of updating of these criteria would need to take place. Because homelessness has come to be primarily a problem of social services and social policy (i.e., our language is instrumental), I assume that any such reworking will entail a taxonomy that breaks along programmatic lines of funding and social services. This point was made at the incipient moment of the social science use of the term *homeless*; Alice Solenberger had one taxonomy for administering services and a second one for analytical purposes. However, developing an instrumental vocabulary for the social service and policy population will most likely mean that the language of homelessness will still be subordinated to the bourgeois interests of managing a population rather than those of the homeless population.

The Family and Cultural Drag

However much I agree with the argument for recognizing the pluralism within the populations considered under the rubric of homelessness, my concern is even more so with the term *homeless* itself. The term carries legacies of theological and cultural critiques of modernity; it posits the idea of a home, which transcends place. The term *homeless* is now posited as one of space (the absence of a fixed shelter), but it has never been divorced from its inheritance of meanings—traces linger in the discourse. The discourse on homelessness is not merely the absence of shelter, nor is it merely the absence of family. These were both derivative from broader concerns about modernization. The discourse is about the collapse of community and the basis of such community; these bases rest on relationships and place, longstanding ties to people and land. But the ways of discussing these places, the language, and symbols that articulate these ties that bind are collapsed. Homelessness is a discourse that contains a longing and a critique—it laments the dissolution of a life before modernization.

I am not positing a pristine *Gemeinschaft*—the discourse on homelessness, however, assumes that such a community existed. But I am positing that a language of loss, even a language of fall, is taken up into the discourse on homelessness. The fin-de-siècle Christian home of the Victorian family already included loss in the concept of home. The meaning embedded in "home" contained the loss of the totality presumed to be in a community. The Lukácsian sense of unity embedded in the idea of the community as a home assumes a homogeneity of population. The mass migrations of the late nineteenth century undermined such perceived homogeneity and thus permanently undermined the possibility of such unity.

With the formation of the homeless city and the homelessness of its residents, the loss of fullness and unity was able to inhabit this negative term. Home could contain all the positive meanings, and the entire history of loss could reside in "homelessness." While home has come to be nearly synonymous with dwelling and homelessness with its absence, all the attendant meanings—like community, family, and nation—still vie within the dialectical pair. Thus the negation of dwelling is a negation of a source of meaning, of community, of metaphysical grounding. As we saw in the previous passage, Kozol's call for a more nuanced language is a recognition of the plurality of social practices subsumed under the guise of homelessness, but he fails to recognize that this pluralism is precisely what created the conditions for a transcendental homelessness. Plurality undermines the unity necessary for the totality of community; the fragmentation of this supposed totality is the problem of transcendental homelessness. The term *homeless* must go, and then a new way of talking about social displacement must replace it. Otherwise, the discourse remains a carrier of critiques of modernity. The bucolic ideals central to the discourse on homelessness do not reflect current cultural commentary on the family; few still long for a small town of kin relationships, and fewer think such an ideal obtainable. Yet our categories of urban social science retain this nostalgia and a lament for the city that ended this community life.

As the urban conditions that gave rise to this transcendental problem now seem like a remote past—as migrations, flows of capital, and the distribution of labor are transformed through ever-changing communications and transportation technologies—a critique of nineteenth-century urbanization seems quaint. Of course, much of our public debate is still wrestling with many of these same issues. Beyond a Horkheimerian cultural lag, the American family values debates and cultural wars of recent decades have established a cultural drag. Max Horkheimer's analysis of family[25] looks not only to the immediate impact of production on social forms but also to how cultural forms, like family, remain connected to older modes and thus lag in changing to reflect current economic circumstances. Because of this cultural lag, these slower-changing institutions, like the family, can sustain a form and rhetoric that reflects older economic conditions. However, I argue that the contemporary debates about family are not a failure to recognize structures changing through shifts in means of production and consumption; a cultural drag is a purposive effort to deny change in order to freeze time while simultaneously lauding or trying to accrue the benefits of the economic shifts. Cultural drag is an effort to bisect cultural politics from political economy. As I have argued elsewhere,[26] the homeless figure wanes as the primary carrier of family anxieties; these are able to become freestanding through processes of the culturalization of politics. Then the cultural drag becomes quite explicit. But even within the discourse on homelessness, the cultural drag begins.

Myth, in the instance of homelessness, has been a tool of cultural drag. Tethering the modern problem to deep culture connects the social practices—whether they be Victorian tramping, fin-de-siècle slum dwelling, or Reagan-era family homelessness in a welfare motel—to a past. These are not of the modern (in the Baudelairean sense) world; to be ever-new would require the cultural form to maintain its pace with the shifting landscape of modernization as it is writ large. The problem thus becomes delinked from the economic system of which the urban lumpen are an unfortunate side effect. This new problem of homelessness is thus rendered as a cultural problem and not an economic one. The latency of myth in the discourse implies an argument that homelessness is still a problem of culture. It is the bourgeois argument that the modern economy is not integral to the formation of homelessness—no overaccumulations of labor, no elimination of housing stock, and no problems with employment contribute to the formation of a homeless figure. The homeless figure is accounted for by explanations of sin appropriately secularized as pathology.

Barthes is, in part, correct—the latency of myth is an argument against an economic underpinning of homelessness. But this presumed bourgeoisness of myth is predicated upon a crude base-superstructure model of Marxism—hardly a compelling read of Marx. And it subordinates the use of myth to its form. The form here contains the bourgeois cultural argument, but the form does not limit the potential deployment. And the bourgeoisness is the result of the exigencies of history—it is a class whose interests are served by the cultural/economic bifurcation. Other classes have been served by such dichotomies, and one can imagine the possibility of another class having such interests. The use and the form of myth do not have to coincide within a particular relationship to capital. But this does not answer our questions about the roles of cultural drag with homelessness.

Why is it useful to think of homelessness as a cultural problem? Why does getting behind sociology and the McKinney Act help us to better understand homelessness? The family has become a symbol of enormous import in American society—it represents the potential for good, for disseminating values and culture. It embodies the organicism of life that we believe once existed. Some lament that as a society, we have tragically undermined the institution of the family through the faux compassion of social work and social services; others fear that it has been undercut by the economic changes that require two incomes; and, again, others fear that it is a shambles because of the selfishness of individualism. The discourse on homelessness helps us to see these debates in relief—the contradictions between our claims about the family come to the fore in this discourse. But the discourse on homelessness is important for more than this heuristic purpose. One could probably study the family in itself to get to many of these questions. But the structure of thought and language, we know, is predicated on categories of difference—words are only understood in negation. Yet we have no word to negate the family—"familyless" does not easily slip off the tongue. Homeless is the closest we have to this negation. By bringing the anxieties about the family into relief and demonstrating how they relate to the social changes wrought by modernization, I am able to demonstrate a sense of the complexity of the relationships between culture, the economy, and social structures. The inability to fully decouple family ideals from the discourse on homelessness reveals the cultural drag of this institution.

The attempted bifurcation of homelessness from family anxieties produced other side effects. For over a century, the discourse on homelessness had been a carrier of anxieties about the social impacts of modernization. Merely because a series of court cases and pieces of legislation redefined homelessness does not mean that anxieties about the family disappeared. In fact, concern for the family was already increasing as evidenced by rising divorce rates, more women entering the workforce, *Roe v. Wade*, and the greater demand for equal rights. There were now anxieties about the family that were originating elsewhere in American society—not merely through urbanization's impact on social structures. While these broader changes in gender and family politics certainly have ties to the same economic shifts informing the discourse on homelessness, the discourse of these newer problems developed independently of that on homelessness. Homelessness thus was not an exclusive carrier of family anxieties. When homelessness became defined as a material condition, much of the family anxiety no longer remained connected to the homeless figure. It was no longer the primary carrier; these anxieties emerged in this other cultural location—the emerging family values movement.

Jonathan Kozol was already starting to see the incommensurability between worries about family values and the discourse on homelessness. In his interventions, he argues that the pathology associated with homeless individuals and, I argue, the implicit familial problems attendant to them cannot cohere to the homeless families. These families are loving, whole, and struggling to remain so in the face of great economic struggle. The problem is not a lack of family values within the family that becomes homeless; it is an insufficient embrace of such values by the institutional apparatus of social service bureaucracies. According to Kozol, any family destruction in those whom he studies is not the cause of homelessness, but rather is the result of being homeless. For him, the idea of disaffiliation cannot reside within the homeless family. Kozol writes the following:

> We may wonder at an agency of government that, even unwittingly, punishes a mother in a time of crisis for her desperation to remain close to the one adult in the entire world who seems to love her. Why would a society alarmed by the decline in family values try to separate a mother from her child's father at the time she needs him most and when he displays that willingness to share responsibility whose absence we repeatedly deplore?
>
> This, then, is a case not of the breakdown of a family but of a bureaucratic mechanism that *disintegrates* the family, tearing apart a mother and father in a time of shared ordeal. Sharing pain does not merely bring relief to people under siege; it often forms a bond that gives them stronger reason to remain together later. So the efforts of the city, as belated as they were, to offer Holly shelter if she would agree to shed her child's father, like its offer to remove her as a parent altogether and to place the child in an institution—not because the child *needed* institutional care but because the city could not give her a safe home—represent destructive social policy on several levels.[27]

The homeless family then is entirely beyond the pale of disaffiliation; it does not deny family values. For Kozol, those values are important and need to exist, but anxiety about the family cannot attach to this new construction of homelessness.[28] Kozol rhetorically establishes a line between the homeless family and the lifestyle homeless—a distinction further legitimated through myth, and thus he does little to challenge prevailing paradigms of the homeless figure as disaffiliated; he merely establishes an outlying group.

So disaffiliation remains a predominant characteristic of the homeless individual. The fracturing of the monolithic consensus of the disaffiliated man did not eliminate disaffiliation as a basic characteristic of the homeless figure; the demographics of disaffiliation merely expanded to include a wider population. No longer just the single, white middle-age man, women and African Americans were now reported in the populations suffering disaffiliation. Even after the advent of the homeless family, disaffiliation remains a basic determinant of the homeless individual; the homeless family thus remains quite distinct. Peter Rossi's late 1980s *Down and Out in America* was the first important work on homelessness after the emergence and bracketing of the homeless family. As such, it is an important text to determine how Kozol's (and other's—he is, after all, emblematic of the process, not its sole advocate) distinction between the homeless family and the individual is assimilated into the discourse. Rossi argues that large-scale changes in the homeless population started in the 1970s. He argues that the structure and nature of homelessness changed so much that we have to distinguish between the "old" homeless and the "new." He wrote the following:

> The "old" homeless may have blighted some sections of the central cities, but from the perspective of urbanites they had the virtue of being concentrated on Skid Row, which one could avoid and hence ignore. Also, must of the old homeless had some shelter, although inadequate by any standards, and very few were literally sleeping on the streets . . . Homelessness began to take on new forms by the end of the 1970s. Although all the researchers found some homeless people sleeping out on the streets or in public places in the 1950s and 1960s, the homeless by and large were familyless persons living in very inexpensive (and often inadequate) housing, mainly cubic and SRO hotels. Toward the end of the next decade, what had been a minor form of homelessness became more prevalent: literal homelessness began to grow and at the same time to become more visible to the public. It became more and more difficult to ignore the evidence that some people had no shelter and lived on streets. The "new" homeless could be found resting or sleeping in public places such as bus or railroad stations, on steam grates in doorways and vestibules, in cardboard boxes, in abandoned cars, or in other places where they could be seen by the public.[29]

The big change with the rise of Rossi's "new homeless" is the formation of a class. The homeless have become the class of the urban displaced—they are the new lumpenproletariat or the urban rabble. Here we see a shift that has long been under way—the "homeless" are now a group; the term *homeless* is no longer an adjective attached to the city or a person but the class of people experiencing a set of circumstances. In Sutherland and Locke, the homeless figure had been constituted as a solitary individual—he was a homeless man. Any semblance of individuality collapses once "the homeless" become a group. The individuality of the earlier homelessness is integrated with the assumption of disaffiliation. The homeless figure was a solitary, modern individual whose significant social relations were torn by the demands of urbanization. With the homeless family, homelessness became a collective act, and the foundational assumption of disaffiliation was brought into doubt. The ability of the discourse and empirical situations to reconcile was brought into question; judicial and legislative actions were necessary for social services to even recognize the empirical shifts. What does it mean that the term *homeless* was now an object and not a condition?

For Rossi, this shift signifies that a new homelessness has come into being. But Rossi's oft-bandied distinction between the old homeless and new homeless—essentially the disaffiliated man on Skid Row versus the shelterless living on sidewalks and in parks and boxes—fails to fully account for how the two conditions are connected. Despite appearing to be quite distinct social problems, the same term was used to apply to both. The practices could not include a complete break, or the new problem could not have so easily assimilated to the old category. He argues for several shifts—most of which deal with demographic changes[30]—but acknowledges a good many continuities. These continuities go to the core of what the discourse assumes homelessness to be. Without some continuity, the two categories would be articulated as distinct social problems. Yet both Rossi's new and the old homeless continued to be considered homeless. Looking at Rossi's outline of continuities helps us see what characteristics are at the core of homelessness. As I pointed out in the introduction, there are no complete breaks. Analyzing the continuities helps us understand the basic assumptions of the discourse. Rossi explains these continuities:

> There are also some continuities from the old to the new homeless. First of all, they share the condition of extreme poverty . . . The new and the old homeless also are alike in having high levels of disability[31] . . . A new twist is drug abuse . . .

A final point of comparability between the old and the new homeless is that both are relatively isolated socially . . . So extensive was the absence of social ties with kin and friends among the old homeless that Caplow and Bahr define homelessness as essentially a state of *disaffiliation*, without enduring and supporting ties to family, friends, and kin. Disaffiliation also characterizes the new homeless, marking the group off from other extremely poor persons.[32]

These continuities account for the reasons that the "new" are still subsumed under the rubric of *homeless*—extreme poverty, disability (pathology), and disaffiliation. At the moment that the social science and policy have supposedly assimilated the homeless family, the discourse cannot move beyond disaffiliation, but rather disaffiliation characterizes homelessness, despite a new policy definition—to which we shall shortly come—based exclusively on where one stays at night. Rossi does not redefine disaffiliation to smooth over this difficulty; it remains for him a state "without enduring and supporting ties to family, friends, and kin."[33] A family without ties to family or kin cannot exist; it is a logical contradiction, for (as we saw in Part II) the discursively presumed family is a nuclear one. Therefore, the discourse de facto separates the homeless family from the category of "the homeless." The discourse on homelessness—which has shaped the social science categories—is very slow to take up the new empirical shifts. Demographic changes are noted, as we see with Rossi, but the basic categories are not questioned. As judicial and legislative action forcibly works against culture, we find the deep cultural bases of the discourse resistant to change. The basic discursive framework remains, despite the change in the legal definition of homelessness.

Even Christopher Jencks's famed summing of the state of the field in his 1994 book *The Homeless*—an implicit statement of who is in the group and who is not—looks at families primarily for the role of changes in marriage in contributing to the problems of homeless. ("The decline of marriage may have been linked to a general weakening of family ties that left more of the very poor without relatives willing to help them.")[34] His summary of the field has the glaring absence of the homeless family; he still studies the family to clarify the role of disaffiliation in the homeless figure.

In earlier periods, *homelessness* was a description of those people who experienced a state or condition of being homeless. In the fin-de-siècle period, the category was a grouping of other categories; these other categories fell out of the discourse by the New Deal era. But by the 1980s, a new shift is well under way from description to objectivation. The constitution of "the homeless" as a mass (as a noun) marks the group of people defined by the discourse; *homeless* as an adjective remains a legal effort to work against the discourse. When Congress defined *homeless* for the purpose of funding and regulating social services,[35] the heading of paragraph 11302 was "general definition of homeless individual." The category is still descriptive. But this definition worked against culture, and policy cannot be effective when working against culture. The discourse maintained the assumption of disaffiliation by constituting a class defined as such. When the discourse on homelessness shifts from a language of description to the formation of a class, a new politics is embedded within the discourse. Is it merely a question of mass formation? Or is something else happening here? Why at this moment did "the homeless" become a mass? What necessitated this grammatical shift?

While this grammatical change in the formation of the homeless is interesting, I am more concerned with how this shift relates to the tensions between the discourse and policy. How does the formation of "the homeless" relate to this? The formation of a mass elides all individuality and personality; within the mass of "the homeless," there is no longer a homeless figure. At the moment when a new empirical definition furnishes the semantic tools for ever-greater individuation, the blindness to a range of demographic variation is seemingly falling away. As legislative fiat provides new categories to avoid reconstituting such blind spots, the mass is formed. The mass empties the collective of all content. "The homeless" are not a composite in which each individual maintains a unique identity; it is a category of the whole—it is not fully formed until each individual figure has been emptied of its content. In his discussion of a different mass formation—the mass ornament of the Tiller Girls, Siegfried Kracauer points out that the formation of the mass indicates a "relapse into mythology":

> It is only remnants of the complex of man that enter into the mass ornament. They are selected and combined in the aesthetic medium according to a principle which represents form-bursting reason in a purer way than those other principles that preserve man as an organic unity.
>
> Viewed from the perspective of reason, the mass ornament reveals itself as a *mythological cult* that is masquerading in the garb of abstraction. Compared to the concrete immediacy of other corporeal presentations, the ornament's conformity to reason is thus an illusion . . . It is the *rational and empty form of the [mythological] cult*, devoid of any explicit meaning, that appears in the mass ornament. As such, it proves to be a relapse into mythology of an order so great that one can

hardly imagine its being exceeded, a relapse which, in turn, again betrays the degree to which capitalist *Ratio* is closed off from reason.[36]

Beyond the necessary caveats—a different mass and a different form of myth than my more narrowly defined deinstitutionalized religious narratives— the structure of a mass formation signaling a return to myth has significant parallels with my argument about the "the homeless." The mass is an elision of the particular; it is the denial of the concrete. It is the formation of a transcendental form in lieu of the plural; it is a category of the total. The mass of "the homeless" rests upon what I call a second order mythologization—the ideological process of mythologizing the family.

The mythologizing of the family runs parallel to the formation of this mass, for the family is itself a collectivity. The return to myth, which envelops the homeless family, takes place through both first order ("Rachel and her children") and second order (collectivity bracketed from "the homeless") processes of mythologizing. The new empirical conditions, which necessitated judicial and legislative interventions, met with superficial integration within much of the social science literature—as we saw with both Peter Rossi and Christopher Jencks. A new taxonomy of new versus old homeless made a nod to the policy fiats, but the cultural logic of the discourse remains. The juxtaposition of the family to the homeless continues within the structure of the discourse. But this family-homeless dialectic takes on a dualness. First, "the homeless" remain the other of bourgeois subjects and their social/familial norms. But a second layer of othering appears with the homeless family—the homeless family becomes an other to "the homeless."

Policy attempts to integrate all of the displaced by redefining the homeless individual by material means created the conditions whereby a family and an individual can all be homeless. This attempt to assimilate the homeless family appears to correct the dialectical relationship (between family and the homeless figure) whose logic had blinded social scientists and service providers to the families needing services. However, this judicolegislative action never fully undid the discursive logic. Rather, the constitution of the collectivity of "the homeless" overwhelmingly failed to integrate the homeless family, as we have seen with Kozol, Rossi, and Jencks. The discourse bracketed the family from "the homeless." Even though legislation established the means whereby the family could be brought under the general rubric of the homeless, it still failed to integrate it. Paragraph 11302 of the US code—which provides the oft-cited HUD definition of homelessness—delineates the "general definition of homeless individual" and goes on to declare the following:

(a) In general

For purposes of this chapter, the term "homeless" or "homeless individual or homeless person" includes—

(1) an individual who lacks a fixed, regular, and adequate nighttime residence; and

(2) an individual who has a primary nighttime residence that is—

(A) a supervised publicly or privately operated shelter designed to provide temporary living accommodations (including welfare hotels, congregate shelters, and transitional housing for the mentally ill);

(B) an institution that provides a temporary residence for individuals intended to be institutionalized; or

(C) a public or private place not designed for, or ordinarily used as, a regular sleeping accommodation for human beings.

While acknowledging that the law needs to define the individual and not a collectivity, such a broad redefinition takes up the uncertainty of the moment in its use of three articulations of *homeless*. Two are clearly still functioning within the longstanding adjectival form of the word—homeless individual or homeless person. The first use of *homeless* ("the term 'homeless'") remains ambiguous—is it a move toward the mass formation of the noun sans the definite article? Or is it merely the adjective without a modifier (homeless X), such as the family? The latter ("homeless individual or homeless person") seems more likely because the subpoints (1) and (2) both assume a modification in the preceding line. The McKinney Act attempts to make space for the homeless family but not as family. "Homeless" are defined as individuals. One's family status is irrelevant to legally constituting an individual as homeless, but the collectivity of the "homeless family" is not taken up within the law, a clarification that federal law waited 25 years to make.

While making it possible for a member of a family to be constituted as homeless, the law, at the same time, circumvents the family tensions by ignoring them. The law does not take on the discursive logic of homelessness; rather, it reasserts an atomized homeless individual when reconstituting homelessness on material grounds. Following this definition, Rachel and her children are homeless not as the collective of the family but as solitary individuals who find themselves in a welfare hotel; their family status would thus only appear in the operational procedure of directing them to the appropriate shelter. By falling back onto a fragmented individual, the law leaves the cognitive space for the reassertion of disaffiliation to greater or lesser extent, such as Rossi's assertion that disaffiliation continues as a defining characteristic of homelessness or Jencks's falling back onto explanatory models, which assume that shifting family structures—like marriage later in life and an increasing divorce rate—create the economic conditions in which people more easily become homeless.

The legal intervention of the McKinney Act (now McKinney-Vento) shifts the primary definer of homelessness from social science to law. The legal definition is now the working definition of service providers (whose funds come from McKinney-Vento budget appropriations) and social scientists. But as we have seen in the representative works of Rossi and Jencks, the material definition is deployed, but the discursive logic of disaffiliation continues. Homelessness continues to be about the family.

The increased ease of becoming homeless, however, is not our primary concern in this chapter. Rather, we have looked at the discursive negotiations of the rise of the homeless family—the concern is one of language and rhetoric and not with the changes in the streets. Those are important for they inflect and interact with the language, but they are not our primary focus. In this chapter, we have seen that the homeless family was semantically bracketed from the disaffiliated men and women on the streets. This bracketing occurred in two forms—myth and sociological explanation. Mythic tropes were invoked to describe the homeless family, while the homeless individual continued to be discussed within the sociological framework of disaffiliation and pathology. Both in the use of myth and in the sociological distinctions, the discourse sustained the basic assumptions about homelessness, which we have had since the fin-de-siècle period—the homeless figure as the other of family. The bracketing of the homeless family was essential to continue with this discursive framework.

This new distinction between the homeless family and the street homeless has parallels in the fin-de-siècle period. As we saw in Part I, Jacob Riis distinguished between the honest poor and paupers, now more commonly distinguished as the working versus undeserving poor. With the bracketing of the homeless family, the street homeless—those paupers (or in Riis's more colorful description, the nether half) who embody the threats and anxieties to home and family—take the position of the other to the family. The street homeless become "the homeless" proper; they are that group Christopher Jencks discusses under that rubric (and that title). Newly constituted as a mass, "the homeless" continue to be the other of bourgeois family norms and take on a new role as other to the homeless family.

The emergence of this homeless family threatened the structure of the discourse. Policymakers did make a seeming break with the past by establishing a new definition of homelessness, which uses the homeless individual's material location as the basis for determining one's homelessness. However, despite this shift in definition, the discursive framework of homelessness as disaffiliation sustained.

Disaffiliation remained the definition of homelessness as long as the category of the nuclear family continued to be fairly stable. The broad framework of disaffiliation and pathology continued to be used by sociologists into the early 1970s, when we start to see journalists documenting new conditions that belied basic assumptions of the discourse. In this part, we saw that the changes in family and social life that began in the 1960s established the conditions for the greatest challenge to the disaffiliation thesis: the homeless family. The logic of the discourse—homelessness as disaffiliation—assumes separation from a family. Before this contradiction comes to the fore, several cracks appeared in understanding the disaffiliation of the homeless man. In this part, we find that the fracturing of a discursive consensus leads to shifts in the gender and racial assumptions of the discourse. No longer was the homeless figure exclusively the (white) man of Skid Row. This opening of the discourse created the possibility for a further opening—the constitution of the homeless family. This period of discursive flux and confusion continues until the McKinney Act fiats a new legal definition of homelessness, which is soon assimilated by scholars and service providers alike.

PART IV

Transforming Homelessness

The bracketing of the homeless family and the rise of a new federal definition of homelessness did not immediately transform the discourse on homelessness. However, they combined with changes in the political economy, urban development, and the state's relationship to social services to give rise to an emptying out of the discourse—no longer was it a critique of modernization, nor a carrier for family anxieties, nor a nostalgic appeal to a simpler rural life. Homelessness has now become a material problem of housing. The lingering disaffiliation thesis continued for some time, as access to shelter and housing was primarily linked to using services, indicating that there was a perceived lack or problem with the person for being homeless. The continuation of this implied pathology began to be challenged in some corners in the 1990s but did not begin to broadly influence the direction of policy and homeless services until the new millennium. The logic of the discourse on homeless continued for some time. But this process of setting aside the disaffiliation thesis comes by finding other places in public life for family anxieties and the appeal of some long lost *Gemeinschaft*; the city transformed to become safe for families.

In Part IV, I analyze the implications of this confrontation between gentrifying demands to clean up the city and the new mass of the homeless. As a mass—signified in the term's grammatical shift from an adjective ("the homeless man") to a collective noun ("the homeless")—the homeless come to represent two threats to the metropolis: danger and violence, on the one side, and the anomie of transcendental homelessness, on the other. These threats of violence were increasingly policed as the homeless spilled out of Skid Row and the middle class poured into the city. As the homeless subject is constituted, the demands to subject these homeless to the state increased. A large federally funded apparatus of service providers expanded, which both offered services and interactions in which subjects could possibly be molded and assimilated into bourgeois norms. These family norms and their role in society emerged as a central political topic with the rise of the family values movement in the 1980s. The discourse on homelessness has since its inception been a carrier of these family anxieties. But through the transformation of the role of family in public life, homelessness returns to a problem of space—where one stays at night. The discourse on homelessness transforms with the neoliberalization of homelessness policy.

CHAPTER 8

The Homeless and the Disneyfication of the City

The new HUD definition of homelessness from 1987's McKinney Act moved homelessness from a condition of social relations to a material condition of where one stays at night. Despite this legislative fiat, the disaffiliation thesis lingered in both sociological analyses of homelessness and the administration of social services. The rise of this new definition atomizes the homeless population as individuals as the new mass category of "the homeless" appears in the public sphere of academia and media. The dual processes of modernization—formations of anonymous individuals and equally anonymous masses—take place simultaneously. While the discourse on homelessness has always posited solitary modern subjects, the mass formation is, in part, new. In this chapter, we briefly look at the changes in urban space and policy that give rise to the formation of this mass.

First, we look at the conditions that increased the visibility of the homeless at a particular historical moment. This increase in visibility was abetted by two processes that significantly increased the encounters between homeless individuals and the middle class: the destruction of Skid Rows and the reentry of the middle class into the city. The deindustrialization of the city rendered metropolitan space more desirable than it had been when it was a locus for factories chugging smoke into the air. The suburbanization trend, which had been in part an attempt to find a small amount of land for the nuclear family, could be reversed. This reversal began gentrifying processes of urban renewal, including the new movement of families back into the city. Thus these returning members of the middle class increasingly encountered the homeless who themselves were moving out of the Skid Row areas and scattering across the metropolis. Together, these formed the conditions in which the homeless became more visible.

This increased visibility prompted a political backlash against the urban poor. This revanchism relegated many of the roles for maintaining social order to the markets and increased policing. Because the homeless represented dual threats of the urban mass—a violent upheaval and the embodiment of transcendental homelessness—they became an object of this increased policing. Gentrifying reclamation of the city required the removal of the homeless to reclaim urban space for the middle-class family.

Gentrification made the American city a space of consumption and no longer a locus of production. These changing economic roles of the American city affected a broader political change, which is integral to the discourse on homelessness—a culturalization of politics. We saw the beginning of this trend in the fin-de-siècle period. Here we look at the impact of the culturalization of politics on the discourse and on ideas of the family. The critique of modernity, which has been at the core of the discourse on homelessness, begins to unwind through this process. As this culturalization becomes more widespread, the homeless figure no longer was the sole carrier of family anxieties; these anxieties developed their own political role without being sublimated to other social concerns. This sets the stage for the decoupling of family anxieties from the homeless. The rise of the homeless family is both the result of these economic shifts and the cause of some of these political changes. Thus we look at some of the negotiations of empirical encounters between the middle class and the homeless.

The new empirical conditions raised questions about the presence of the homeless family. The existence of displaced families is nothing new with the 1980s. Whether called families in crisis or transition, Okies or the tribe of Ishmael, families have been displaced throughout American history. But at particular moments, they become visible. In any moment, the ways in which sociologists have operationalized studies of homelessness have produced blind spots—we saw that with Howard Bahr. Yet in other moments, the previously unseen becomes apparent; the obscure becomes visible. These moments of visibility appear at those times when the concerns of bourgeois subjects are empirically confronted with some form of displacement; the ability to overlook becomes impossible, and the discourse must meet this new challenge. The logic of homelessness assumes that solitary figures reside in populations that can be managed; after all, the constitution of a homeless figure only took place through the ghettoization of the disaffiliated man into the social service system in Skid Row. But the homeless are encountered as a mass, one that cannot quietly be managed.

What, however, enables these moments of visibility? Why, as Joel Blau calls them, do the homeless become the visible poor?[1] Why does the middle class suddenly find themselves confronted by the homeless population? Broader shifts in urban life brought previously segregated populations into proximity. The changes in the urban landscape that had first given rise to Rossi's new homeless—conditions that increased the visibility of the homeless—ran their course. Industry's abandonment of city centers,[2] the loss of jobs in downtown areas,[3] the destruction of SROs as the bottom rung of the housing market,[4] and other major shifts had followed the suburbanization movements of the 1950s and 1960s. Suburban flight exacerbated urban problems, which became de facto invisible to most middle-class culture safely tucked away in their bedroom communities. These urban changes just beginning in the 1960s created conditions for an increase in the homeless population—in particular, job loss, the elimination of the cheapest housing, and personal negotiations of frustrations arising from job and housing shortages (i.e., substance abuse). (After all, Freud has pointed out that intoxicating substances are one of the three primary palliative measures for dealing with misery—the other two being deflections and substitutive satisfactions.[5])

The ghettoization of disaffiliated men in Skid Row areas collapsed with the destruction of the SROs over the 1970s. The spatial segregation that had been necessary to constitute the homeless man was suddenly lost; homeless populations began to spill throughout the city. But if the majority of the middle class remained safely ensconced in their suburban homes, they would remain blissfully ignorant of the urban changes. Certainly, many commuted into the city during work hours before an evening retreat beyond the reach of public transit. In the daytime hours, many may have sensed the encroachment of homeless individuals into their views of the city. The city of a suburban commuter is often a narrow swath from the parking lot (or commuter rail station) to the office to nearby restaurants; a segregated homelessness would remain invisible. But a panhandler or two en route to the office is hardly grounds for action.

The problem arises with more systemic interactions—the longstanding problem of homeless services: NIMBYism (Not In My Back Yard). Middle-class homeowners, business owners, or convention bureaus do not want homeless people to congregate near their homes, workplaces, or convention centers. When daily life begins to intersect urban issues, those issues can potentially become problems. Gentrification began bringing many middle-class Caucasians (of course, we are all aware of the racializing of the politics of gentrification) back into the city. But such movements into neighborhoods come with the expectation that "problems" will be cleaned up. Atlanta's recent (2005) antibegging statute coincided with the reentry of capital and tourist dollars into a downtown corridor. The final impetus to the Atlanta City Council came in a public nudge from Bernie Marcus, the billionaire cofounder of Atlanta-based retailer The Home Depot and donor of $250 million for downtown's latest attraction—the largest aquarium in the world. Gentrification is about movements of capital, as much as it is about those of people. The discourse on homelessness burst onto the stage of public notice at the moment when the city began to become a destination rather than a locus of flight. In the 1980s, when the gentrification processes began to bring a large enough mass of middle-class returnees, the homeless problem became increasingly visible. Studies proliferated, services increased, and explanations for causes and numbers increased. Much of the sociological work in the decade from the mid-1980s into the early 1990s, including Rossi and Jencks, focused on identifying demographics of the populations, probable causes, and a census count for the numbers. For a long time, the most frequently cited number was the two million figure put forth by Mitch Snyder, an outspoken homeless advocate and founder of the Washington, DC–based Community for Creative Non-Violence. It was the standard number until it was discovered that the count was not even a ballpark figure but a symbol of a large problem. Many had gone along with the number because it served the mutual interests of social activists and new urban pioneers who wanted the problem to seem like a mass one, so they could better demand policy changes.

After the demise of Snyder's figure of two million homeless, studies wanted to better document numbers and demographics to determine the scale of the problem and to direct the funds made available from the McKinney Act to the appropriate places. A decade and a half of creative torpor in social science work on homelessness led to a great deal of census, demographics, and program evaluation with little substantive change in services or in the discourse on homelessness. Only in the new century have sociologists, anthropologists, and political scientists stepped back from the immediate problems to contextualize homelessness within broader histori-cal and social arcs.

The changes in the 1980s American city were driven by gentrifying urban revitalization efforts led in part by initiatives like James Rouse's developments including Faneuil Hall Marketplace in Boston, South Street Seaport in New York City, or Harborplace in Baltimore, which established urban shopping malls under the guise of historic preservation. These devel-opments could only work if people felt "safe" to spend their time and, more importantly, money in the spaces claimed for urban reclamation. From the 1960s, capital reinvestments began to be made in dilapidated housing near central business districts (CBD).[6] But these programs of rehabilita-tion by wealthy professionals took place alongside a broader "deterioration of inner-city housing, disinvestments in the CBD, and suburbanization of most new housing construction for the private market."[7] The conditions were established to bring the extremely poor urban populations, whose inner-city housing was being increasingly eliminated, in proximity to upper-income populations. Yet this newfound proximity does not reverse socioeconomic and racial tensions within the city.[8] The dual claims on urban space by the homeless poor (whose spatial delimitation in Skid Row collapsed with the demise of SRO motels) and the urban upper classes (who moved into neighborhoods with previously deteriorating housing) led to tensions. And despite the efforts of advocates, the interests of the upper income carried greater political weight with city halls. Thus by the 1990s, the Disneyfication of CBDs was well under way, which included significant capital investments on the part of commercial interests, the urban appear-ance of suburban megastores and "family friendly" spaces.[9] As a scholar of gentrification, Neil Smith points out that this disappearance of homeless people from certain urban districts and the rise of suburban chain stores is not merely a coincidence: "Suburban cool—the suburbanization of the city—is precisely the point of the multibillion-dollar Disney mother colony in Times Square. The central areas cleared of homeless people are now open for business. The dynamic geographies of culture, real estate capital, and revanchism seem perfectly synchronized."[10]

The processes of gentrification thus had a twofold contribution to the visibility of the homeless—increasing dispersion of homeless individuals through the metropolis and increasing the number of upper-income indi-viduals residing in urban areas who could encounter the homeless. The destruction of Skid Rows and SROs—which increased the dispersion of the homeless—was itself part of the gentrifying process; the motels were torn down or rehabilitated for a land use, which yielded greater value and thus greater tax revenue for the municipality. Thus the process that, in part, put far more people onto the streets by eliminating the bottom rung of the housing market also created the demand for eliminating this population from public spaces. But these urban changes involved broader shifts in the functions of the metropolis from the 1970s to the present; the shifts in urbanization, themselves, rest upon the changes in capital—the basic changes linked to globalization and flexible accumulation. David Harvey points out that the employment base of urban areas faced many pressures with these economic changes: "A combination of shrinking markets, unemployment, rapid shifts in spatial constraints and the global division of labor, capital flight, plant closings, technological and financial reorganization, lay at the root of that pressure."[11] Such changes set the stage for class, race, and spatial stresses between those benefiting from a shift in urban employment from industrial labor to financial services, as well as the spatial tensions arising from the large increase in urban poverty in the middle of spectacular displays of wealth.[12] Those who were the target audience of the urban spectacle of festival market places wanted spaces reserved for themselves— oases of consumption should not be spoiled by the blight of the homeless. Neil Smith points out that the 1990s revanchism of New York City—like its nineteenth-century Parisian namesake—"blends revenge with reaction."[13] The overwhelming withdrawal of state programs to manage social reproduction (e.g., the end of welfare entitlements) led to the dual forces of the market, on the one hand, and policing, on the other, to establish and maintain social norms.[14] Beyond New York—as we saw with Atlanta's urban spectacle of tourist consumption in the world's largest aquarium—the same demands of the market are enforced through increased policing over the last decade and a half in the American metropolis.

This reactionary turn, however, had to identify a clear target for policing—a population had to receive the brunt of aggressive tactics, or else the vigorous efficacy of policing falls apart. In his plan for New York— published as *Police Strategy No. 5*—Giuliani identified a range of homeless by their status (without shelter) or their activities (like panhandling or squeegee cleaning). Neil Smith writes the following:

"The downward spiral of urban decay" was real enough, but what Giuliani achieved in *Police Strategy No. 5* was two things: first, a visceral identification of the culprits, the enemies who had indeed stolen the city from the white middle class; and second, a solution that reaffirmed the rights of the white middle class to the city. Rather than indict capitalists for capital flight, landlords for abandoning buildings, or public leaders for a narrow retrenchment for class and race self-interest, Giuliani led the clamor for a different kind of revenge. He identified homeless people, panhandlers, prostitutes, squeegee cleaners, squatters, graffiti artists, "reckless bicyclists," and unruly youth as the major enemies of public order and decency, the culprits of urban decline generating widespread fear. "Disorder in the public spaces of the city" presented "visible signs of a city out of control, a city that cannot protect its space or its children."[15]

The aesthetic removal of the homeless, street merchants, and squeegee cleaners, among others, was an incomplete fixing of homeless policy into market forces. This 1990s policing strategy popularized in New York under the Giuliani administration was predicated on then (and now recently returned under Mayor de Blasio) New York Police Commissioner William Bratton's subscribing to the broken windows theory of law enforcement, in which the police target small petty crimes and perceived antisocial behavior to deter escalation into larger crimes.[16] Bratton and Mayor Giuliani were concerned about the 60 percent of polled New Yorkers who felt "that dirt, graffiti, homeless people, noise, panhandlers and beggars have reduced the quality of life for themselves and their families" and wanted to reduce crime and fear in the city and to systematically "reduce the level of disorder in the city."[17] Making the city safe for families became intertwined with an anti-homeless sentiment. While a range of urban poor are implicated in *Policy Strategy No. 5*, the homeless in particular were thought to be the problem. Smith goes on to make this point:

> The brunt of 1990s revanchism was borne by homeless people. The antihomeless antagonism that smouldered in the 1980s burst into flame as official urban policy in the early 1990s. For New York City's homeless population, numbering as many as 100,000, the beginning of the decade brought a crippling combination of economic depression, public attack, and the evaporation of public sympathy. Evictees from the private and public housing markets inhabiting the barest interstices of public space quickly passed from being front-page news in the late 1980s to public blight number one in the 1990s.[18]

But how do these urban processes of increasing density and changing the city's relationships to capital relate to my more particular concerns with the homeless figure, modernization, and the family?

In some ways, gentrification is the about-face of suburbanization—it is a refusal to cede the city to homelessness, which is a homelessness in the anomic, transcendental sense. Harvey points out that the shifts in spatial arrangements of the city to accommodate flexible accumulation undermine those processes that enable the urban poor to construct any sense of community; the collapse of these processes entail "an increase in individual anomie, alienation, and all of the antagonisms that derive therefrom."[19] His argument implies that the problems of the urban poor amount to a Mertonian acute anomie. But this claim is an inversion of my argument that the discourse of homelessness arose with the problem of transcendental homelessness—or acute anomie—among the bourgeoisie. The problems of the fin-de-siècle city were thought to be caused by the poor (quite similar to the 1990s revanchism), but the class whose fears and sense of loss were categorized as anomic has shifted, along with the form of anomie. But of course, this is a bit of a red herring. The bourgeois discourse on homelessness does not worry with the community structures among the poor. The social networks of hobos appeared as insufficient social mooring because the ties necessary to bind the mobile labor force were conjugal or natal relations, not hobo unions. The family was the necessary source of social structure. The problems of the urban poor, the mass of "the homeless," were those not sufficiently integrated into family structures. Thus Harvey's claim remains—transcendental homelessness of the fin-de-siècle era remains a lingering fear.

It lingers because the city does not lose its complexity; it continues to augment the pace of life and fragment social relations. The vibrant street life—which probably fostered a far greater sense of community than a nuclear family retreating into a walk-up—was greatly tamed by Riis and other reformers. Streets teeming with people always present anxieties to the agents of social control—the surveillance tactics used by the American urban police after the 1999 World Trade Organization protests in Seattle include limiting rights to assembly to maintain control of the streets; these tactics demonstrate a continuing anxiety about masses in the city. Baron Haussmann and Robert Moses both restructured spaces for greater urban control—to prevent the formation of a mass. The 1970s–1980s upsurge in homeless individuals on the streets marked the first time since the fin-de-siècle reactions to urbanization that the streets and sidewalks had a marked increase in disorder. The discourse on homelessness readily furnished language—that of "the homeless" as a mass—to marginalize the populations and establish the population as a threat, and once marginal, policies and policing were able to redress the situations.

The homeless thus embody the dual threats of the urban mass: violent upheaval and the embodiment of transcendental homelessness. A fear of the former has probably lain latent among metropolitan authorities since at least the storming of the Bastille; the latter problem drove the formation of the discourse on homelessness. Volunteer Special, Jacob Riis, and Frank Laubach all expressed fears of the city's potential for violent political upheaval; much of the last century and a half has done much to mitigate this threat. But this amelioration rests upon the assimilation of populations into institutions—random hordes on streets are not integrated into the bourgeois institutions of social welfare, charities, and schools. A homeless individual on the street is not undergoing a shelterization process. But this threat can be addressed—coercing or compelling individuals into institutions and penal systems or shipping them out of town. The latter threat—a transcendental homelessness—is a more difficult problem to rectify. It evokes a fear that life in the modern world cannot be grounded. As Edward Said has pointed out, Lukács's transcendental homelessness pervades the world through an unnaturalness and unreality. The tension between nature—both in the sense of God-given forces and creations and in the normal naturalness of cultural hegemony—and the modern world pits the discourse on homelessness against metropolitan extremes. Transcendental homelessness emerges through the dual collapse of nature, when technology destroys the God-given and the resulting social changes undermine cultural assumptions. The acute anomie arising from modernizing urban processes evoked affirmations of nature—the development of parks and green space, on the one hand, and the use of myth, on the other. Myth is an affirmation of both parts of nature. But with the constant subordination of life to technology, with the global urbanization of populations in the new millennium—most of the world's population now resides in the city; the nature that is affirmed increasingly becomes the cultural one, rather than the environmental one. In his discussion of the modern mass, Kracauer realized that myth increasingly legitimates nature in the modern world:

> The process of history is a battle between a weak and distant reason and the forces of nature that ruled over heaven and earth in the myths. After the twilight of the gods, the gods did not abdicate: the old nature within and outside man continues to assert itself. It gave rise to the great cultures of humanity, which must

die like any creation of nature, and it serves as the ground for the superstructures of a *mythological* thinking which affirms nature in its omnipotence. Despite all the variations in the structure of such mythological thinking, which changes from epoch to epoch, it always respects the boundaries that nature has drawn. It acknowledges the organism as the ur-form; it is refracted in the formed quality of what exists; it yields to the workings of fate. It reflects the premises of nature in all spheres without rebelling against their existence. Organic sociology, which sets up the natural organism as the prototype for social organization, is no less mythological than nationalism, which knows no higher unity than the unison of the nation's fate.[20]

Myth becomes the means to reaffirm both senses of nature, after the twilight of the gods. Myth is now a form of cultural legitimation in a seemingly secular world. It is the last way to sustain and affirm meaning by imbuing the social with an organic naturalness.

The acute anomie of transcendental homelessness, as we saw with fin-de-siècle urbanization processes, arose through the subordination of life to instrumental reason; modernization transformed the distribution of populations, their relationships to space, and thus those who occupy that space. Ties to land eroded, and the family became articulated as the sole social unit still bound together by more than the instrumentality of economics, but once individuals left their natal family, they were unbound until conjoined into a conjugal one. The family became a way to stave off the overwhelming threats the city brought to social relationships. These social shifts with the rise of the industrial city are well known. But that this acute anomie lingered within a discourse on the homeless figure was not previously known. This figure became a carrier of Victorian anxieties. The homeless figure becomes this lens because it embodies that which seems unnatural—disaffiliation and social isolation. These problems arise with the city, which is not thought to be an organic formation. Within the discourse on homelessness, bourgeois subjects (and their family norms) are posited as a natural, normal form of subjectivity that might be temporarily exiled from the community, which is its natural habitat.

Suburbanization was in many ways an attempt to reclaim some modicum of land for the bourgeois family. Gentrification was the reclaiming of urban spaces to make them safe for the family—to make possible a Disney Store or Virgin Megastore (I'm sure its name meets with great approval from the guardians of family values.) in Times Square. Modernization created a homeless city—some middle-class families fled, and others brought aspects of the country (e.g., parks and green spaces)—into the city. Values of cleanliness (it is next to godliness, after all), hard work, and thrift were inculcated through the modern institutions of schools and social work. Once the battle with the slums pushed the tenement into retreat and a middle class was firmly ensconced, small enclaves were set aside for those individuals whose social patterns kept them from assimilating into bourgeois family and social norms. The city became an ordered space. The security of the city barely lasted beyond the Second World War. The tensions and anxieties generated by homelessness led to the discursive practice of othering the homeless figure and a parallel spatial practice of separating the homeless men into Skid Row areas. From the spatial delimitation of Skid Row (ghettoization), to suburban flight, to gentrifying demands for removal,[21] the discourse on homelessness has had an integral relationship with urban spatial distribution.

The discourse is also central to a broader trend in American life—the culturalization of politics. Technological changes in communication and transport enabled urbanized capital to begin the geographical separation of production and consumption, which in earlier stages of industry needed spatial proximity. This bifurcation has led to a society that increasingly is blind to processes of production other than the occasional antiglobalization protest. In the absence of large-scale production—and the mass of the proletariat that it brings into being—politics have increasingly shifted to problems of culture, which in many ways function as surrogates for the economic and class problems of yesteryear. Although the formation of the homeless figure is certainly intertwined with shifts in urban capital, the discourse shifts the debates to problems of culture. The homeless of the 1980s and 1990s do not present the same threats as the homeless city and its residents. Violent, or revolutionary, political upheavals were the latent cauldron thought to be lingering among the fin-de-siècle urban lumpenproletariat—thus, so the argument went, whenever a social problem arose, the city exploded in the Haymarket, Draft, and Tompkins Square riots. This systemic threat is not that which the 1990s revanchists are trying to roll back; they want an uninterrupted possibility of consumption—a Times Square in which all the family can safely shop, a Centennial Olympic Park in which tourists may spend millions at conferences, aquariums, concerts, and sporting events. The discourse on homelessness began in response to overaccumulations of labor for production—the dense concentrations of an urban proletariat created the conditions for the city to be regarded as homeless. It now most frequently appears in discussions of urban commercial, business, and tourist districts—how can the problem of homelessness be minimized so that consumption can best take place? This consumption can happen at the level of shopping in stores, attending the theater, or in purchasing a home. A mayor can call for the removal of these homeless "signs of disorder," these neighborhood problems, because the bourgeois response has always regarded the homeless figure as a threat to order. Riis called for reigning in the city and subjecting it to an order, which ensured proper protocols and behaviors were observed by the poor; reforms were necessary to both ensure and enable the assimilation of the immigrant poor. Housing codes, schools, public parks, and social workers all disseminated social norms and acculturated to some middle-class Protestant ideals of social behavior. These ideals were legitimated through turns to deep culture.

The culture wars of the last two decades have been a long time coming; the current debates have a lineage that goes back to fights about the fin-de-siècle city and the havoc that it brought to life. In the 1980s and 1990s, discursive negotiations of changing empirical conditions became intertwined in other cultural movements. The discursive crisis that arose with the homeless family was primarily about establishing and legitimating the bourgeois subject and its familial norms. Concerns about the family as an institution frequently surface at times of social change—it is that last institution by which to bind society. With new fears of waning civil society—itself a problem to family in the fin-de-siècle era—the family discursively becomes the binding social unit against threats of complete atomization into solitary individuals. Against threats from supposedly solipsistic pleas for freedom, the family is held up as the great white hope. As the last remnant of *Gemeinschaft*, family becomes a bulwark against modernization and the anonymity of solitary life or transactional relationships.

This ostensible remnant of *Gemeinschaft* looks very different as it moves back into the city. The family that embraces the city is not the same family trying to be protected by its vagaries in the fin-de-siècle period. In part, the city is quite different, but even more so—as we shall see in the next chapter—the family is quite different. In this chapter, we saw that increased encounters between middle-class families and the homeless in the newly gentrifying city provoked political reaction. The space of the city shifts from one of production to one of consumption; thus the city needed to be safe for tourists and new residents to shop, stroll, and enjoy the urban amenities. These changes in urban space integrate with broader economic shifts from an industrial to an information economy and with broader political changes to a culturalization of politics. The discourse on homelessness is imbricated in these large social changes. The discursive negotiations of the post-Fordist city presage the denouement of our discussion of homelessness—the rending of the family from the homeless figure.

CHAPTER 9

A Decoupled Homelessness
Changing Signification

Family anxieties are never fully decoupled from the discourse on homelessness, but the homeless figure is no longer a primary carrier of these social fears. The culturalization of politics processes enable the family anxieties to become relatively freestanding as part of the family values movement. But in this separation from the discourse on homelessness, the family also loses its role as the last remnant of *Gemeinschaft*. The idea of home—which the discourse on homelessness has legitimated through the process of negation—also decouples from the discourse on homelessness. "Home" becomes significantly reinforced in public discourses, as threats to homeland security emerge as a substantial concern. Relatively emptied of its signification, the category of homelessness transforms from the mid-1990s to the present to become primarily a material condition of where one stays at night. Though mostly shorn of the century-plus discourse, the transformation of homelessness into a housing problem is not without some difficulties to which we shall turn.

The formation of "the homeless" as a mass in the 1990s is the last remnant of the homeless as the other to middle-class family norms. The discourse fractures as the family-*Gemeinschaft* dyad is broken, and those bifurcated concerns are taken up elsewhere in public discourses. The threat to some romanticized lost *Gemeinschaft* slips away from the discourse on homelessness, as urban space is embraced by the returning middle class. The family ideal no longer reflects the fin-de-siècle antiurban sentiment. Widespread 1990s gentrification counterintuitively inverts its etymological roots in land; instead, it reflects a middle class claiming urban territory. This gentrification does not reflect the nineteenth-century desire to bring elements of the countryside into the city with parks and fresh air into tenements—it is the suburbanization of the city with megastores and shopping malls.

Progressive-era interventions in urban life produced successes in improving conditions for many poor in the tenements. As we have seen, the other half retrenched to the smaller group residing in Skid Row. Effective muckraking and policy advocacy led to a de facto ghettoization of the homeless; there was almost an expectation that if the public sector has responded to the problem, then the middle class should not have to be confronted with the lingering presence of homeless men. The 1980s advocacy to address homelessness culminated in 1987's Stewart B. McKinney Act. The success bred a similar expectation that the problem should be managed (and thus relatively out of sight). The return of a Republican to New York City's Gracie Mansion in the 1990s brought a municipal administration to the nation's largest city that was happy to comply with the demand to hide the homeless. This expunging of the homeless, squeegee boys, and other street denizens was part of a new urban policing to bring back a middle class to the city as tourists, residents, and most importantly, as consumers.

In this chapter, we look at the devolution of the discourse on homelessness and how this breaking up of the assumptions related to a broader neoliberalization of social policy. The changes in the discourse on homelessness have unfolded with a restructuring of the spaces, language, and institutions of homelessness; this trinity of characteristics, which have demarcated populations as homeless, has shifted tremendously over the last several decades. Gentrification of urban spaces, linguistic decoupling of family concerns from homelessness and a subsequent public reappropriation of the category of home, and the change in policy (and thus service institutions) addressing homelessness gave rise to the rapid policy change to Housing First over the last decade.

In this chapter, we return to a debate we have seen earlier and I have discussed in depth elsewhere[1]—the relationship between family and civil society. In Part I, these issues came to the fore, as Jacob Riis lamented the rise of volunteer associations. We again encountered the contradictions between these two different social structures in the Part II discussion of the limits of hobosociality for social mooring. In that discussion, we saw that the associational life of the hobo community was inadequate for social life; the family was to be the proper foundation for society. I analyze how this debate reappears in its most recent incarnation—the assimilation of the family anxieties to those of social capital. The former clash between these social structures has now become one of partnership. This section unravels the cognitive contradictions necessary to create an instrumental politics to preserve the supposedly organic form of the nuclear family.

The struggle to define America is much older than the coming of age of the baby boomers. Since its Victorian inception, the discourse on homelessness has intertwined with broader culture wars over the class, ethnic, and religious configurations of the nation. For the making of Americans, Jacob Riis calls for hackneyed Protestant values of thrift, orderliness, hygiene, hard work, and dedication to family; he combined these with a desire for small-town values, a normative assumption of language (English), and expectations of cultural assimilation for the "other half." For his prescription for social integration, he has received homage from contemporary religious right figures, such as the founder of modern "compassionate conservatism," Marvin Olasky.[2] He wrote of the need to preserve the family and home three-quarters of a century before James Dobson called for a focus on the family or the Family Research Council gave Reagan administration officials a forum for further politicizing of the family.[3] The previous fin-de-siècle *kulturkampf* now became an issue of policy—the culture wars spread from the way institutions function and disseminate norms to legislative and executive actions. The tenor of the culture wars took a new pitch.

The discourse on homelessness has always been one front in a much larger struggle over American identity in response to modernization— proper types of individual subjects and proper social structures. But as the repository of all the urban threats to bourgeois life—the expansive array of political radicalism, public disorder, homosexuality, filth, crime, and a mobility that resists civilizing impulses for roots—the homeless figure has been a particularly efficacious rejoinder to urban life. The 1980s bubbling up of the politicization of the family, at the moment that the discourse on homelessness reached a crisis with the forced acknowledgement of the homeless family, provoked realignments on several positions within both this discourse and the camps of the culture wars. Jacob Riis had drawn the lines clearly between the family and civil society—these were antagonistic social structures. He worried that after a day of work, either in the marketplace or in the realm of domesticity, the family would not gather in the home but rather take care of the demands of civil society by spending their evenings in their voluntary associations. We have already seen how the formerly antagonistic social structure (civil society) supplanted the category of community and then appropriated the language of community.

The religious right has in recent years joined this anxiety with a new rhetoric of loss—social capital—irrespective of the tensions between the two social structures. While the tendency to join family anxieties with the rhetoric of declining civil society is widespread, former senator Rick Santorum's book *It Takes a Family: Conservatism and the Common Good* is a particularly good example of this propensity. The two movements (family values and social capital) both decry a loss of social relations, and both argue that society is better maintained, better facilitated with stronger social relations. Thus far, they reach similar diagnoses. However, the prescriptions are at odds. They fail to distinguish types of social relations, they fail to see how social forms are shaped by historical conditions, and they fail to see contradictions in their respective solutions. As I have written elsewhere, the family values movement has now inverted the concept of family from its claimed Victorian roots:

> This family of the new millennium attempts to keep the form of family without the same internal principles structuring it. Implicit is a sense that there has been a foreclosure of the sentiment relations of *Gemeinschaft*—it becomes irretrievable. The family, which was articulated as its last remnant, no longer seems to exist; it has to have a new means to bolster it. The exhortations for protection of the family from policy and legislation inserts instrumentality into the institution of the family—it has become, in Tönnies' sense, a *Gesellschaft* structure. The collapse between the movements of family values and social capital marks a second acquiescence—the family has been irredeemably changed by modern life. The family of the family values movement is a shell institution from which the previous content has been emptied.[4]

The family values movement is very much a political movement and, as such, grounded in instrumentality. The primarily evangelical movement[5] has to legitimate its decision to shed its centuries-old commitment to a Troeltschian sectarianism vis-à-vis the state. The de facto withdrawal from concerns of temporal power has been foresworn through the classic moves of *ressentiment* politics. With the decline of unions and other voluntary life, religious institutions remain a primary locus of vibrant social capital. The religious right has a comparative advantage over its political opponents because of this built-in infrastructure into which it can tap. Thus it assimilates social capital to its political goals of "family values," however ambiguously defined.

But the functioning of the religious right is not our concern here. The assimilation of family values rhetoric to the concerns of social capital signals a rapprochement between social conservatism and modernity. As economic shifts push the nation into a globalized, postmodern culture, positions of bourgeois embrace no longer hearken back to the simple times of *Gemeinschaft* ideals. It is too remote a past to be viable; thus there is an acquiescence to modernity.

The discourse on homelessness has since its inception been a carrier for anxieties about the family and critiques of modernization. The modern family values movement spurns its Victorian roots by maintaining the nostalgic language for a life and family of old, built around a Christian home, while embracing means and institutions and, even more important, a form of family, which belies the nostalgia.

The family is now but a remnant of the social institution it once was, but this shrinking has taken place at the hands of its defenders. In this section, we saw that the religious right has integrated its concerns for family with those for a waning civil society. By entirely subordinating the rhetoric of community to civil society, the religious right is able to assimilate the last remnant of community (i.e., the nuclear family) to social capital. The family now becomes an instrument of civil society rather than its antagonist. While the discourse on homelessness need no longer be a carrier of these anxieties, it was in many ways a far more capable protector of the family. The family values movement has embraced modernization and thus accepted its impacts on the family. It nominally protects the family while primarily working for the cause of capital and its bourgeois social structure—civil society.

Marvin Olasky's branch of the family values movement and social conservatism was popularized by George W. Bush in his 2000 presidential bid. His administration came into office in early 2001 with much fanfare from the acolytes of this compassionate conservatism. The new president established the White House Office of Faith-Based and Community Initiatives to oversee the institutionalization of this conservatism and installed John Dilulio as its director. The hopes for this initiative and its support within the White House soon waned and entirely floundered after the attacks of September 11 later in that first year of the new administration. When Dilulio wrote a public letter in *Esquire* explaining why he was the first senior advisor to leave the administration, he said that he had been unable to get any policies on the compassionate conservatism agenda through. And now that concerns for homeland security occupied the agenda, he saw little chance.[6] While the rhetoric of homeland security is not our primary concern, its emergence reconstituted the category of home in public discourses and completed the process of emptying the discourse on homelessness of its Victorian roots. Anxieties about family made their way to politicized religious debates about family values, and the rural ideal of a life rooted in land became a metonym for a nation with homeland security. The fears taken up in the discourse on homelessness were to avert the perils of and to ensure the preservation of the Protestant Christian home. The nativist sentiment in the rhetoric of homeland security posits a foreign other to the nation as home.[7]

Homeland Security

The rise of the Department of Homeland Security and its role in the war on terror derailed a domestic focus on compassionate conservatism and also completed the decoupling of homelessness from family anxieties. In the discourse on homelessness, the homeless figure was the other to the norm of the middle-class family, but that family had a metonymic relationship with the broader idea of *Gemeinschaft*—that is, social relations rooted in place and familial relations. Writing on the rhetorical advantages of using *home* in *homeland security*, J. Patrick Dobel wrote the following: "Home offers a space where relationships connect humans to the sustaining world around them. Normally home involves a location. But physical location is not essential; often 'home' involves a gathering of individuals together in safety and interdependence. The safety of home fosters relationship of intimacy and production where people live with intimate, make a life, raise children, and 'hand on' or 'hand down' things (stories, traditions, material things, etc.) to successive generations. A home protects and enables growth."[8] This private *Gemeinschaft*-like home became imbricated with the public policy concern of national security. While the migration of family concerns to the family values movement need not empty the discourse of its relationship to this ideal of social relations, the rise of cultural concern with the homeland (and threats to it) completed the transformation of the language of homelessness.

The new department reshaped the notion of the state in ways tied to land and roots; as Amy Kaplan has pointed out, "homeland connotes an inexorable connection to a place deeply rooted in the past."[9] This invocation of a *Gemeinschaft*-type sense of being rooted in land harkens back to the fin-de-siècle nativist sentiment whence the discourse on homelessness began. However, it is now taken up into a rhetoric of nation that excludes the immigrant—who had, after all, ostensibly been the source of the internal threat to the homeland.[10] Much like in the fin-de-siècle period, there were fears of the foreign other that was in some way radicalized. A couple months after the advent of homeland security into popular nomenclature and into debates about anxieties from threats both foreign and domestic, *New York Times* columnist William Safire wrote about the history of the term *homeland* in his "On Language" column. He wrote the following: "'Home on the range, home of the brave, hometown boy,' wrote John Mullan in Britain's Guardian. 'Perhaps "home" is an easier word for patriotic Americans than it would be for us. Homeliness is at a premium in such anxious times . . . a word was wanted that sounded reassuring but unaggressive. Americans have become more sensitive or more wary about the homeliness of their geopolitical talk.' In referring to their place of origin, speakers of British English prefer *this country* to *homeland*."[11] While he gestures here to the idea of land in the reference to the lyrics of "The Star-Spangled Banner" (the land of the free and the home of the brave), the invocation of "Home on the Range" simultaneously invokes the openness of the plains (it is the state song of Kansas)—"a home where the buffalo roam / Where the deer and the antelope play"—and affirms the juxtaposition of this ideal land to the city in the second verse—"I would not exchange my home on the range / For all of the cities so bright." The gesture toward the *Gemeinschaft*-like connotations of the concerns with homeland security invokes an implicit antiurban sentiment (which remains necessarily latent, since the attack on the homeland most often invoked was the destruction of the Twin Towers of New York's World Trade Center) and a sense of place.

This rhetoric of homeland security decoupled the category of home from that of family and completed a process of emptying the discourse on homelessness of its roots in fin-de-siècle anxieties about the impact of urbanization on the middle-class family. This evacuation left homelessness both as a rather marginal place in public discourses and without any major signification. Emptied of signification, the discourse was enabled to take on a Zeligian capacity for transformation. Over the last decade and a half, the discourse has transformed more than in the preceding century. The spatial changes in American cities, from processes of gentrification, and the linguistic changes, in the discourse that emptied the term *homeless* of its signification of threats to family and community ideals, abetted these rapid changes. Though the sentiments reflected in earlier stages of the discourse still appear from time to time, the emptying of the family and *Gemeinschaft* ideals from the discourse presaged a major transformation in understandings of homelessness as well as policy and institutional changes in social services.

Housing First

These institutional changes to a Housing First approach to homelessness did not transpire in either a policy or economic vacuum. Two earlier trends in social services are in the background for developing the Housing First model—the 1980s move to community-based mental health services and the 1990s public housing move to vouchers and mixed-income developments over large congregate housing projects like Atlanta's Techwood Homes or Chicago's Cabrini-Green. The move to community mental health centers (CMHCs) provided a model for treatment separated from residential provision.[12] The deinstitutionalization of state mental hospitals led to an increase in the numbers of homeless mentally ill because the mentally ill were moved out of state hospitals as the Reagan administration cut federal funding for the CMHCs. The delinking of housing and mental health services left the mentally ill vulnerable when funding for services was cut—a shift in policy, which greatly increased the chronically homeless in the 1980s. Housing was removed, and few services were available. For the homeless, Housing First assures housing and then, instead of the more passive approach of CMHCs, aggressively seeks formerly homeless residents to get them into services; the services are there in the community to be accessed, if interested.

The second change in services that presaged the shift to Housing First was the move from large congregate housing to scattered-site or mixed-income communities in public housing. This change in public housing began before research substantiated the benefits of it.[13] While studies eventually indicated some gains made—albeit with a net reduction in the number of subsidized units available—the move toward this policy was not based on evidenced-based research that is touted as the impetus for the changes in homeless policy. The changes grew out of a retreat of the public sector from large-scale domestic policy; similar neoliberalization of housing policy began gaining headway globally in the 1980s and eventually made its way into American housing and homelessness policy. Though Housing

First did not become the basis of US homelessness policy until the 2000s, the discursive and institutional shifts began earlier.

On a cold January morning in 1996, I caught the subway to Boston's Park Street and wandered into the Episcopal Diocesan offices where the nonprofit Social Action Ministries (SAM), where I was a student intern, had donated space. The big event for later in the day—a ceremony recognizing then-HUD secretary Henry Cisneros—was moved up a few hours to be earlier in the day, and hundreds of attendees had to be notified. Our board president's staff at his nonprofit, Greater Boston Housing and Shelter Alliance (GBHSA), around the corner of the Boston Commons at Park Street's Paulist Center (where the ceremony was to take place), are already on the phones. I scurried over to get a list of numbers yet to call and joined in. SAM Board President and GBHSA Director Philip Mangano checked in to see where we were on the call lists, and SAM Executive Director Brian Kelley coordinated with the secretary's staff for the latest updates. Former Texas representative Barbara Jordan had died, and Secretary Cisneros was the most senior Texan in the Clinton administration, so he was to go to Texas for the funeral. The presentation of the Canon Brian S. Kelley Public Servant Award to the secretary in recognition for his innovative contributions to homeless services, for implementing the continuum of care model of homeless services, would be made, though an hour or two earlier in the day.

Only a decade later, the lauded continuum of care model of homeless services was falling from favor, Secretary Cisneros had long since returned to the private sector, and Philip Mangano had moved on to Washington as the federal homelessness czar, serving as the executive director of the US Interagency Council on Homelessness (USICH). An approach to homeless services that inverted the continuum of care model had become the new direction for policy, funding, and services. After stepping down from the USICH, Mangano reflected on this shift: "We changed the equation of homelessness. We used to think that people had to earn the right to go into housing, when they finally got to a certain level of moral goodness, a certain level of sobriety. Let's get people into housing, the central antidote to homelessness, just as quickly as possible. Then, in the stability and security of that place to live, let's deliver services."[14] Experiments with this new Housing First model had begun in the 1990s and started producing new data in the early 2000s that indicated greater cost effectiveness and improved outcomes for keeping chronically homeless individuals housed.

In the fall of 2007, HUD issued its first report on Housing First programs—*The Applicability of Housing First Models to Homeless Persons with Serious Mental Illness*—with a positive assessment. This model that had been pioneered by organizations like Pathways to Housing in New York and the Downtown Emergency Service Center in Seattle inverted the older continuum of care model of housing readiness. The disfavored linear model[15] consists of a process involving a series of steps to bring the program participant to a point of housing readiness. The homeless person would enter a shelter and then graduate into transitional housing and finally move into some permanent housing. Along each step of the assembly line, the homeless person was being "readied" for housing through mandatory treatments for mental health and substance abuse. Most of these programs have policies of abstinence or low tolerance for substance abuse lapses.

The Housing First model removes the programmatic and compliance barriers to housing—the homeless persons seeking assistance first receive housing. HUD identifies four basic features of Housing first approaches: (1) directly placing (or nearly so) the homeless population into permanent housing; (2) not requiring participation in services to stay in housing; (3) using assertive outreach to engage residents in services for mental illness, substance abuse, and so on; and (4) continuing to offer case management and to hold spaces for program participants, even if they leave their housing for brief periods.[16] Recent data indicate some better success in keeping people housed and relatively little difference in drug and alcohol consumption between the two populations.[17]

Our concerns here are neither the debates of evidence per se nor the comparisons between the different program structures. Rather, we are looking to what were the conditions giving rise to the changes in rhetoric and policy, as well as possible implications of these changes. The ideas of home that have lingered in the discourse on homelessness no longer hearken back to the fin-de-siècle Christian home family ideal. The family anxieties that created the blind spot around the possibility that one could be homeless *and* with one's family slip into other public discourses, and the discourse on homelessness reduces to the material condition of where one sleeps. The recent redefinition of homelessness in the HUD HEARTH (Homeless Emergency Assistance and Rapid Transition to Housing) Act now allows that one can be staying at a family member's house and still be legally homeless. This materialization of homelessness, the elimination of the disaffiliation thesis, and the emptying of signification takes place through a series of policy and discursive steps. The social anxieties find homes elsewhere in public discourses, and the discourse on homelessness de facto invokes the minimal understanding of homelessness embodied in Charles Loring Brace's nineteenth-century formulation *houseless*.

This rearticulation of homelessness, however, overly reduces it to this minimal material condition—having no fixed place to stay. The changes in policy fragment housing off from a broader social context and political economy. The discourse on homelessness had embedded displacement within a context of bigger social and cultural issues of immigration, urban overpopulation, and migratory labor. The narrowed focus on housing creates a vacuum seemingly unencumbered by the political economy in which the housing market works. The sloughing off of questions of labor markets, urban development, and criminal justice systems, among others, arises from a broader restructuring of the public sector—a retrenchment that we saw beginning in Chapter 8—making the city safe for consumption. But the neoliberal turn in housing and homelessness policies is broader than the embrace of gentrification and the requisite displacement of the homeless, street vendor, squeegee boys, bike messengers, and other ostensible undesirables. *Police Strategy No. 5* and its broken window theory are but a small part in the retreat of the public sector in housing.

The changes in policy over the last decade and a half from Cisneros's accolades to the embrace of Housing First are the result of the disembedding of policies on homelessness from broader discourses, as those social anxieties find prominent new homes in the public sector, and changes in roles of government in providing housing. The introduction of consumer choice with Housing First seemingly gives greater dignity to the homeless, while at the same time locating them squarely within the capitalist system, to which the homeless had earlier been regarded as a dangerous outside. They are both consumers and participants in a housing market in ways that the linear model of homeless services does not afford.

This disembedding arises from not only a fragmenting of the homeless subject but also a commensurate fragmenting of the fabric of a social welfare system that had been established with the New Deal and strengthened with the 1960s War on Poverty. The systematic integration of housing, unemployment, social security, food, health, and disability fracture into distinct programs. The neoliberalization of housing (and subsequently homelessness) policy took place with great rapidity alongside the transitions of the discourse on homelessness and thus enabled the dismantling of that discourse.

The neoliberalization of homelessness policy began in 1990s as cities across the United States began to overhaul central business districts to make cities safe for consumption. Global changes in housing policy toward privatization and market forces can be traced to at least the 1970s overhauling of housing policy in Pinochet's Chile under the advisement of University of Chicago-trained economists.[18] In the mid-1970s, the United Kingdom began the process of redirecting its social housing: "The task of the Public Sector Housing Group was to align privatization within a wider austerity and pro-property agenda by assessing . . . How to re-orientate public sector housing policy to ensure . . . substantial reduction in public expenditure whilst ensuring those unable to provide for themselves are looked after [and] impetus . . . to the growth of owner occupation (Conservative Research Department, 1976:1)."[19] Increasing reliance on market forces to provide housing and dependence on the private nonprofit sector and on faith-based organizations to furnish services is part of a broader dismantling of the welfare state apparatus. The large infrastructures of public housing complexes have been taken down and replaced with voucher programs that place the recipient of subsidized housing into the private real estate market with the government underwriting the expense—it is the privatizing of public dollars.

The self-evidence of the neoliberalization of homelessness policy is not so much our concern—this has been a decades-long global trend in economic restructuring. Housing theorists David Clapham and Susan Smith summarize the broad outlines of the neoliberal turn:

> Neo-liberalism places emphasis on the market as the principal mechanism for distributing services and resources, and on the family or the voluntary sector for providing social and material support. The reduction of direct state intervention this implies is justified by appeal to both economic and moral arguments. From an economic perspective, neo-liberals regard the market as the most effective and the only efficient, system of resource allocation . . . From a neo-liberal (and libertarian) perspective, the market model is also seen as morally desirable. Whereas state provisioning is condemned for producing a poorly motivated "dependency culture," subsuming individual integrity within collective indecision, the market is promoted as source of incentive and drive, dispensing individual rewards for individual effort and widening individuals' choices.[20]

The moralizing of the market model has entered into the restructured discourse on homelessness. The Housing First model has much to recommend it—greater dignity for the homeless individual, a possible step en route to recognizing housing as a basic right, and elimination of the imputation of pathology through lingering traces of the disaffiliation thesis. Theoretically, Housing First has much that improves it over the older disaffiliation thesis, but it is a poor fix. The rhetoric of Housing First is that of abolition—ending homelessness. That should be the goal, and yet placing someone into housing does not address the supply of new people becoming homeless. It is a backward policy but one amenable to market forces. Instead of eliminating the conditions giving rise to homelessness (lack of affordable housing, living wages, education, and so on), it places the solution in the government's hands to shove someone into housing. The homeless subject may no longer be in the classical form of interpellation—the person is (ideally) placed into housing quickly and, thus, is no longer legally a homeless subject.

The discourse on homelessness became a systematic codification of norms through the creation of a homeless subject. A process that began with Sutherland and Locke's Depression-era study *Twenty-Thousand Homeless Men*, the forming of homeless subjects reached its culmination in the 1980s. The *McCain v. Koch* lawsuit against New York City had families internalizing the appellation of homeless and suing to be recognized as such. And with the McKinney Act, services and funds became available on a large-scale basis to those identifying as homeless (i.e., interpellating the subjectivity). But the formation of homeless subjects had de facto been realized through the population accessing shelters for decades.

The formation of homeless subjects through processes of shelterization, as we saw in Chapter 4, enabled the management of individual men living in Skid Row areas of town. As the homeless population increased exponentially in the 1980s and spread across central business districts and other parts of cities beyond the Bowery, the need to manage the homeless population expanded from individuals, who were a threat to social norms, to a single group. The formation of this group was abetted through legislation and studies that began to look at "the homeless." No longer an adjectival marker of men, families, or people, *homeless* became a noun; a new mass formation of "the homeless" emerged. This Foucauldian shift from individuals to a mass and the practice of discipline to those of biopolitics established the homeless as a mass to be regulated and contained. Foucault articulated this shift in his lecture series *Society Must Be Defended* at the Collège de France:

> Disciplines, for their part, dealt with individuals and their bodies in practical terms. What we are dealing with in this new technology of power is not exactly society (or at least not the social body, as defined by the jurists), nor is it the individual-as-body. It is a new body, a multiple body, a body with so many heads that, while they might not be infinite in number, cannot necessarily be counted. Biopolitics deals with the population, with the population as political problem, as a problem that is at once scientific and political as biological problem and as power's problem.[21]

This new technology of biopolitics is for regulating a mass—not the individual radical of the fin-de-siècle period—with "much more subtle mechanisms [than charitable institutions] that were much more economically rational than an indiscriminate charity."[22] Integrating the homeless into the political economy instead of marginalizing them in Skid Row areas necessitates new solutions to the problem of this varied group. The formation of this mass is part of subordinating these social arrangements to the economic and thus bringing them under broader forces of governing the population.

The formation of "the homeless" was initially embraced by those working with and in behalf of the homeless. Early advocacy organizations included the National Coalition for the Homeless formed in 1982 and incorporated in 1984. The Coalition for the Homeless in New York was a few years earlier. In Mitch Snyder and Mary Ellen Hombs's 1982 publication by the Community for Creative Non-Violence *Homelessness in America*, they use the mass formation of "the homeless" in their preface.[23] Forming this homeless mass was for the advocates a concomitant part of establishing the large scope of the homeless problem along with the large figure of two million homeless people invoked by Mitch Snyder. Increasingly, this new mass showed up in 1980s policy documents[24] but became so much a part of common parlance by the early 1990s that Christopher Jencks's sympathetic survey of the state of research on homelessness carried the simple title *The Homeless*.

Advocates successively established the homeless mass as a widespread concern meriting policy responses, which culminated in the McKinney Act. But once a mass, it was an entity to be regulated and controlled—not a docile population of the shelterized; the economic cannibalizing of social problems was part of this control. Foreclosing an outside to the economic sphere limits the range of possible policy and service obligations; a social good is only good insofar as it accomplishes an economic goal. Services become but means to integrating the homeless into the economy, rather than regulating social relations; hobosociality and alternate communities are no longer the concern. The institutional imperatives transform to meet these demands. The movement of the definition of homelessness from disaffiliation to one's placement in the housing market is also a part of this subordination of the social to the economic.

This reach of economics into spheres once beyond its purview, though not unique to homelessness, has changed meanings of language, uses of space, and ways in which services are provided. This rationalization of the world reduces the social to the quantifiable. Problematic traces of deep culture might be expunged but for policies and institutions, as antiseptic as the Disneyfied Times Square. Between the insufficient disenchantment, which gave rise to the discourse on homelessness, and the evisceration of nuance and significance, with the neoliberalizing of space and social services, the former posits a world in which complexity is implicitly acknowledged—the turn to myth is a recognition that social conditions are not fully articulable—but the latter neoliberalizing is embraced for an ease of governance.

The discourse on homelessness is a frail shell of its once complex (and admittedly problematic) way of articulating social life. Stripped first of any connection to social anxieties of the middle-class family and subsequently of some nostalgia for a lost *Gemeinschaft*, the discourse is now a quantifiably rationalized series of policy imperatives to increase the income and return to independence. Fears of the uncertain social arrangements of alternative communities cede to desires to render each homeless person a cog in the political economy. Housing First is the programmatic way to begin this process.

CHAPTER 10

Conclusion

The prominence that attached to homelessness as a social problem in the 1980s has waned. No advocates like Mitch Snyder occupy news programs or have television cameras recording their congressional testimony on homelessness. The crisis of homelessness has seemingly subsided into banality. Certainly people still go without shelter in the United States; each year more than six hundred thousand Americans find themselves without a fixed place to stay at night. But homelessness is no longer a national crisis. Much like a century earlier, urban order has been restored; this order always comes with an element of acquiescence—in this case, to the idea that we shall have people living on the streets of American cities. A new focus on permanently housing these homeless appears, but there is little talk of restructuring housing and economic conditions contributing to people becoming homeless. In policy talk, ending homelessness means moving those who are homeless into housing, not keeping them from becoming homeless in the first place.

A semblance of order has come to the city and to social services. Homeless advocacy has undertaken the common professionalization of activists with a revolving door between political appointments and positions of leading advocacy groups. Along with this professionalization, there has come an increasing willingness of homeless service agencies and advocacy groups to partner with business, civic, and municipal leaders. This seemingly new partnership is merely a return to the practices at the formation of the discourse on homelessness. Then early advocates, like Jacob Riis, wanted business to take the lead in responding to homelessness—he did, after all, regard business as the Haussmann of the American city. Municipal leaders were to pass laws that facilitated the restoration of order to the city. The American city is increasingly an antiseptic space to accommodate the gentrifying demands of young professionals and urban families.

From its beginnings, the discourse on homelessness has been concerned with making the city safe for the family. At the turn of the last century, New York came to be called the "homeless city" because its slums threatened the home, which simultaneously fostered the family and citizens. This dual fostering highlights a contradiction that was long latent in the discourse but only came to the fore with the advent of the family values movement: the instrumentality of social policy and activism to foster the supposed organicism of community and family. Early in the fin-de-siècle rise of the discourse on homelessness, the family (in its emerging nuclear form) was presumed a naturally given social formation. Mythologizing processes of constructing the Christian home and the constitution of an other—the homeless figure—furnished a naturalizing overlay to the family. Through this mythologization, the family transcended the historical moment and became the natural foundation for social order.

But the state (of which one is a citizen) and civil society are not natural. Again, at the turn of the last century, Jacob Riis was alarmed by the increasing presence of the voluntary associations of civil society; these associations were destroying the family. The state, however, was a reformer's ally; it was a necessity. Statist institutions became allies in bringing changes to daily lives. The reach of these state institutions was not (primarily) to go into the family but to create spaces in which the family could flourish. Zoning laws, building codes, and housing ordinances established a literal framework to which the family could retreat from the fast-paced life of the city. This pace was augmented by technology, demands from work, and demands from civil society associations. The state could help protect the family, while associations were merely a distraction. The eventual integration and subordination of the concerns for the family to those of civil society and social capital introduced instrumentality into the family and not merely into the creation of spaces for this social foundation. The discourse on homelessness arose because of social and political anxieties about the impact of modernization on the family.

In Part I, I argued that the emergence of the concept of homelessness was integrated with the mythologizing process of family legitimation. The industrializing city transformed social life and rent longstanding ties to places and people; it became a locus defined by the acute anomie of transcendental homelessness. The concept of homelessness was developed as part of a semantic process, which combined with spatial and institutional processes to bring order to the chaos of the city. One form of social norms had collapsed without a new order being in place to regulate the city— these processes of ordering were to extend rationalization (*logos*) over the metropolis. In this process of ordering, the concept of homelessness became the other both to the family and to order, since the family was to be the basis for social order.

Fin-de-siècle commentators turned to deep culture in their linguistic processes of ordering. They deployed ancient tropes of a quintessential other in Western culture—"the Jew." These anti-Semitic tropes furnished a constellation of meanings and juxtapositions—Christian/non-Christian, family/individual, wandering/unsettled, radical/bourgeois—which began to shape the nascent discourse on homelessness. This deployment of anti-Semitic tropes rendered homelessness as a problem of culture. In the Cain story—whose mark, according to Riis, defaces the modern urban slums— the founding of the Ur-city took place within his lineage responsible for technological development. The city was only founded when Cain was cut off from nature, from the soil. The homeless figure is an inherently urban formation and so embodies that which is unnatural about the metropolis. As deinstitutionalized religious narratives, the Cain story and other mythic tropes carried anxieties about the family and grounded social life in deep culture. As part of a semantic ordering process, myth became an instrument of rationalization; myth's deployment is an early turn to a culturalization of politics, which became important in the more recent incarnations of the discourse on homelessness.

In the interim, which I deal with in Part II, myth and culture recede in the discourse on homelessness. Social and semantic stabilities combined with an acquiescence to metropolitan life; the urgency of fin-de-siècle anxieties faded as some order came to the city. Though the *Gemeinschaft* ideal was inevitably not established, some form of social order was in place. With a relative social order, social science was able to more clearly distinguish populations and groups—new taxonomies also made their way into the discourse on homelessness. The earlier mythic tropes had established a framework for the discourse; sociology consolidated these basic characteristics into taxonomies and definitions.

In this period of stability, the homeless man was consolidated as the normative category of social displacement. Before this consolidation took place, an urban population was segregated from the broader (and in one sociologist's phrase "normal") population. These men were distinguished by spatial, linguistic, and institutional limits—these residents of Skid Row areas of town came to be the homeless men. This constitution of the category of the homeless man integrated efforts from social service providers and sociologists. The consolidation of this category came about through the marginalization of the competing category of the hobo. The homeless man was the Skid Row man who went through a shelter, while the hobo was a free spirit who did not remain long in one place. The hobo had his own institutions and associations; the homeless man was shorn of significant social relations.

The discursive role of homelessness as the other of the family continued into this new sociological category. The assumption that the family was the only legitimate basis for social order moved from fin-de-siècle activists to the Chicago School sociologists. The widespread hobo associations were not legitimate society. Family relations were central to sociological studies; social workers attempted to integrate the homeless back into their families. The thriving hobo community was disparaged—the associational life of the poor, working men was an insufficient form of society and failed to allay social and political anxieties.

These anxieties had lost the fevered pitch of earlier decades; they slowly subsided into a sense of social worry. The homeless figure came to be defined as the disaffiliated man, as the midcentury appearance of the category of the nuclear family integrated with the sociological fad of loneliness studies. Anxieties about revolution were now worries about loneliness—the family was the panacea for both. The language of homelessness was no longer deployed to describe threats to the Christian home ideal; it became the mere absence of such a home.

The cultural logic of homelessness was completely integrated with family legitimation—the homeless man was the other of the family. The assumption was so integrated into the sociological work on homelessness that enormous blind spots developed within sociological studies. The spatial location was an enormous part of this limitation—sociologists studied homelessness in those Skid Row areas where they found the homeless, white men outside of family life. The disaffiliation thesis could easily sustain, since only disaffiliated populations were studied. This spatial limitation to sociological work had a series of consequences: most importantly, the displaced people outside of these urban regions were not considered homeless. Racial and gender blind spots became increasingly glaring over the late 1960s and early 1970s; a decade later, other such blind spots began to appear.

In Part III, I argue that the discourse on homelessness faced a moment of crisis with the emergence of the contradiction of the homeless family. The logic of the discourse and the role of the homeless figure as a primary carrier of social anxieties about the family were brought into tension with empirical realities. The discursive logic had already obscured the presence of homeless women and African American men—journalists had to document their appearance on the streets before social scientists noticed them. Women and African Americans did not make their way into the discourse until after the mid-1960s pathologization of the African American family in the Moynihan Report and the rise of second-wave feminism. The race and gender blind spots were small by comparison to that of the homeless family.

Displaced families were known to exist—they were called families in crisis or transition. But they logically could not be homeless, since they were still together with their family. The *McCain v. Koch* lawsuit resolved this problem and established the homeless family. The de facto bracketing of this group with monikers like *families in crisis* took on a new form—myth. The deployment of mythic tropes bracketed the homeless family—they were distinct from the other street homeless. This homeless figure became dually juxtaposed—first to bourgeois family norms and then to the homeless family. The basic framework of disaffiliation continued to define the street homeless, while the homeless family became bracketed from the assumptions of disaffiliation and pathology. A new legal definition of the homeless individual—one without a fixed place to stay at night—rendered homelessness as a material condition. However, the discursive logic continued within sociological work. The material definition was deferred to, while disaffiliation remained a basic assumption.

In Part IV, we looked at the restructuring of the language, space, and institutions of homelessness as the discourse is emptied of much of its signification. The street homeless remained a point of urban concern and frustration. As middle-class families returned to city centers to visit or reside in gentrified shopping and residential districts, they increasingly encountered the homeless on the streets. These same gentrifying trends also destroyed old Skid Row areas and tore down SROs. More people were turned into the streets to spread across the city as middle-class families were increasingly in urban areas; as a result, there were increased demands for policing to make the metropolis safe for consumption. This figure continued to be a threat to the family.

But the usefulness of the homeless figure as a primary carrier for family anxieties was severely compromised. The primary cultural locus for these anxieties shifted to the emerging family values movement. But this movement accommodates itself to the call for increasing social capital. The family ideal in the discourse on homelessness is mythologized—it assumes an organic naturalness. The artificial relations based on capital are antagonistic to the family ideals in the earlier discourse—therefore, the family ideal has to transform in this new cultural locus.

The family in the discourse on homelessness had to be shielded from the modern world—its pace and pressures were threats to the family. Deep culture was part of this legitimation of the family—it became a transcendental form and thus could stand, in part, outside of modernity. The homeless figure embodied the threats of modern life: unsettled states, movement, the absence of family, and a life that is always already urban. The deployment of myth to other this figure (and later to bracket the homeless family) is a turn to deep culture to solve the problems of the day. A family ideal integrated into the civil society structures of social capital implicitly assumes that modernity can solve these problems.

The homeless figure became "the homeless"—this mass first needed help but soon became a mass to be regulated and governed. With housing and homelessness policy participating in global neoliberalizing trends, this homeless mass became increasingly integrated into market forces. This subordination to the economic made the discourse on homelessness irrelevant as a carrier of social anxieties. The discourse was emptied of its signification; no longer did it embody anxieties about the family and nostalgia for a lost *Gemeinschaft*. Homelessness became a material condition, which policymakers and service providers alike thought should be addressed through reintegration into the housing market. The discourse on homelessness was no longer an expression of fears of modernization.

Modernity is not the object of this project—it is a backdrop that has receded. The modern city was thought to be destroying social life; the family was ostensibly the last hope to preserve it. The *Gemeinschaft* ideals that were foisted onto the family are no longer heralded as a model for society—modernity is too much with us. The family can now accommodate itself to the modern world. Homelessness is doubly marginal. Homeless figures are marginal in society, and the discourse is no longer central to public life. When aggressive panhandlers too often confront conventioneers or tourists, convention bureaus and newspaper columnists will still call for action. But the issue soon fades. While pundits still fear threats to the family, it is not an urban camper who is first invoked as such a threat. Policing has mitigated this possibility.

The discourse on homelessness arose through problems in establishing the American city as the primary locus of production; the homeless figure remained a problem as the city became the primary locus of consumption. Is the homeless figure, then, just a heuristic to look at shifts in the American city, family, and society? It is that, but it is also more. Is the homeless figure, in the face of gentrification, merely a more contemporary story of the arcade projects of Second Empire Paris? Is it a problem to, but not of, consumption? Does the homeless figure merely undermine the security of spaces of consumption? Is it merely a disorder to be rectified so the locus of consumption is able to receive both financing and customers? But the homeless figure is more than a heuristic or an example; it is intertwined with American attempts to wrestle with modernization. As American life has urbanized,[1] social life has transformed. In each incarnation of the city, the ability of the urban commentators to make sense of the day has been stretched. In periods of great change, such commentators often could not articulate new social structures—the modernity of the city was too much to legitimate within the means available to the day, thus the turn to deep culture in the form of myths. The metropolitan myths coalesced around homelessness—an inherently new and modern form of urban life thought to threaten dominant social structures. The homeless figure often resists recalibration in the face of empirical shifts because it is constructed by myth; disaffiliation lingers despite shifts in demographics, geographical distribution across the city, and underlying economic concerns. In the discourse on homelessness, the figure is constituted as the modern instantiation of ancient perils to the preservation of the home. The homeless figure becomes a repository of all that is undesirable of the modern city, while the bourgeois subject may enjoy the urban parks, museums, and cultural life—in short, the metropolitan amenities.

Urban life is now quite orderly. The contemporary American city has little resemblance to the fin-de-siècle homeless city with its throngs spilling from sidewalks into the streets. The American city is no longer a location of production; consumption (and services) is now its primary economic functions and lifeblood. The city of consumption has to be kept orderly to abet the movements and safety of the consumers. American cities have now been thoroughly rationalized, and even more so, they are sanitized.

Notes

Introduction

1. US Department of Housing and Urban Development, *Homelessness: Programs and the People They Serve, Findings of the National Survey of Homeless Assistance Providers and Clients Highlights* (Washington, DC: US Department of Housing and Urban Development Interagency Council on the Homeless, December 1999).
2. For instance, see Larry Logue, *To Appomattox and Beyond: The Civil War Soldier in War and Peace* (Chicago: Ivan R. Dee, 1996).
3. Kenneth L. Kusmer, *Down and Out on the Road: The Homeless in American History* (Oxford: Oxford University Press, 2002), chapter 3.
4. Early taxonomies of the displaced distinguished categories with two criteria: work and motion. Tramps remained in motion wandering from place to place but did not work. Hobos also wandered, but they did work. Bums neither wandered nor worked.
5. Cities that had already been growing for decades boomed over the waning of the nineteenth and opening of the twentieth centuries. For instance, according to US census data, Chicago grew 246 percent from 1890 to 1920. Over the same period, New York City grew 371 percent, Detroit 482 percent, and Los Angeles 1144 percent.
6. Daniel Patrick Moynihan, "The Negro Family: The Case for National Action," in *The Moynihan Report and the Politics of Controversy*, ed. Lee Rainwater and William L. Yancey (Cambridge, MA: MIT Press, 1967).
7. According to Ferdinand Tönnies, a *Gemeinschaft* is an association based on organic life, growing out of familiar, comfortable, and exclusive social existence. His theory of *Gemeinschaft* posits a complete unity of wills in an original, or natural, state. This collapse of the value systems of a society is a condition that sociologist Robert Merton calls acute anomie. In critiques of modernity, this strong anomie appears as a sense that modernization destroyed a sense of being at home in the world and established a condition—in György Lukács's phrase—of "transcendental homelessness." For more on *Gemeinschaft*, see Ferdinand Tönnies, *Community and Civil Society*, trans. José Harris (Cambridge, MA: Cambridge University Press, 2001). For more on acute anomie, see Robert Merton, *Social Theory and Social Structure* (Glencoe, IL: Free Press, 1963). For more on transcendental homelessness, see Georg Lukács, *The Theory of the Novel:*

A Historico-Philosophical Essay on the Forms of Great Epic Literature (Cambridge, MA: MIT Press, 1999).

8. William Dean Howells and Jacob Riis, among others, called New York a homeless city.

9. In July 1863, a week of urban violence broke out, releasing a range of class and racial tensions. Because the first draft act in America included a provision that let someone pay $300 to avoid the draft, the perception developed that the poor were being sent off to fight a war from which the wealthy were exempt. Thousands rioted a few days after the first names were drawn in New York City.

10. The Paris Commune was the short-lived rule of a left worker's government in the spring of 1871. These socialists and anarchists briefly seized power following French defeat in the Franco-Prussian War.

11. The McKinney Act contained emergency relief measures, preventive measures, and long-term solutions to homelessness. Most importantly, it established a federal, legal definition of homelessness.

12. Roy Lubove, *The Professional Altruist: The Emergence of Social Work as a Career, 1880–1930* (New York: Atheneum, 1983).

13. Recent changes with the federal Homeless Emergency Assistance and Rapid Transition to Housing (HEARTH) Act simplify this process by broadening the definition of homelessness to include those obscured under McKinney-Vento: "unaccompanied youth and families with children and youth who are unstably housed." While the definition of homelessness in McKinney-Vento did not recognize this group as homeless, statutes like the Runaway and Homeless Youth Act (42 U.S.C. 5701 *et seq.*), the Head Start Act (42 U.S.C. 9831 *et seq.*), subtitle N of the VAWA (42 U.S.C. 14043e *et seq.*), section 330 of the Public Health Service Act (42 U.S.C. 254b), the Food and Nutrition Act of 2008 (7 U.S.C. 2012(m)), the Child Nutrition Act of 1996 (42 U.S.C. 1786(b)(15)), and subtitle B of title VII of the McKinney-Vento Homeless Assistance Act (42 U.S.C. 11431 *et seq.*) See Federal Register/ Vol. 76, No. 233 / Monday, December 5, 2011 / Rules and Regulations 76001. This outlier of the homeless family and unaccompanied youth (i.e., children without parents) is reflective of a propensity to bracket the homeless family from the rest of the homeless population once the category of the homeless family becomes discursively possible in the 1980s, an issue to which we shall return in Parts III and IV.

14. For instance, Peter Rossi and Kenneth Kusmer both begin their histories in colonial towns governed by Elizabethan Poor Laws, even though the category of homelessness does not appear until the latter half of the nineteenth century. Peter H. Rossi, *Down and Out in America: The Origins of Homelessness* (Chicago: University of Chicago Press, 1989), chapter 2.

15. National Alliance to End Homelessness, "Organizational Change: Adopting a Housing First Approach," August 24, 2009, 1.

16. Charles Loring Brace, *The Dangerous Classes of New York, and Twenty Years' Work among Them* (New York: Wynkoop and Hallenbeck, 1872), 97.

Chapter 1

1. In the early 1850s, Baron Haussmann was commissioned by Napoleon III to modernize Paris. He built large avenues and shopping districts. In part, the goal was to break up the poor, working-class neighborhoods in which the uprisings of 1848 began. The wider streets would both facilitate troop movements and make barricade-building more difficult for those hoping to start future uprisings. The changes implemented by Haussmann transformed the urban landscape and scattered the poor from the previously overcrowded, labyrinthine neighborhoods.

2. Geographer and urban analyst David Harvey talks about the contradictory impacts of industrializing the city—the rationalization of certain bureaucratic structures, while also unleashing the chaotic problems of unemployment, inadequate housing, and ethnic and class factionalism, which arise from the overaccumulation of labor in cities. For a discussion of the urbanization of capital, see David Harvey, *The Urban Experience* (Baltimore: Johns Hopkins University Press, 1989), especially 17–34.

3. William Dean Howells, *A Hazard of New Fortunes* (New York: Modern Library, 2002), 302.

4. According to Jacob Riis, "The tenements to-day are New York, harboring three-fourths of its population. When another generation shall have doubled the census of our city, and to that vast army of workers, held captive by poverty, the very name of home shall be as a bitter mockery what will the harvest be?" Jacob Riis, *How the Other Half Lives: Studies among the Tenements of New York* (New York: Penguin Books, 1997), 20. Because my project is a study of the discourse on homelessness, I am not concerned with attempting to determine the seeming accuracy of Riis's numbers. Rather, I want to look at how the city, its life, and its problems were being thought about and discussed.

5. Howells, 64–65.

6. Colleen McDannell, who has undertaken several studies of the Christian home, describes its central importance as a social institution:

   > During the nineteenth century, good family life was seen as the means by which the nation and its religion were maintained. Americans believed the home to be the nursery of both patriotism and piety. Home life taught the mutual dependence and reciprocal responsibility of each citizen. By connecting the individual to the community at large, the family instilled notions of morality, order, stability, education, purity, refinement, and discipline. Although the church also played an important role in creating good Christians, the Victorian preoccupation with the family saw home life as the more crucial purveyor of ethics and piety.

   Colleen McDannell, "Parlor Piety: The Home as Sacred Space in Protestant America," in *American Home Life, 1880–1930: A Social History of Spaces and Services*, ed. Jessica H. Foy and Thomas J. Schlereth (Knoxville: University of Tennessee Press, 1992), 164.

7. McDannell, 173.

8. The nondenominational Protestant American Sunday School Union was founded in 1824 out of some earlier institutions for the evangelical purpose of establishing Sunday schools in places of destitution.

9. "In most great cities there are districts in which the families are few in comparison with the number of individuals. Such districts are commonly the haunts of criminals, and even the value of the property is usually lowered as the result. In such places there are houses but not homes, dwellings but not families." John Hall, *A Christian Home: How to Make and How to Maintain It* (Philadelphia: American Sunday-School Union, 1883), 11–12.

10. In particular, the Draft Riot of 1863 and the Tompkins Square Riot of 1877 (also Chicago's Haymarket Riot of 1886) exacerbated anxieties. I argue that these earlier riots (and the Paris Commune) become markers of lingering dangers. In the 1880s and 1890s, they are discussed with great alarm not as history but as possible futures. Volunteer Special's *The Volcano Under the City* (pseudonymously published in 1886 by William Stoddard—formerly one of President Lincoln's personal secretaries) argues that the potential for urban explosion continues to lurk under the city. Jacob Riis calls for social change to avert another Tompkins Square incident. Later in 1916, large vagrant populations are cited as a source of a New York threat much like the extensive vagrant involvement in the French Revolution. See Volunteer Special, *The Volcano under the City* (New York: Fords, Howard, and Hulbert, 1887); and Frank Laubach, *Why There Are Vagrants, a Study Based upon a Examination of One Hundred Men* (New York: Columbia University Press, 1916). Jacob Riis in *How the Other Half Lives, Battle with the Slum*, and *The Peril and Preservation of the Home* also repeatedly cites these riots as possible urban futures.

11. The early 1890s' responses to the poverty of industrialized cities were not only important in the United States. Pope Leo XIII began the modern tradition of social encyclicals with 1891's *Rerum Novarum*, which tried to speak against the excesses of capitalism, tempered with even more alarming critique of communism. This tendency to acknowledge problems from the overquick industrialization of cities and to call for incremental changes to avert the more sweeping (and atheistic) social transformations offered by anarchists and communists also marked the calls for reform in the United States.

12. Arthur Schleslinger Jr., "Introduction," in Howells, xi.

13. Howells, 67.

14. Ibid., 67.

15. Ibid., 68.

16. For instance, see Jürgen Habermas, *The Structural Transformation of the Public Sphere: An Inquiry into a Category of Bourgeois Society*, trans. Thomas Burger with Frederick Lawrence (Cambridge, MA: MIT Press, 2000).

17. Howells, 308–9.

18. Ibid., 309–10:

> He was working up a branch of inquiry which had so long occupied him, in the libraries, and studying the great problem of labor and poverty as it continually presented itself to him in the streets. He said that he talked with all sorts of people

whom he found monstrously civil, if you took them in the right way; and he went everywhere in the city without fear and apparently without danger. March could not find out that he had ridden his hobby into the homes of want which he visited, or had proposed their enslavement to the inmates as a short and simple solution of the great question of their lives; he appeared to have contented himself with the collection of facts for the persuasion of the cultivated classes.

19. Ibid., 147.
20. Ferenc M. Szasz and Ralph F. Bogardus, "The Camera and the American Social Conscience," *New York History* 55, no. 4 (1974): 422.
21. See Charles Loring Brace, *The Dangerous Classes of New York, and Twenty Years' Work among Them* (New York: Wynkoop and Hallenbeck, 1872), 97. Riis was certainly familiar with this text. He alludes to it in *How the Other Half Lives* as well as numerous magazine articles and books. Riis, *Other Half*, 197.
22. For discussions of these texts and their influence on Riis, see Louise Ware, *Jacob A. Riis, Police Reporter, Reformer, Useful Citizen* (New York: D. Appleton-Century, 1938), 49; and James B. Lane, *Jacob A. Riis and the American City* (Port Washington, NY: Kennikat Press, 1974), 52–53.
23. Lane, 53.
24. The "Bread or Blood" riots were a series of uprisings from primarily industrial workers, starting in 1830s Britain. Riis, as was typical of his day, dismissed any social or political discontents as anarchists and relegated them to the status of criminal elements or rowdies (rather than as offering social critique).
25. For an example of his take on Tompkins Square, see Riis, *Other Half*, 124; or Riis, *The Peril and the Preservation of the Home: Being the William L. Bull Lectures for the Year 1903* (Philadelphia: George W. Jacobs, 1903), 184.
26. Riis, *Other Half*, 124.
27. Jacob A. Riis, *The Making of an American* (New York: Macmillan, 1925), 272.
28. For a similar point, see also Lewis F. Fried, *Makers of the City* (Amherst: University of Massachusetts Press, 1990), 21.
29. Edwin G. Burrows and Mike Wallace, *Gotham: A History of New York City to 1898* (New York: Oxford University Press, 1999), 794.
30. Ibid., 795. Burrows and Wallace continue with this: "Doubting that the park's deep structure would sufficiently discipline the unruly, Olmsted established regulations that, in marked contrast to the laissez-faire streets of the city, soon blanketed the park terrain with 125 varieties of directive and injunctive signs and posters. He also instituted park police—'keepers'—who would 'respectfully aid an offender toward a better understanding of what is due to others, as one gentleman might manage to guide another.'" Burrows and Wallace, 795.
31. For this point, see Terence Young, "Modern Urban Parks," *Geographical Review* 85, no. 4 (October 1995), 535–51.
32. See Young, "Modern Urban Parks," 537.
33. For instance, see Jane Addams, *The Spirit of Youth and the City Streets* (New York: Macmillan, 1914).
34. Riis, *Other Half*, 7.

35. "The tenements to-day are New York, harboring three-fourths of its population. When another generation shall have doubled the census of our city, and to that vast army of workers, held captive by poverty, the very name of home shall be as a bitter mockery what will the harvest be?" See Riis, *Other Half*, 20.

36. Initial rules required parental acknowledgement of age, and when that proved to be easily perjured, additional requirements like birth certificates were mandated.

37. See Robert H. Wiebe, *The Search for Order: 1877–1920* (New York: Hill and Wang, 1967).

38. Karl Marx calls these the catchphrases of the old society. They were the slogan for the conservative alliance formed between Catholic and monarchist elements in 1848 France; this group was sometimes called the Party of Order. See Karl Marx, "The Eighteenth Brumaire of Louis Bonaparte," in *Surveys from Exile: Political Writings Volume II*, ed. David Fernbach (New York: Vintage Books, 1974), 155. Louis Bonaparte and his reactionary program of order (i.e., Haussmannization) were lauded by Jacob Riis as a model for how to respond to the problems of urbanization.

39. Riis, *Other Half*, 146.

40. Jacob A. Riis, *The Children of the Poor* (New York: Garrett Press, 1970), 65.

41. Riis, *Other Half*, 137.

42. Ibid., 5.

43. Ibid., 5; emphasis in the original.

44. Riis, *Other Half*, 5:

> Long ago it was said that "one half of the world does not know how the other half lives." That was true then. It did not know because it did not care. The half that was on top cared little for the struggles, and less for the fate of those who were underneath, so long as it was able to hold them there and keep its own seat. There came a time when the discomfort and crowding below were so great, and the consequent upheavals so violent, that it was no longer an easy thing to do, and then the upper half fell to inquiring what was the matter. Information on the subject has been accumulating rapidly since, and the whole world has had its hands full answering for its old ignorance.

Riis's demand to know the other half to avert such disasters is emblematic of broader outcries. For instance, see Volunteer Special, *Volcano*. Stoddard (Volunteer Special) argues that the Draft Riots broke out precisely because the public (i.e. the bourgeois public) were unaware of the simmering conditions among the poor. To avert further explosions, the poor must be monitored and controlled; the "powers that be" must be aware of the conditions.

45. Riis, *Other Half*, 39.

46. Ibid., 87–88.

47. Riis, *Children*, 56. See also Riis *Children*, 18–19. The value of cleanliness was so important that New York reformers set up associations (e.g., the Citizens Council on Hygiene) for the sole purpose of ensuring that the value and methods of hygiene were taught to and implemented by the poor. For discussions of these, see Jacob A. Riis, *Peril*, 71; or Jacob A. Riis, *The Battle with the Slum* (Mineola, NY: Dover, 1998), 19, 81.

48. Riis, *Battle*, 75.
49. Ibid., 53.
50. Riis, *Children*, 51.
51. Though, he does note here that some institutions (i.e., churches) have the ability to inspire a certain cleanliness in its older members, though not as a systemic way of life.
52. Riis, *Other Half*, 139.
53. The greater ease of forming a character than reforming one is a refrain of his career. "Where it would have been—is—so easy to *form* character, we have been laboring with such infinite toil to *reform* it. It would have formed itself had we left the boy the home, for that is where character grows. The loss of it thrust a hundred problems upon us of finding props to take its place. All the labor of forty years has been directed to that end." Riis, *Peril*, 181–82. The props include the fresh air holidays, boys' clubs, kindergarten, cooking class, the social settlement, etc. Riis, *Peril*, 182–87.
54. Riis, *Other Half*, 146.
55. Ibid. Much of the anxiety about the Five Points area stemmed from the midcentury rapid demographic changes. In the decade from 1846 to 1855, nearly a half dozen Protestant churches shuttered their doors to be replaced by two Catholic parishes and several Jewish congregations in the surrounding area. Methodist minister Lewis Pease established projects to develop job skills among the immigrant poor and to address issues of poverty. However, the more evangelically inclined Missionary Society backing the ventures wanted emphasis on proselytizing among the Catholics. Pease turned to wealthier Episcopalian backers to sponsor his social ministry. See Tyler Anbinder, *Five Points: The 19th-Century New York City Neighborhood That Invented Tap Dance, Stole Elections, and Became the World's Most Notorious Slum* (New York: Penguin Books, 2001), 241ff.
56. See, especially, Addams, *Spirit*. Here she discusses the necessity to properly guide the impulses of youth to avoid the impulses misdirecting youth into vice.
57. Riis, *Other Half*, 184–85.
58. Ibid., 185.
59. Ibid., 184.
60. Ibid., 120.
61. See, for example, Riis, *Children*, 38ff.
62. "I have the authority of a distinguished rabbi, whose field and daily walk are among the poorest of his people, to support me in the statement that the moral tone of the young girls is distinctly lower than it was. The entire absence of privacy in their homes and the foul contact of the sweaters' shops, where men and women work side by side from morning till night, scarcely half clad in the hot summer weather, does for the girls what the street completes in the boy [that is, corrupt their morals]." Riis, *Children*, 43.
63. Riis, *Other Half*, 101.
64. Kathryn Kish Sklar, *Catharine Beecher: A Study in American Domesticity* (New York: W. W. Norton, 1976), 12–13.

65. Catharine E. Beecher and Harriet Beecher Stowe, *The American Woman's Home: Or, Principles of Domestic Science; Being a Guide to the Formation and Maintenance of Economical, Healthful, Beautiful, and Christian Homes* (New York: Arno Press, 1971), 434.

66. "The hardest work of all is to restore a guilty, selfish, hardened spirit to honor, truth, and purity; and this is the divine labor to which the pitying Saviour calls all his true followers; to lift up the fallen, to sustain the weak, to protect the tempted, to bind up the broken-hearted, and especially to rescue the sinful. This is the peculiar privilege of woman in the sacred retreat of a 'Christian home.'" Beecher and Stowe, 433.

67. Beecher and Stowe, chapter 38.

68. Riis, *Other Half*, 81. Both the Naturalization Act of 1870 and the Chinese Exclusion Act of 1882 restricted the presence of women in the Chinese community. The early Chinese male immigrant as a threat to the home and the sanctity of white, middle class American women is a long-standing cultural trope. Its most recent appearance was in the 2002 Broadway adaptation of the 1960s film *Thoroughly Modern Millie*.

69. Riis, *Battle*, 40.

70. Riis, *Other Half*, 61.

71. Stephanie Golden, *The Women Outside: Meanings and Myths of Homelessness* (Berkeley: University of California Press, 1992), 126ff.

72. Riis, *Other Half*, 60.

73. Beecher and Stowe, chapter 1.

74. Riis, *Peril*, 187–88.

75. For instance, see Riis, *Children*, 92–117; Riis, *Battle*, 31.

76. Riis, *Children*, 92.

77. Ibid., 93.

78. For instance, see Riis, *Peril*, 180.

79. See Riis, *Children*, 116–17.

80. Riis, *Other Half*, 201. Also, he argues that private enterprise must do the lion's share and must make it unprofitable to own a bad tenement. Riis, *Other Half*, 210–11.

81. Ibid., 183.

82. Ibid., 191. This nether half, I argue, invokes the diabolic connections of wandering. Not only does he use a term that conveys an explicit reference to the lowest levels of existence and evokes ideas of the netherworld, but also he claims that the nether half hides its deformity—a probable reference to a cloven foot. Diabolic connections to wandering are long lived. For instance, see Daniel Defoe, *The History of the Devil* (Totowa, NJ: Rowman and Littlefield, 1972). In Chapter 2, we shall see that the diabolical underpinnings of both the idea of wandering and anti-Semitism remain latent within this discourse on homelessness.

83. Riis, *Other Half*, 191.

84. Ibid., 196.

85. Riis, *Battle*, 54:

> Meanwhile, philanthropy is not sitting idle and waiting. It is building tenements on the humane plan that lets in sunshine and air and hope. It is putting up hotels

deserving of the name for the army that but just now had no other home than the cheap lodging houses which Inspector Byrnes [Chief of detectives from 1880–1895] fitly called "nurseries of crime." These also are standards from which there is no backing down, even if coming up to them is slow work: and they are here to stay, for they pay. That is the test. Not charity, but justice,—that is the gospel which they preach.

86. His arguments for justice are still motivated by fear; he believes that if a more just system is not set up, there will be violent upheaval. He criticized a report from the Association for Improving the Condition of the Poor (AICP), which expressed the fear "that reform may come in a burst of public indignation destructive to property and to good morals." He argued against this report: "They represented one solution of the problem of ignorant poverty *versus* ignorant wealth that has come down to us unsolved, the danger-cry of which we have lately heard in the shout that never should have been raised on American soil—the shout of 'the masses against the classes'—the solution of violence. There is another solution, that of justice. The choice is between the two. Which shall it be?" Riis, *Other Half*, 196. The AICP was founded by the New York City Tract Society to be the social wing distinguished from the evangelical Tract Society's more explicitly religious work among the poor of the Five Points area. Anbinder, 243–44.

87. Riis, *Other Half*, 197.

88. Riis, *Peril*, 130. Initially, he seems to call for a five percent return. Riis, *Other Half*, 198. Perhaps he comes to realize that business investors need more than that, so he ups it to seven in his later book.

89. "[New York] has often sadly missed a Napoleon III, to clean up and make light in the dark corners." Riis, *Other Half*, 199.

90. Ibid., 201.

91. Riis, *Children*, 1–2.

92. See note 86 of this chapter.

93. Laubach, 5. Laubach goes on to draw historical parallels to the French Revolution to make his case for the potential violence: "How pernicious the influence of his vast army of vagrants might become, should the class struggle develop, is suggested by the following description of conditions just before the French Revolution." Laubach then cites a long passage from Taine's "L'Ancien Régime" in which he describes vagabond vermin as criminal elements who "were the leaders or supernumeraries of the Revolution." Laubach, 6. Taine's conclusions are the same ones reached by Stoddard, Riis, and others about the New York City riots—criminal elements with no justifiable social critique.

Chapter 2

1. An earlier version of this chapter was published in Philip Webb's "Anti-Semitic Roots of Homelessness: Myth, Exile and Radicals in American Homelessness," in *Jewish Images in the Media*, ed. Martin Liepach, Gabriele Melischek, and Josef

Seethaler, 39–60. *Relation: Communication Research in Comparative Perspective*, n.s., vol. 2 (Vienna: Austrian Academy of Sciences Press, 2007).

2. McDannell, 173.

3. Sander Gilman and Steven Katz argue that this traditional view fails to understand the nineteenth century secularization of religious models in the biological sciences; they argue that the racialized pathologies attributed to Jews in the newer anti-Semitic categories were secularizations of older tropes from the religious traditions. My argument, however, is slightly different from this secularization thesis. Sander L. Gilman and Steven T. Katz, eds., "Introduction," in *Anti-Semitism in Times of Crisis* (New York: New York University Press, 1991), 1–2.

4. I will, thus, use the term anti-Semitism to discuss these tropes, except for those few cases when I am talking explicitly about an ancient theological tradition.

5. I use the category of myth to identify those images that are used as cultural forms and not as explicitly religious discourse.

6. Gilman and Katz, 4–5.

7. Amos Warner, *American Charities: A Study in Philanthropy and Economics* (New York: Thomas Crowell, 1894), 183. As the standard textbook for social work in its day, it continued into multiple editions over the next three decades and even, somewhat curiously, warranted a 1989 reprint edition with an introduction by social work historian Mary Jo Deegan. By the time of a posthumously revised edition in 1919, the book was already seemingly quite dated:

> The book is hardly of sufficient contemporary interest for the general reader, but for the social worker it is instructive and entertaining—and somewhat bewildering . . . One puts down this book with the sense that admirable as were the motives of the revisor in devotedly attempting to perpetuate the memory of a pioneer in social work, the net result falls short of justice to a man who was a progressive spirit in his time and who if he had lived today would have written a book radically different from anything that can be made out of his work of a generation ago.

This quote is from an unsigned review, "Review of 'American Charities,'" *The Dial* 67, August 23, 1919, 164. Unfortunately, the hordes clamoring for *compassionate conservatism* are unable to see the datedness of the book that was already quite evident within a couple of decades of its initial publication. Marvin Olasky—the former American Enterprise Institute fellow who derived the late twentieth-century concept of *compassionate conservatism* from figures like Riis—likewise greets the work of Warner with encomiums. Olasky concludes that the lessons of *American Charities* are the following: "The goal of charity workers, therefore, was not to press for governmental programs, but to show poor people how to move up while resisting enslavement to the charity of governmental or private masters. Charity leaders and preachers frequently spoke of freedom and showed how dependency was merely slavery with a smiling mask." Marvin Olasky, *The Tragedy of American Compassion* (Washington, DC: Regnery Gateway, 1992), 100. Thus this foundational text of social work, like Riis, gives rise to a discourse of home, family, and homelessness that emerges generations later as our contemporary rhetoric of family values.

8. Warner, 182–83.

9. He does not refer to historical identifications of the apostle Stephen as the Christian protomartyr; this recognition was longstanding—no one need look for this protomartyr. Rather, the protomartyr inspiration refers to attempts to understand the modern world. In the eighteenth and nineteenth centuries, new political and social movements identified their protomartyrs as part of grounding modern movements and ideas.

10. Warner, 183.

11. Ibid.

12. In his 2002 history of homelessness, Kenneth Kusmer invokes Amos Warner's idea of Cain as a prototramp to explain the idea that the "vagabond life is depicted as synonymous with a life of crime." See Kusmer, 44 and 263n25. With the emergence of the post-Civil War tramp in the 1870s and 1880s, criminality and immigrant background, along with laziness, were perceived as major aspects of the homeless man. Kusmer, 46.

13. Riis, *Other Half,* 9.

14. Ibid., 17.

15. Ibid., chapter 1.

16. Ibid., 16.

17. Riis, *Battle,* 7; Riis, *Peril,* 13 and 162.

18. Riis, *Peril,* 49–50.

19. "They are many and complex in the setting forth of them, I suspect: the hurry of our modern life, the new freedom that makes little minds think themselves bigger than their maker, the *de*-moralization of the public school, the pressure of business,—it is hard to get the family together—which is merely setting up the fact of the scattering of the home in the defense of it. The causes are many, but the result is one: the wreck of the home." Riis, *Peril,* 50.

20. For a fuller discussion of Riis's use of the Cain story in legitimating the family, see my "Family Values, Social Capital and Contradictions of American Modernity," *Theory, Culture & Society* 28, no. 4 (July 2011): 96–123, 102ff.

21. Riis, *Peril,* 80.

22. In a diatribe against the Pharisees, Jesus charges that the blood of all the righteous from Abel (the first victim of murder in the Hebrew Bible) to Zechariah (the last victim of murder) rests upon them (Matthew 23:35). The diatribe opens with Jesus saying that "the scribes and Pharisees sit on Moses' seat" (Matthew 23:2); he connects them—as murderers of Abel—with the leadership of the Jewish people.

23. Ambrose is a fourth century Bishop of Milan.

24. Ambrose, *Saint Ambrose: Hexameron, Paradise, and Cain and Abel,* trans. John J. Savage (New York: Fathers of the Church, 1961), 360.

25. Ibid., 362.

26. Dan Cohn-Sherbock, *The Crucified Jew: Twenty Centuries of Christian Anti-Semitism* (Grand Rapids: Wm. B. Eerdmans, 1997), 29:

> In Aphrahat's writings the statement in John 8:44, "Your father was a murderer from the beginning," was identified with Cain. Ephrem also identified the Jews with

Cain: "Today the glory has passed from the people of Israel and they stand among the nations ashamed as Cain was, at the unnatural deed." In the fourth century, Prudentius maintained that the Jew was the murderous brother who now wanders the face of the earth: "From place to place the homeless Jew wanders in ever-shifting exile, since the time when he was torn from the abode of his fathers and has been suffering the penalty for murder and having stained his hands with the blood of Christ whom he denied, paying the price of sin."

27. Augustine, *Concerning the City of God against the Pagans*, trans. Henry Bettenson (New York: Penguin Classics, 1984), 606.
28. Anti-Semitism is usually taken to be an anti-Jewish attitude. But historically, Arabs have also been classified as Semites. Ishmael is the legendary progenitor of the Arab people.
29. This paper was published three years later.
30. "You were an Ishmaelite, and there was a savage satisfaction in feeling that all the world had its hand raised against you, and yours against the world. Indeed, to tell the truth, you were not far from desperate deeds. The step from poverty to crime is a short one—if poverty, *itself*, be not a crime. A man without money feels an ownership in every one else's property an ownership where Might becomes an agent of Possession." William Staats, *A Tight Squeeze; Or, the Adventures of a Gentleman Who on a Wager of Ten Thousand Dollars, Undertook to Go from New York to New Orleans in Three Weeks without Money as a Professional Tramp* (Boston: Lee and Shepard, 1879), 23–26, in Todd DePastino, *Citizen Hobo: How a Century of Homelessness Shaped America* (Chicago: University of Chicago Press, 2003), 40.
31. M. W. Law, "Our Ishmael," *American Journal of Sociology* 8, no. 6 (May 1903): 838–51.
32. For a discussion of the relationship of modern illegitimacy to this tradition, see John Witte Jr., "Ishmael's Bane: The Sin and Crime of Illegitimacy Reconsidered," *Punishment and Society* 5, no. 3 (2003): 327–45.
33. With the mark, the wandering, and the association with Christ—Abel as Christ—the legend borrows a great deal from the Cain story. George K. Anderson, *The Legend of the Wandering Jew* (Providence, RI: Brown University Press, 1965), 3.
34. Ibid., 11.
35. Eugene Sue, *The Wandering Jew* (London: Dedalus, 1990), 1.
36. As we have already noted, this possible conflation between the Wandering Jew and diabolism probably develops because of the traditions of wandering associated with Satan. For instance, in his *The History of the Devil*, Daniel Defoe argues that the Devil's banishment from heaven is a state of wandering: "In short, the true account of the Devil's circumstances, since his fall from heaven, is much more likely to be thus: That he is more of a vagrant than a prisoner, that he is a wanderer in the wild unbounded waste . . . Satan being thus confined to a vagabond, wandering, unsettled condition, is without any certain abode . . . This is his present state, without any fixed abode, place, or space, allowed him to rest the sole of his foot upon." Defoe, 94–95.

37. *Deseret News* 17 (1856), in Rudolf Glanz, "The Wandering Jew in America," in *The Wandering Jew: Essays in the Interpretation of a Christian Legend*, ed. Galit Hasan-Rokem and Alan Dundes (Bloomington: Indiana University Press, 1986), 108–9. For an account of the "veritable Wandering Jew" in New York City, see *Deseret News* 7 (1856), in Glanz, 108.

38. Sue, 1.

39. Ibid., 846.

40. Ibid.

41. As I shall show later, the discourse of Jewish radicalism most frequently cites threats from Russian Jews. Though this is three-quarters of a century before the Bolshevik revolution, we already see a Jew bringing radicalism by entering the American shores from Russia.

42. Susannah Heschel, "The Exile of Redemption in Judaism," in *Religions of the Book*, ed. Gerard Sloyan (Lanham, MD: University Press of America, 1996), 4.

43. Ibid.

44. Riis, *Other Half*, 87.

45. Because the threats of homelessness include a class dimension of poor laborers, the famous Shylock stereotype has no significant role in the discourse on homelessness.

46. Georg Simmel, "The Stranger," in *Georg Simmel: On Individuality and Social Forms*, ed. Donald N. Levine (Chicago: University of Chicago Press, 1971), 143.

47. Ibid., 144.

48. Maxwell Sommerville, *A Wanderer's Legend* (Philadelphia: Drexel Biddle, 1902), 151.

49. See also Glanz on this point; Glanz, 110–11:

    > Here we find the wandering Jew already in transition to a new motif. He has already acquired a secular purpose, while it had been the very essence of his previous distinction that he did not trade, and that his long bag served only to illustrate his long travels. But on the long way across the American continent the resemblance of his bag to the peddler's bag of the German-Jewish immigrant continuously increases, and we have already found this hinted in our poem. If we take this as our point of departure, we come to understand why the legendary features of the wandering Jew blend so fully with those of the traveler for temporal gain in the figure of the Jewish peddler that has been treated so often in the literature, that in the end the long bag full of the sufferings of the eternal wanderer is forgotten over the peddler's bag.

50. Chinese immigrants were another such group. But as we saw in the Chapter 1, laws inhibiting their immigration kept their total numbers comparatively low in New York.

51. *Life* 71, no. 1860 (June 20, 1918): 983.

52. Ibid.

53. *Life* 71, no. 1858 (June 6, 1918): 915.

54. In the latter part of this period of the long fin-de-siècle, the targeting of Russian Jews increased in particular because of the Bolshevik Revolution and, perhaps, because of Trotsky's time in New York shortly before the revolution. However,

even before 1917, they were sometimes singled out as being especially prone to radicalism.

55. *Life* 71, no. 1860 (June 20, 1918): 983.

56. Both the Hobo College and the closely connected hobo union called the International Brotherhood Welfare Association were founded and funded by James Eads How (the so-called hobo millionaire) who recruited the garrulous Reitman to coordinate many of the organizations' Chicago activities.

57. For instance, the 1918 Kansas City conviction of Rose Pastor Stokes—whose Russian-Jewish background was a central concern—under the new wartime Espionage Act provoked *Life* magazine to recall her past activism in behalf of Paterson, New Jersey, silk-workers who participated in a 1913 strike organized by the IWW.

58. Michael Dobkowski, "Ideological Anti-Semitism in America: 1877–1927" (PhD diss., New York University, 1976), 486.

59. "Emma Goldman and her companion [fellow anarchist Alexander Berkman] were not workers at Homestead—in fact, they are not workers anywhere. They are butters-in, outsiders, who agitate, vex, annoy and stir up strife and discontent. Samuel Gompers, kin by racial blood-ties and social sentiment, represents the same type Gyp the Blood, Lefty Louie, and their confreres . . . They toil not, they do not build, they do not create. Their tendency is to destroy, tear down, uproot." Elbert Hubbard, *The Philistine* 37, no. 2 (July 1913): 53–54.

60. Ibid., 55.

61. Ibid., 63.

62. While not Jewish, Tolstoy was a very public face of Russian radicalism. Also, Hubbard had already derisively discussed the exported Russian anarchists in America—the Jewish radicals Emma Goldman and Alexander Berkman. Tolstoy was the internationally public face of Russian anarchism, while Goldman and Berkman were the American faces.

63. *Life* 71, no. 1860 (June 20, 1918): 983.

64. While his essay on the hobo mind does not explicitly use anti-Semitic symbols for representing, the structure is present. Elsewhere in his oeuvre, Park's analyses do appear to be tinged with anti-Semitism. For instance, he says, "From the standpoint of organization the Jews are the most interesting of the immigrant groups. There is among them, indeed a great variety of disorder and personal demoralization—gambling extortion, vagabondage, family desertion, white slavery, ordinary and extraordinary crime." Robert E. Park and Herbert A. Miller, *Old World Traits Transplanted* (New York: Harper and Brothers, 1921), 237.

65. Robert E. Park, "The Mind of the Hobo: Reflections upon the Relation between Mentality and Locomotion," in *The City*, eds. Robert E. Park, Ernest W. Burgess, and Roderick D. McKenzie (Chicago: University of Chicago Press, 1925), 156.

66. For instance, Freud interprets this ambition to create a dwelling as a substitution for the mother's womb: "the dwelling-house was a substitute for the mother's womb, the first lodging, for which in all likelihood man still longs, and in which he was safe and felt at ease." Sigmund Freud, *Civilization and its Discontents*, trans. James Strachey (New York: W. W. Norton, 1962), 38.

67. Park, "Mind of the Hobo," 158.
68. Ibid., 159.
69. Gilman and Katz, 5.
70. Charles Monroe Sheldon, *In His Steps* (Philadelphia: John C. Winston, 1937).
71. The more contemporary *What Would Jesus Do* movement, which has devolved into primarily a marketing campaign for bracelets, bumper stickers, hats, t-shirts, and other paraphernalia, was inspired by the Sheldon novel.
72. Mike Hertenstein, "What Would Jesus Do? The Settlement House Movement and *In His Steps*," *Cornerstone Magazine*, 1997, 39.
73. Riis, *Battle*, 23.
74. Marx, "Eighteenth Brumaire," 146.
75. Ernst Cassirer, *The Myth of the State* (New Haven, CT: Yale University Press, 1946).
76. Ibid., 280.
77. Ernst Cassirer, *The Philosophy of Symbolic Forms, Volume 2: Mythical Thought* (New Haven, CT: Yale University Press, 1955).
78. Roland Barthes, *Mythologies* (New York: Hill and Wang, 1987).
79. Gorki, in Raymond Williams, *Culture and Society, 1780–1950* (New York: Columbia University Press, 1983), 279.

Chapter 3

1. An earlier version of this chapter appeared in Philip Webb, "Discourse and Subjectivation in American Homelessness," *Queen: A Journal of Rhetoric and Power* 5, no. 2 (Fall 2009), special issue on the rhetoric of place.
2. Burrows and Wallace, 178. The following discussion of the Bowery's history primarily draws upon Burrows and Wallace and David Levinson, "The Bowery," in *Encyclopedia of Homelessness, Volume I*, ed. David Levinson (Thousand Oaks, CA: Sage, 2004), 32–35.
3. See George Chauncey, *Gay New York: Gender, Urban Culture, and the Making of the Gay Male World 1890–1940* (New York: Basic Books, 1994), chapter 1. He discusses the Bowery as an object of spectacle for the slumming curious.
4. Levinson, 33:

> In 1873, the YMCA opened a branch on the Bowery, the first lodging houses opened the following year, and the Bowery Mission opened in 1879. In 1878, elevated railroad tracks were erected over the sidewalks, making the street unattractive for pedestrians. In 1890, the Salvation Army opened four facilities, and by 1900, there were 100 lodging houses lining the street. The living facilities were soon neighbors to labor halls, secondhand stores, cheap restaurants, pawnshops, brothels, and saloons. In 1916, the Third Street El (elevated railroad tracks) was built over the street itself, blocking out sunlight (until removed in the early 1960s). The population was composed almost entirely of men, including those who lived there year-round, day laborers, hoboes, and tramps.

5. "Concentrations of facilities which catered to homeless men came to be called 'Skid Rows,' the name deriving from the skidways on which lumberjacks in the

Northwest transported logs. In Seattle the lodging houses, saloons, and other estab-lishments were contiguous to the 'skid road' running from the top of the ridge down to Henry Yesler's mill, and the term 'skid road' was applied to the com-munity of the homeless. Transferred to other urban enclaves of homeless men, it became 'Skid Row.'" Howard M. Bahr, *Skid Row: An Introduction to Disaffilia-tion* (New York: Oxford University Press, 1973), 32.

6. Donald J. Bogue, *Skid Row in American Cities* (Chicago: Community and Family Study Center, University of Chicago, 1963), 1.
7. Ibid., 2.
8. Ibid.
9. Ibid.
10. Sinclair Lewis, "Hobohemia," *Saturday Evening Post*, April 7, 1917, 4.
11. Lewis, 6.
12. First of all, Manhattan already had such a location—the Bowery. Second, the Greenwich Village of Mabel Dodge, John Reed, and Max Eastman was a world of wealthy (or comfortable) radicals. The Ivy League and émigré Bohemians were a different class than the Bowery man. When "Hobo King" Ben Reitman accompanied his anarchist lover Emma Goldman to New York on their speech tours, the working class doctor repeatedly felt ill at ease. The political radicals from bourgeois families frowned at his coarse wit, licentious comments, and his inability to expound on political theory. His unpublished autobiography is replete with the discomforts of the class chasm between the hobo and the Bohe-mian radical. See Ben Reitman, "Following the Monkey, Unpublished Autobi-ography," box 1, Ben Reitman Papers, University of Illinois at Chicago Special Collections.
13. Lewis, 126.
14. "Committee's Preface," in Nels Anderson, *The Hobo: The Sociology of the Home-less Man* (Chicago: University of Chicago Press, 1923), ix.
15. Robert Park, "Editor's Preface," in Anderson, *Hobo*, v.
16. Anderson, *Hobo*, 4.
17. Bogue, 4.
18. Ibid., 2.
19. Anderson, *Hobo*, 9.
20. Most likely the name came from New York's Bohemian Greenwich Village, which is frequently known by this abbreviated name.
21. Anderson, *Hobo*, 9.
22. In the six years intervening between Sinclair Lewis's short story and Nels Ander-son's monograph, American Bohemianism was dealt some significant blows. When the United States entered the First World War, a number of Greenwich Village's bohemian stalwarts abandoned their radicalism to endorse the US inter-vention. The US entry into the war and the Bolshevik's October Revolution spawned the 1917 Espionage Act, the 1918 Sedition Act, and the Palmer Raids of 1919 into the early 1920s. Factional disarray, deportation as enforcement of antiradical legislation, and disillusionment spawned by both domestic and inter-national radicals left much of the Bohemian left a bit shattered.

23. Anderson, *Hobo*, 14–15.

24. Jack Kerouac, "The Vanishing American Hobo," *Holiday*, March 1960.

25. "*One Thousand Homeless Men* is the name of a worthwhile human study made of the denizens of West Madison Street. In this canyon stretching across the great west side from the Lake, through the Loop and on toward the setting sun, flow never-ceasing streams of humanity, the largest number of homeless and hungry men that have ever been brought together anywhere in our land." Frank O. Beck, *Hobohemia* (Rindge, NH: Richard R. Smith, 1956), 13.

26. Anderson, *Hobo*, 5.

27. Beck, 76. This description of the hobo mind is quite reminiscent of Robert Park's analysis of the same three decades earlier: "The hobo, who begins his career by breaking the local ties that bound him to his family and his neighborhood, has ended by breaking all other associations. He is not only a 'homeless man,' but a man without a cause and without a country." Park, "Mind of the Hobo," 159.

28. Beck, 77.

29. Anderson, *Hobo*, 5.

30. Ibid., 87ff.

31. Ibid., 89; emphasis mine.

32. Ibid., 87.

33. Ibid.

34. This discussion falls in part 2 of *The Hobo*—"Types of Hobos," in which Anderson looks at "Why Do Men Leave Home?" (chapter 5), "The Hobo and the Tramp" (chapter 6), "The Home Guard and the Bum" (chapter 7), and "Work" (chapter 8).

35. "The distinctions between the seasonal worker, the hobo, and the tramp, while important, are not hard and fast. The seasonal worker may descend into the ranks of the hobos, and a hobo may sink to the level of the tramp . . . Significant, also, but not sufficiently recognized, is the difference between these migratory types and the stationary types of homeless men, the 'home guard' and the 'bum.'" Anderson, *Hobo*, 95.

36. Edwin H. Sutherland and Harvey J. Locke, *Twenty Thousand Homeless Men: A Study of Unemployed Men in the Chicago Shelters* (New York: Arno Press, 1971), 174.

37. Ibid., 175.

38. While the term *homeless* is used here as a noun to signify the mass formation of a group of homeless men, this practice remains very rare until the 1980s. Homeless is almost always used adjectively until that time—a point to which we shall return.

39. Alice Willard Solenberger, *One Thousand Homeless Men: A Study of Original Records* (New York: Survey Associates, 1914), 1.

40. She subsumes all categories of beggars or tramps under the rubric of "homeless" and then argues that we have always had beggars. Whereas, I contend that though beggars may have always existed, the homeless man is a very modern form of social displacement, predicated upon several discursive (as well as historical and economic) conditions. Merely because the older categories are subsumed

under a newer one at a particular historical moment does not enable the anachronistic attribution of the new term and the figure it signifies.

41. Solenberger, 3.

42. Bahr and Caplow's 1973 study continued this disaffiliation theme, writing, "Homelessness is a condition of detachment from society characterized by the absence or attenuation of the affiliative bonds that link settled persons to a network of interconnected social structures." They continued, saying, "the man who occupies the same lodging on Skid Row for forty uninterrupted years is properly considered homeless. The essence of the concept goes beyond residential arrangements. Homelessness is best visualized as a relationship to society at large." Howard Bahr and Theodore Caplow, *Old Men Drunk and Sober* (New York: New York University Press, 1973), 5 and 7.

43. Solenberger, 3–4.

44. Ibid., 9–10.

45. Ibid., 11–12.

46. Ibid., 12.

47. See Reitman, "Following the Monkey."

48. While Ben Reitman was not a social scientist, he worked for a period at the Chicago Department of Health, and he served on the Committee on Homeless Men that commissioned Anderson's *The Hobo*. (Anderson even included one version of Reitman's taxonomy in the study.) The activism of Reitman and other directors of the Hobo College had an open line of communication with the sociologists at the University of Chicago. Many of the early taxonomies from these hobos appeared in Anderson's book. Robert Park famously takes up the idea of motion as defining the hobo in his essay on the hobo mind, which came out two years after Anderson's book.

49. Hobo is used as the term for a particular form of homeless men, a broader term for the three categories of migratory workers, and the metacategory for all types of the unattached and outcasts. A former head of Chicago's Hobo College makes this point explicit. Anderson cites St. John Tucker's analysis that all the forms of migratory workers are hobos: "A hobo is a migratory worker. A tramp is a migratory non-worker. A bum is a stationary non-worker. Upon the labor of the migratory worker all the basic industries depend. He goes forth from the crowded slavemarkets to hew the forests, build and repair the railroads, tunnel mountains and build ravines. His is the labor that harvests the wheat in the fall and cuts the ice in the winter. All of these are hobos." St. John Tucker quoted in Anderson, *Hobo*, 87. Likewise, M. Kuhn (author of "The Hobo Problem"), Nicholas Klein (president of the Hobo College), and Roger Payne (self-proclaimed hobo philosopher) all subsume all types of migratory workers under the term of hobo. Anderson, *Hobo*, 88ff.

50. I have already noted that Anderson's study was a University of Chicago collaboration with the Chicago Council of Social Agencies and that Solenberger studied applicants to the Chicago Bureau of Charities. Sutherland and Locke's study was likewise a collaboration between the University of Chicago and the Illinois Emergency Relief Commission.

51. Bahr, *Skid Row*, 17ff.
52. The local government—town, county, or parish—was made responsible for its poor with the 1601 Elizabethan code. Kusmer, 20.
53. This discussion of colonial charity borrows significantly from Rossi, 17ff.
54. Peter Rossi points out that this colonial-era settlement requirement to receive public assistance lingered for most of the nation's history until a 1969 ruling by the Supreme Court "declared unconstitutional the length-of-residence restrictions that states and local communities ordinarily placed on eligibility for benefits." Rossi, 18.
55. Kusmer, 21.
56. Roy Lubove, *The Professional Altruist: The Emergence of Social Work as a Career, 1880–1930* (New York: Atheneum, 1983), 2. The following discussion of the fin-de-siècle rise of charity organizations draws extensively from Lubove.
57. J. J. McCook, "Charity Organization and Social Regeneration," in *Lend-a-Hand* 13 (1894): 461–69, in Lubove, 5.
58. F. J. Kingsbury, "Charity Organization a Necessity of Modern Conditions," in *Lend-a-Hand* 14, no. 1 (1895): 3–9, 7.
59. Lubove, 14.
60. Theodore Roosevelt, *Theodore Roosevelt: An Autobiography* (New York: Charles Scribner's Sons, 1920), 199.
61. Sutherland and Locke, 148–49.
62. Sutherland and Locke, 144–45:

> The process of shelterization is organically related to attitudes and behavior patterns acquired previous to life in the shelter. Shelterization, in fact, is adaptation not only to the shelters but to the total situation in which a man find himself. The total situation includes being unemployed and dependent on public relief, living in the slum area of the city, being isolated from former social and economic contacts, having disheartening experiences with employment agencies and business concerns, and either being or approaching the age when re-employment in industry is unlikely.
>
> These prior experiences form a preliminary step in the shelterization process. The men had undergone such disheartening experiences as being out of work and being unsuccessful in the search for jobs. They had lost confidence in themselves and in their social world. Many of them had gone to the extent of pawning clothes, borrowing money from friends, going hungry, and sleeping in parks or hallways for a few days. The decision to enter a shelter was in many cases the surrender of a man's highest values and was made as a last resort.

63. For instance, many New Deal programs like the Federal Emergency Relief Administration or the Works Progress Administration settled unemployed migratory laborers and provided jobs. But the Second World War did the most to settle the hobo populations. About this trend, Peter Rossi writes,

> The outbreak of World War II drastically reduced the number of the homeless, absorbing them into the armed forces and into mushrooming war industries. The permanent unemployed that worried Nels Anderson virtually disappeared, almost within months. The WPA public works employment projects were terminated after 1943 and relief programs were drastically reduced as employment opportunities increased and men

went into the armed forces. Municipal lodging houses and emergency shelters were closed; what remained of the local and transient homeless were apparently left to forage on Skid Row, the bottom tier of the private housing market. (Rossi, 27)

64. Sutherland and Locke, 10–11.
65. Anderson, *Hobo*, 15.
66. Early in my career in homeless services, I had a homeless, mentally ill man—I'll call him David—whom I was trying to get into a facility for this specific population. Coordinating a meeting time with a caseworker for the facility and David who had no watch, no calendar, and no fixed place for me to find him (on top of his mental health problems) was obviously difficult. After the initial meeting and a preliminary indication of David's eligibility for the facility, he was placed on a six-month waiting list. Keeping track of this unsettled person over this course of time was not easy. I had to tell him to drop in to my office at least once every two weeks so that when his name did come up on the waiting list, he might not lose his space. I did have an approximate idea of the location of David's urban campsite, where I could seek him out, if he stopped following up regularly. Multiply this incident by the thousands of homeless, and the problem of mobility becomes seemingly insurmountable. When clients wander from city to city, most efforts to engage them in some social service are pointless.
67. Warner, 183.

Chapter 4

1. "The salaries of the staff members were paid by the Illinois Emergency Relief Commission, and the other expenses of the project by the Social Science Research Committee of the University of Chicago. The authors of this book were connected with the University of Chicago during the period of the study." Sutherland and Locke, v, n1.
2. Ibid., 186.
3. Ibid., 49.
4. "After a man had used up most of his money, he felt the necessity of selling or pawning his extra suits of clothes, watch, and suitcase. In many cases these material possessions were of critical importance as class symbols and their loss resulted in a feeling of degradation." Sutherland and Locke, 88.
5. For example, see Chapter 3, note 63.
6. Sutherland and Locke, 14.
7. Ibid., 15.
8. Social relations began to mimic capital because capital was shaping them—as Marx said, social capital is both a prerequisite for and result of production. In his third volume of Capital, Marx analyzes the social character of capital in which these social relations both enable production and result from it.
9. Robert D, Putnam, *Bowling Alone: The Collapse and Revival of American Community* (New York: Simon and Schuster, 2000), 18–19.
10. Anderson, *Hobo*, 92.
11. Bahr, *Skid Row*, 11–12.

Chapter 5

1. Earlier versions of some sections of this chapter appeared in Webb, "Family Values."

2. Wood explains these distinctions:

> In the category of interest relations the selection of contacts is made from the point of view of the service the relations may render toward the realization of some dominant interest; thus such relations are means to other ends rather than ends in themselves. For example, considerations of personality, group membership, and social status are of secondary importance in business relations, relations between employer and employee, lawyer and client, and so forth. On the other hand, relations in which sentiment takes the place of calculation are ends in themselves. They comprise the great number of relationships in which the satisfaction of the desire for affectionate response is the main purpose. They are characterized by intimacy, mutual attachment, and sympathy. Such, for example, are the relationships established in acquaintance, friendship, and love.

Margaret Mary Wood, *Paths of Loneliness: The Individual Isolated in Modern Society* (New York: Columbia University Press, 1960), 10.

3. Theodore Abel, "The Significance of the Concept of Consciousness of Kind," *Social Forces* 9, no. 1 (October 1930): 7. Abel does slightly steer aside from entirely mapping sentiment relations onto *Gemeinschaft* by arguing that he grounds them in a "consciousness of kind" rather than Tönnies's *Wesenswille*. For our purposes, however, this distinction is irrelevant. First, Wood does not even go into it—she does not even mention Tönnies. Second, it is these basic social relations and not their grounding that is crucial to Wood's analysis. Abel acknowledges that the basic distinctions in these relations are those of Tönnies.

4. Wood, 23.

5. Ibid., 24.

6. Ibid., 27.

7. Ibid., 31.

8. Park, "Mind of the Hobo," 158.

9. Often debates at some of the hobo gathering locations at the Hobo College, Bughouse Square, or the Dill Pickle Club are described as rowdy and sometimes lewd. These did not serve a "civilizing" function.

10. Nels Anderson takes a middle ground between Wood and Park in finding that the hobo's mobility renders him unable to participate in organized associations: "The mobility and instability of the hobo or tramp, which is both cause and consequence of his migratory existence, unfits him for organized group life." Anderson, *Hobo*, 248.

11. "He [the hobo] is propertyless, and therefore the incentive of fixed ownership and fixed residence to remain faithful to any institution is gone. While the man of property secures himself best by associating with his neighbor and remaining in one locality, the hobo safeguards himself by moving away from every difficulty. Then, too, the hobo is without wife and child. His womanless existence increases his mobility and his instability." Anderson, *Hobo*, 248–49.

12. Park, "Mind of the Hobo," 159.

13. Theodore Caplow, "The Sociologist and the Homeless Man," in *Disaffiliated Man: Essays and Bibliography on Skid Row, Vagrancy, and Outsiders*, ed. Howard M. Bahr (Toronto: University of Toronto Press, 1970), 7.
14. Caplow, Bahr, and Sternberg, 494–99.
15. Theodore Caplow, Howard M. Bahr, and David Sternberg, "Homelessness," in *International Encyclopedia of the Social Sciences* 6, ed. David L. Sills (New York: Crowell Collier and Macmillan, 1968), 494.
16. Howard M. Bahr, "Family Size and Stability as Antecedents of Homelessness and Excessive Drinking," *Journal of Marriage and the Family* 31, no. 3 (August 1969): 477–83.
17. This Homelessness Project was conducted from 1965 to 1968 at the Bureau of Applied Social Research, Columbia University with support from the National Institutes of Health. Bahr, "Family Size," 477. I will refer to this study, as Bahr and Caplow often do, as the "Bowery Project."
18. Bahr, "Family Size," 477.
19. Bogue, 353.
20. I assume that by a good home, he must be following the sociological conventional wisdom of the time, meaning an unbroken home (i.e., both parents in the household) with relatively little strife.
21. Anderson, *Hobo*, 149:

> In his sex life, as in his whole existence, the homeless man moves in a vicious circle. Industrially inadequate, his migratory habits render him the more economically inefficient. A social outcast, he still wants the companionship which his mode of life denies him. Debarred from family life, he hungers for intimate associations and affection. The women that he knows, with few exceptions, are repulsive to him. Attractive women live in social worlds infinitely remote from his. With him the fundamental wishes of the person for response and status have been denied expression. The prevalence of sexual perversion among the homeless men is, therefore, but the extreme expression of their unnatural sex life. Homosexual practices arise almost inevitably in similar situations of sex isolation. A constructive solution for the problems of the sex life of the homeless man strikes deeper into our social life than this study can carry us.

22. Bogue, 371.
23. Bogue opens his chapter on marriage and family life of men on Skid Row with two questions:

> The topic requires two separate inquiries:
>
> a. Why didn't the single men ever marry? Did these men ever participate in a courtship, and if they did, why did it not culminate in marriage?
> b. What caused the marriages of the separated and divorced men to fail? In what ways are these failures related to the presence of these men on Skid Row? (Bogue, 355)

24. Wood, 29–30:

> Without the satisfactions of home life and socially approved contacts with women, soldiers and sailors, like other sexually segregated groups of men, tend to find an

outlet for their craving for emotional stimulation in ways which society condemns. Their behavior, seen as a response to a normal social environment, appears abnormal. Viewed, however, in relation to the segregated conditions under which they live, it is not. It is, on the contrary, a natural response to the particular environmental conditions which have called it forth. It is an adaptation to the isolation of a socially segregated environment which is as normal in its way as in the socially approved behavior of persons who are more fortunately placed.

25. Anderson, *Hobo*, 18.
26. Howard M. Bahr and Theodore Caplow, "Homelessness, Affiliation, and Occupational Mobility," *Social Forces* 47, no. 1 (September 1968): 29.
27. Ibid.
28. For instance, F. Ivan Nye, "Child Adjustment in Broken and in Unhappy Unbroken Homes," *Marriage and Family Living* 9, no. 4 (November 1957): 356–61; or Lee G. Burchinal, "Characteristics of Adolescents from Unbroken, Broken, and Reconstituted Families," *Journal of Marriage and the Family* 26, no. 1 (February 1964): 44–51.
29. Bahr points out a range of synonymous labels for a Skid Row man: "homeless man, derelict, unattached man, urban nomad, vagrant, and tramp." Bahr, *Skid Row*, 27.
30. James F. Rooney, "Societal Forces and the Unattached Male: An Historical Review," in Bahr, *Disaffiliated Man*, 18.
31. Bahr, *Skid Row*, 13.
32. Ibid., 11.
33. I use the Catholic Worker as an example of positions outside the predominant assumptions of the sociological literature of the time but do not mean to imply that they were the only position beyond the normative disaffiliation thesis.
34. In Lubove, 10.
35. Day also participates in the 1950s infatuation with loneliness.
36. Dorothy Day, *The Long Loneliness: The Autobiography of Dorothy Day* (New York: HarperCollins, 1981), 179.
37. Day, *Loneliness*, 223–24.
38. Ibid., 195.
39. Dorothy Day, "The Scandal of the Works of Mercy," in *Dorothy Day: Selected Writings*, ed. Robert Ellsberg (Maryknoll: Orbis Books, 1993), 98–99.

Chapter 6

1. Both the *Oxford English Dictionary* and *Merriam-Webster* date the phrase "bag lady" to 1972. It starts appearing in newspaper and magazine accounts of the city at this time. The first monograph on homeless women was the final publication from the Bowery Project. See Howard M. Bahr and Gerald R. Garrett, *Women Alone: The Disaffiliation of Urban Females* (Lexington, MA: Lexington Books, 1976).
2. Rossi, 39.
3. For instance, see Bogue, 2–4.

4. Bahr cites shelter caseworkers on alcohol use among women in the shelter. "Most caseworkers estimated at least half of the Shelter clients were chronic alcoholics, and the substantial majority had experienced some type of acute drinking problem earlier in their lives. In fact, caseworkers assigned special significance to excessive drinking as a cause of the predicament of Shelter women." Bahr, *Skid Row*, 210. His informants identify only about half as being alcoholics, and the number seems to increase to a substantial majority only when the homeless woman's entire life history is considered, indicating that a substantial number of the homeless women do not have a drinking problem at the time that they are homeless.

5. Bahr argues that the literature on alcoholic women is relevant in two ways. First, it is a serious problem among Skid Row women (as well as a popular stereotype), and second, "most of the research on female subjects even roughly comparable to homeless women has been research on drinking behavior." Bahr, *Skid Row*, 193. He does not explain in what ways the material is comparable (class, personal pathology, etc.).

6. Bahr, *Skid Row*, 175–76.

7. This seeming conflation points to an early propensity in the literature to collapse all types of substance abuse. Thus the 1980s advent of the crack epidemic produces a form of the homeless figure easily assimilable to the extant literature on winos.

8. Jane Addams, "The Sheltered Woman and the Magdalen," *Ladies Home Journal*, November 1913, in Jane Addams, *The Jane Addams Reader*, ed. Jean Bethke Elshtain (New York: Basic Books, 2002), 264–69.

9. Bahr, *Skid Row*, 181.

10. Ibid., 187.

11. Ibid., 97ff.

12. Not to be disingenuous in my critique, Bahr and his coauthor Gerald Garrett do undertake some of these questions several years later in their monograph *Women Alone*. Nonetheless, we are left with the situation that the first significant work on homeless women cannot get past alcohol as an explanatory mechanism.

13. Bahr, *Skid Row*, 193.

14. Ibid., 176.

15. Gentrification in the post-Fordist city made a double contribution to homelessness: (1) dispersion of people across the city through the destruction of Skid Row areas and (2) bringing middle class people back into the city for consumption.

16. For instance, see Stephanie Golden.

17. Alix Kates Shulman, "Preface," in Ann Marie Rousseau, *Shopping Bag Ladies: Homeless Women Speak about Their Lives* (New York: Pilgrim Press, 1981). The Jennifer Hand citation is from Jennifer Hand, "Shopping Bag Ladies: A Study in Interstitial Urban Behavior" (paper presented at the Society for the Study of Social Problems, New York, August 1976), cited in Rousseau, 6.

18. "Shopping bag ladies: Aging women with swollen ankles and ulcerated feet, toting bags, shuffling slowly across the street, poking into garbage cans, slumped on a park bench, dozing in doorways, sprawling across library steps, huddled among

their possessions in the dreary waiting rooms of train and bus stations. Poor, sick, lonely, old, afraid." Shulman, 10.

19. Ibid., 12.
20. For instance, see Bahr, *Skid Row*, or Golden.
21. Neil Smith, "Giuliani Time: The Revanchist 1990s," *Social Text* 57 (Winter 1998): 9.
22. Ibid., 10.
23. Daniel Patrick Moynihan, "The Negro Family: The Case for National Action," in *The Moynihan Report and the Politics of Controversy*, ed. Lee Rainwater and William L. Yancey (Cambridge, MA: MIT Press, 1967).
24. Moynihan, 63.
25. Dipesh Chakrabarty, *Provincializing Europe: Postcolonial Thought and Historical Difference* (Princeton, NJ: Princeton University Press, 2000).
26. Moynihan, 75.
27. Ibid.
28. "The Tangles of Pathology" is the title of the chapter in which Moynihan blasts the matriarchal structure of the African American community.
29. Moynihan, 51.

Chapter 7

1. Jonathan Kozol, *Rachel and Her Children: Homeless Families in America* (New York: Fawcett Columbine, 1988).
2. Despite his Jewish background, his sprinkling of the text with biblical allusions is not limited to the Hebrew Bible (as evidenced by the Lazarus reference). The overall biblical framing—beyond Rachel, Lazarus, and this opening with a carpenter, "He was a carpenter" (Kozol, 1)—includes references to Saint Paul ("Be not forgetful to entertain strangers for thereby some have entertained angels unawares." Kozol, 180), Matthew ("I was hungry and you gave me not food . . ." Kozol, 144), and the idea of common Judeo-Christian roots. Kozol, 137.
3. Kozol, 2.
4. The idea of wandering and language of refugees appears several times throughout the text. For instance, see Kozol, 155 or 180.
5. Kozol, 3.
6. He makes the case that childhood homelessness is a likely indicator of adult homelessness.
7. Kozol, 133.
8. Ibid., 142.
9. Ibid., 120.
10. For instance, Kozol, 144 and 180.
11. For an analysis of myth as argument, see Laurie L. Patton, *Myth as Argument: The Brhaddevata as Canonical Commentary* (New York: Walter de Gruyter, 1996). For an analysis of myth as culture, see Gananath Obeyesekere, *The Work of Culture: Symbolic Transformation in Psychoanalysis and Anthropology* (Chicago: University of Chicago Press, 1990).

12. Kozol, 20–21.
13. For some of the monikers since lumpenproletariat, see Kim Hopper, "A Quiet Violence: The Homeless Poor in New York City, 1982," in Mary Ellen Hombs and Mitch Snyder, *Homelessness in America: A Forced March to Nowhere* (Washington, DC: Community for Creative Non-Violence, 1986), 61–68.
14. For instance, see Kozol, 129 or 171ff.
15. For example, see Kozol, 42, 135, or 177.
16. Brendan O'Flaherty, *Making Room: The Economics of Homelessness* (Cambridge, MA: Harvard University Press, 1996), 68.
17. Ibid., 69.
18. The recent 2011 HEARTH Act had to clarify ways in which McKinney-Vento still obscured homeless families in its definition because of this continuing discursive bracketing.
19. As I write this, one of the programs that I run includes both groups. However, the services provided for each group are usually quite distinct.
20. Kozol, 32ff.
21. Ibid., 92.
22. "Kim is a lively woman with an angry and investigative zeal. But none of her anger is turned in upon herself. It is turned out; and in that turning out, that venting of a well-defined and well-supported rage, she finds a fair degree of energy and health." Kozol, 99.
23. Ibid., 93.
24. Ibid., 92.
25. Max Horkheimer, "Authority and the Family," in *Critical Theory: Selected Essays*, trans. Matthew J. O'Connell (New York: Continuum, 1999), 47–128.
26. Webb, "Family Values."
27. Kozol, 123.
28. Throughout *Rachel and Her Children*, Kozol returns to this theme that anxieties about family destruction cannot properly be connected with the homeless family. For instance, "There is a wealth of literature about the loss of certain values that provide cohesion for the family in American society. Less is written of the role played by society itself in the undoing of those decent family ties that do somehow prevail in even the most damaging conditions of existence. How do bureaucratic regulations in themselves conspire to annihilate a family?" Kozol, 47. See also Kozol, 49 or 57.
29. Rossi, 34.
30. Ibid., 38–40:

> A major difference between the old and the new homeless is that the old homeless routinely managed somehow to find shelter indoors, while a majority of the new homeless in most studies are out on the streets. As far as shelter goes, the new homeless are clearly worse off. In short, homelessness today means more severe basic shelter deprivation . . . A second major contrast is the presence of women among the homeless . . . A third contrast with the old homeless is in age composition . . . A fourth contrast is in employment status and income . . . A final contrast is presented by the ethnic composition of the old and new homeless populations. The old homeless were

predominantly white—70% on the Bowery and 82% on Chicago's Skid Row. But the new homeless are recruited heavily from among ethnic minorities: in Chicago 54% were black, and in New York's shelters more than 75% were black, a proportion that has been increasing since the early 1980s.

31. By disability, Rossi includes mental illness, physical disability, alcoholism, and the newer problems of drug use. Rossi, 42–43. With the possible exception of physical disability, these other problems are the standard categories of pathology.
32. Rossi, 40–43.
33. Ibid., 43.
34. Christopher Jencks, *The Homeless* (Cambridge, MA: Harvard University Press, 1994), 59–60.
35. US Code Title 42. Chapter 119. Subchapter I § 11302.
36. Siegfried Kracauer, *The Mass Ornament: Weimar Essays*, trans. Thomas Y. Levin (Cambridge, MA: Harvard University Press, 1995), 83–84.

Chapter 8

1. Joel Blau, *The Visible Poor: Homelessness in the United States* (New York: Oxford University Press, 1992).
2. For discussions of changes in urban relations to capital, see David Harvey, *The Condition of Postmodernity: An Enquiry into the Origins of Cultural Change* (Oxford: Blackwell, 2000), chapter 9.
3. For discussions, see William Julius Wilson, *When Work Disappears: The World of the New Urban Poor* (New York: Alfred A. Knopf, 1997).
4. O'Flaherty, 4ff.
5. Freud, 22.
6. Sharon Zukin, "Gentrification: Culture and Capital in the Urban Core," *Annual Review of Sociology* 13 (1987): 130.
7. Zukin, 132. See also P. L. Clay, *Neighborhood Renewal* (Lexington, MA: D. C. Heath and Company, 1979).
8. See Zukin, 132 for a list of citations.
9. See David Harvey for an analysis of the urban trend "to capture consumer dollars to compensate for de-industrialization." Harvey, *Urban*, 270ff.
10. Smith, 7.
11. Harvey, *Urban*, 259.
12. Ibid., 272ff.
13. Smith, 1.
14. Ibid., 11.
15. Ibid., 3.
16. George L. Kelling and James Q. Wilson, "Broken Windows: The Police and Neighborhood Safety," *Atlantic Monthly*, March 1, 1982, accessed January 5, 2014, http://www.theatlantic.com/magazine/archive/1982/03/broken-windows/304465/.
17. Rudolph W. Giuliani and William J. Bratton, *Police Strategy No. 5: Reclaiming the Public Spaces of New York* (New York: Office of the Mayor, 1994), 6–7.
18. Smith, 4–5.

19. Harvey, *Urban*, 273.
20. Kracauer, 79–80.
21. Without explaining how he planned to do so, Mayor Giuliani planned to eliminate much of the population of the urban poor. "Shrinkage of the poor population in general, including homeless people, is 'not an unspoken part of our strategy,' the mayor once explained at a 'confidential' meeting of newspaper editors. 'That is our strategy.'" Smith, 8.

Chapter 9

1. Webb, "Family Values."
2. See Marvin Olasky, *The Tragedy of American Compassion* (Washington, DC: Regnery Gateway, 1992); or Marvin Olasky, "Giving That Worked," *World Magazine*, 2009, accessed March 2009, http://www.worldmag.com/articles/15070.
3. Focus on the Family was founded in 1977 by psychologist and family counselor James Dobson. Dobson was also involved in setting up the Washington, DC–based Family Research Council in 1983. Its first two directors—Gerry Regier and Gary Bauer—were former Reagan administration officials.
4. Webb, "Family Values," 113–14.
5. Senator Santorum represents the social conservatism alliance between evangelicals and Catholics. With longstanding traditions of subsidiarity from Catholic social teaching, the Catholic Church is easily integrated into a concern with civil society.
6. John Dilulio, "John Dilulio's Letter," *Esquire*, October 24, 2002, accessed July 16, 2013, http://www.esquire.com/features/dilulio. David Kuo, who also worked in the White House Office of Faith-Based and Community Initiatives, also recounts the waning interest in compassionate conservatism in the Bush White House following the 9/11 attacks. David Kuo, *Tempting Faith: An Inside Story of Political Seduction* (New York: Free Press, 2006), chapter 12.
7. "Let me point out in general that the notion of the nation as a home, as a domestic space, relies structurally on its intimate opposition to the notion of the foreign. *Domestic* has a double meaning that links the space of the familial household to that of the nation, by imagining both in opposition to everything outside the geographic and conceptual border of the home." Amy Kaplan, "Homeland Insecurities: Reflections on Language and Space," *Radical History Review*, no. 86 (Winter 2003): 82–93, 86.
8. J. Patrick Dobel, "The Rhetorical Possibilities of 'Home' in Homeland Security," *Administration & Society* 42, no. 4 (2010): 6.
9. Kaplan, 84.
10. For instance, see Kaplan: "Homeland thus conveys a sense of native origins, of birthplace and birthright. It appeals to common bloodlines, ancient ancestry, and notions of racial and ethnic homogeneity." Kaplan, 86.
11. Emphasis mine. William Safire, "The Way We Live Now: ON LANGUAGE; Homeland," *New York Times Magazine*, January 20, 2002, accessed July 19,

2013, http://www.nytimes.com/2002/01/20/magazine/the-way-we-live-now-01 -20-02-on-language-homeland.html.

12. As Christopher Jencks has pointed out, there have been a series of periods of dein-stitutionalization from the 1940s onward. The move to CMHCs was one of the final phases. Jencks, chapter 3.

13. "Although scattered-site public housing has been promoted as an alternative to large projects that concentrate poverty and problems, little systematic infor-mation is available about its characteristics and performance." This is on the Huduser site marketing the 1996 study *Scattered-Site Housing: Characteristics and Consequences* (November 1996), accessed July, 22, 2013, http://www.huduser. org/publications/pubasst/scatter.html.

14. Philip Mangano, "Abolishing Homelessness in Ten Years," interview by David Neff, *Christianity Today* 53, no. 5 (May 2009): 52, accessed July 19, 2013, http:// www.christianitytoday.com/ct/2009/may/30.52.html.

15. Often the linear model is called by its original name: the continuum of care model. However, the Continuum of Care has evolved to become a local planning council, which also serves as a funding vehicle for HUD to channel money to local nonprofits. Because of the dual role of funding and planning in the present moment and the historical role of a service arrangement, I follow after Stefan G. Kertesz, et al., and use the term *linear model* to avoid confusion between the his-torical and present uses of "continuum of care." Stefan G. Kertesz, et al., "Hous-ing First for Homeless Persons with Active Addiction: Are We Overreaching?" *Milbank Quarterly* 87, no. 2 (June 2009): 495–534.

16. *The Applicability of Housing First Models to Homeless Persons with Serious Mental Illness* (Washington, DC: US Department of Housing and Urban Development, Office of Policy Development and Research, 2007), 2.

17. Sam Tsemberis, Leyla Gulcur, and Maria Nakae, "Housing First Consumer Choice, and Harm Reduction for Homeless Individuals with a Dual Diagnosis," *American Journal of Public Health* 94, no. 4 (April 2004): 651–56.

18. Alan Gilbert, "Power, Ideology and the Washington Consensus: The Develop-ment and Spread of Chilean Housing Policy," *Housing Studies* 17, no. 2 (2002): 305–24.

19. Stuart Hodkinson, Paul Watt, and Gerry Mooney, "Introduction: Neoliberal Housing Policy—Time for a Critical Re-appraisal," *Critical Social Policy* 33, no. 3 (2013): 6.

20. David Clapham and Susan J. Smith, "Housing Policy and 'Special Needs,'" *Pol-icy and Politics* 18, no. 3 (1990): 195.

21. Michel Foucault, *Society Must Be Defended: Lectures at the Collège de France, 1975–76*, trans. David Macey (New York: Picador, 2003), 245.

22. Ibid., 244.

23. Mary Ellen Hombs and Mitch Snyder, "Homelessness and the Hundredth Mon-key: A Preface," in *Homelessness in America: A Forced March to Nowhere*, ed. Mary Ellen Hombs and Mitch Snyder (Washington, DC: Community for Creative Non-Violence, 1986), viii.

24. For instance, *A Report on the 1988 Survey of Shelters for the Homeless* (Washington, DC: US Department of Housing and Urban Development, 1989); or *Report to the Secretary on the Homeless and Emergency* Shelters (Washington, DC: US Department of Housing and Urban Development, 1984).

Chapter 10

1. While not all the populations live in metropolitan areas, the processes of urbanization are impacting people beyond the perceived barriers of city limits. "Moreover, as anthropologist Gregory Guldin has emphasized, urbanization must be conceptualized as structural transformation along, and intensified interaction between, every point on an urban-rural continuum. In Guldin's case study of southern China, he found that the countryside is urbanizing *in situ* as well as generating epochal migrations; 'Villages become more like market and *xiang* towns, and county towns and small cities become more like large cities.' Indeed, in many cases rural people no longer have to migrate to the city: it migrates to them." Mike Davis, *Planet of Slums* (London: Verso, 2006), 8–9.

Bibliography

Abel, Theodore. "The Significance of the Concept of Consciousness of Kind." *Social Forces* 9, no. 1 (1930): 1–10.

Addams, Jane. "The Sheltered Woman and the Magdalen." *Ladies Home Journal*, November 1913. In *The Jane Addams Reader*, edited by Jean Bethke Elshtain, 264–69. New York: Basic Books, 2002.

———. *The Spirit of Youth and the City Streets*. New York: Macmillan, 1914.

Althusser, Louis. *For Marx*. Translated by Ben Brewster. London: Verso, 2005.

Ambrose. *Saint Ambrose: Hexameron, Paradise, and Cain and Abel*. Translated by John J. Savage. New York: Fathers of the Church, 1961.

Amster, Randall. *Lost in Space: The Criminalization, Globalization, and Urban Ecology of Homelessness*. New York: LFB Scholarly, 2008.

Anbinder, Tyler. *Five Points: The 19th-Century New York City Neighborhood That Invented Tap Dance, Stole Elections, and Became the World's Most Notorious Slum*. New York: Penguin Books, 2001.

Anderson, George Kumler. *The Legend of the Wandering Jew*. Providence, RI: Brown University Press, 1965.

Anderson, Nels. *The Hobo: The Sociology of the Homeless Man*. Chicago: University of Chicago Press, 1923.

———. *Men on the Move*. Chicago: University of Chicago Press, 1940.

Arnold, Kathleen R. *Homelessness, Citizenship, and Identity: The Uncanniness of Late Modernity*. Albany: State University of New York Press, 2004.

Augustine. *Concerning the City of God against the Pagans*. Translated by Henry Bettenson. New York: Penguin Classics, 1984.

Bahr, Howard M., ed. *Disaffiliated Man: Essays and Bibliography on Skid Row, Vagrancy and Outsiders*. Toronto: University of Toronto Press, 1970.

———. "Family Size and Stability as Antecedents of Homelessness and Excessive Drinking." *Journal of Marriage and the Family* 31, no. 3 (1969): 477–83.

———. *Skid Row: An Introduction to Disaffiliation*. New York: Oxford University Press, 1973.

Bahr, Howard M., and Theodore Caplow. "Homelessness, Affiliation, and Occupational Mobility." *Social Forces* 47, no. 1 (1968): 28–33.

———. *Old Men: Drunk and Sober*. New York: New York University Press, 1974.

Bahr, Howard M., and Gerald R. Garrett. *Women Alone: The Disaffiliation of Urban Females*. Lexington, MA: Lexington Books, 1976.

Barthes, Roland. *Mythologies*. Translated by Annette Lavers. New York: Hill and Wang, 1987.

Beck, Frank Orman. *Hobohemia*. Rindge, NH: R. R. Smith, 1956.

Beecher, Catharine E. *A Treatise on Domestic Economy, for the Use of Young Ladies at Home, and at School*. New York: Source Book Press, 1970.

Beecher, Catharine E., and Harriet Beecher Stowe. *The American Woman's Home: Or, Principles of Domestic Science; Being a Guide to the Formation and Maintenance of Economical, Healthful, Beautiful, and Christian Homes*. New York: Arno Press, 1971.

Behrends, A. J. F., ed. *My Brother and I: Selected Papers on Social Topics*. New York: Hunt and Eaton, 1895.

Benjamin, Walter. *The Arcades Project*. Translated by Howard Eiland and Kevin McLaughlin. Cambridge, MA: Belknap Press of Harvard University Press, 1999.

Berger, Peter L., Brigitte Berger, and Hansfried Kellner. *The Homeless Mind: Modernization and Consciousness*. New York: Random House, 1973.

Berman, Marshall. *All That Is Solid Melts into Air: The Experience of Modernity*. New York: Penguin Books, 1988.

Bertha, Boxcar. *Boxcar Bertha: An Autobiography, as Told to Ben Reitman*. New York: AMOK Press, 1988.

Blau, Joel. *The Visible Poor: Homelessness in the United States*. New York: Oxford University Press, 1992.

Bogue, Donald B. *Skid Row in American Cities*. Chicago: Community and Family Study Center, University of Chicago, 1963.

Boyse, Samuel. "The Triumphs of Nature." *Gentleman's Magazine* 12: 1749, 324.

Brace, Charles Loring. *The Dangerous Classes of New York, and Twenty Years' Work among Them*. New York: Wynkoop and Hallenbeck, 1872.

Bruns, Roger. *The Damndest Radical: The Life and World of Ben Reitman, Chicago's Celebrated Social Reformer, Hobo King, and Whorehouse Physician*. Urbana: University of Illinois Press, 1987.

———. *Knights of the Road: A Hobo History*. New York: Methuen, 1980.

Buk-Swienty, Tom. *The Other Half: The Life of Jacob Riis and the World of Immigrant America*. Translated by Anette Buk-Swienty. New York: W. W. Norton, 2008.

Burchinal, Lee G. "Characteristics of Adolescents from Unbroken, Broken, and Reconstituted Families." *Journal of Marriage and the Family* 26, no. 1 (1964): 44–51.

Burrows, Edwin G., and Mike Wallace. *Gotham: A History of New York City to 1898*. New York: Oxford University Press, 1999.

Caplow, Theodore. "The Sociologist and the Homeless Man." In *Disaffiliated Man: Essays and Bibliography on Skid Row, Vagrancy, and Outsiders*, edited by Howard M. Bahr, 3–12. Toronto: University of Toronto Press, 1970.

Caplow, Theodore, Howard M. Bahr, and David Sternberg. "Homelessness." In *International Encyclopedia of the Social Sciences*, vol. 6, edited by David L. Sills, 494–99. New York: Crowell Collier and Macmillan, 1968.

Cassirer, Ernst. *The Myth of the State*. Translated by Charles William Hendel. New Haven, CT: Yale University Press, 1946.

———. *Philosophy of Symbolic Forms, Volume 2: Mythical Thought*. Translated by Ralph Manheim. New Haven, CT: Yale University Press, 1955.

Chakrabarty, Dipesh. *Provincializing Europe: Postcolonial Thought and Historical Difference*. Princeton, NJ: Princeton University Press, 2000.

Chauncey, George. *Gay New York: Gender, Urban Culture, and the Making of the Gay Male World 1890–1940*. New York: Basic Books, 1994.

Clapham, David, and Susan J. Smith. "Housing Policy and 'Special Needs.'" *Policy and Politics* 18, no. 3 (1990): 193–205.

Clay, P. L. *Neighborhood Renewal*. Lexington, MA: D. C. Heath and Company, 1979.

Cohn, D'Vera, and Jeffrey S. Passel. *U.S. Population Projections: 2005–2050*. Washington, DC: Pew Research Center, 2008.

Cohn-Sherbock, Dan. *The Crucified Jew: Twenty Centuries of Christian Anti-Semitism*. Grand Rapids, MI: Wm. B. Eerdmans, 1997.

Coontz, Stephanie. *The Way We Never Were: American Families and the Nostalgia Trap*. New York: Basic Books, 1992.

Crane, Stephen. *Maggie, a Girl of the Streets, and Other New York Writings*. New York: Modern Library, 2001.

Davis, Mike. *Planet of Slums*. London: Verso, 2006.

Dawson, William Harbutt. *The Vagrancy Problem. The Case for Measures of Restraint for Tramps, Loafers, and Unemployables: With a Study of Continental Detention Colonies and Labour Houses*. London: P. S. King and Son, 1910.

Day, Dorothy. *Dorothy Day, Selected Writings: By Little and by Little*. Maryknoll, NY: Orbis Books, 1992.

———. *The Long Loneliness*. San Francisco: Harper, 1997.

Deegan, Mary Jo. *Jane Addams and the Men of the Chicago School*. New Brunswick, NJ: Transaction Books, 1988.

Defoe, Daniel. *The History of the Devil*. Totowa, NJ: Rowman and Littlefield, 1972.

DePastino, Todd. *Citizen Hobo: How a Century of Homelessness Shaped America*. Chicago: University of Chicago Press, 2003.

Deseret News 7, 1856. In Glanz, Rudolf. "The Wandering Jew in America." In *The Wandering Jew: Essays in the Interpretation of a Christian Legend*, edited by Galit Hasan-Rokem and Alan Dundes, 105–18. Bloomington: Indiana University Press, 1986.

Deseret News 17, 1856. In Glanz, Rudolf. "The Wandering Jew in America." In *The Wandering Jew: Essays in the Interpretation of a Christian Legend*, edited by Galit Hasan-Rokem and Alan Dundes, 105–18. Bloomington: Indiana University Press, 1986.

Dickens, Charles. *American Notes for General Circulation and Pictures from Italy*. London: Chapman and Hall, 1910.

———. *Dombey and Son*. Oxford: Oxford University Press, 1987.

Dilulio, John. "John Dilulio's Letter." *Esquire*, October 24, 2002. Accessed July 16, 2013. http://www.esquire.com/features/dilulio.

Dobel, J. Patrick. "The Rhetorical Possibilities of 'Home' in Homeland Security." *Administration & Society* 42, no. 5 (2010): 1–25.

Dobkowski, Michael Nachin. "Ideological Anti-Semitism in America: 1877–1927." PhD diss., New York University, 1976.

Durkheim, Emile. "Anomic Suicide." In *Suicide, a Study in Sociology*, edited by George Simpson, translated by John A. Spaulding and George Simpson, 241–76. Glencoe, IL: Free Press, 1951.

Elshtain, Jean Bethke. *Jane Addams and the Dream of American Democracy: A Life*. New York: Basic Books, 2002.

———, ed. *The Jane Addams Reader*. New York: Basic Books, 2002.

———. *Public Man, Private Woman: Women in Social and Political Thought*. Princeton, NJ: Princeton University Press, 1981.

Feldman, Leonard C. *Citizens Without Shelter: Homelessness, Democracy, and Political Exclusion*. Ithaca, NY: Cornell University Press, 2004.

Foucault, Michel. *Discipline and Punish: The Birth of the Prison*. Translated by Alan Sheridan. New York: Vintage Books, 1979.

———. *Society Must Be Defended: Lectures at the Collège de France, 1975–76*. Translated by David Macey. New York: Picador, 2003.

Freud, Sigmund. *Civilization and Its Discontents*. Translated by James Strachey. New York: W. W. Norton, 1962.

Fried, Lewis F. *Makers of the City*. Amherst: University of Massachusetts Press, 1990.

Gibson, Campbell. "Population of the 100 Largest Cities and Other Urban Places in the United States: 1790 to 1990." Washington, DC: US Bureau of the Census Population Division, 1998.

Gillin, J. L. "Vagrancy and Begging." *American Journal of Sociology* 35, no. 3 (1929): 424–32.

Gilman, Sander L., and Steven T. Katz, eds. *Anti-Semitism in Times of Crisis*. New York: New York University Press, 1991.

Gilmore, Harlan W. *The Beggar*. Chapel Hill: University of North Carolina Press, 1940.

Giuliani, Rudolph W., and William J. Bratton. *Police Strategy No. 5: Reclaiming the Public Spaces of New York*. New York: Office of the Mayor, 1994.

Glanz, Rudolf. "The Wandering Jew in America." In *The Wandering Jew: Essays in the Interpretation of a Christian Legend*, edited by Galit Hasan-Rokem and Alan Dundes, 105–18. Bloomington: Indiana University Press, 1986.

Glazer, Nathan, and Daniel Patrick Moynihan. *Beyond the Melting Pot: The Negroes, Puerto Ricans, Jews, Italians, and Irish of New York City*. Cambridge, MA: MIT Press, 1963.

Golden, Stephanie. *The Women Outside: Meanings and Myths of Homelessness*. Berkeley: University of California Press, 1992.

Gowan, Teresa. *Hobos, Hustlers, and Backsliders: Homeless in San Francisco*. Minneapolis: University of Minnesota Press, 2010.

Habermas, Jürgen. *The Structural Transformation of the Public Sphere: An Inquiry into a Category of Bourgeois Society*. Translated by Thomas Burger with Frederick Lawrence. Cambridge, MA: MIT Press, 2000.

Hall, John. *A Christian Home: How to Make and How to Maintain It*. Philadelphia: American Sunday-School Union, 1883.

Halmos, Paul. *Solitude and Privacy: A Study of Social Isolation, Its Causes and Therapy*. London: Routledge and Kegan Paul, 1952.

Hand, Jennifer. "Shopping Bag Ladies: A Study in Interstitial Urban Behavior." Paper presented at the Annual Conference of the Society for the Study of Social Problems, New York, September 1976.

Harris, Lee O. *The Man Who Tramps: A Story of Today*. Indianapolis: Douglas and Carlon, 1878.

Harvey, David. *The Condition of Postmodernity: An Enquiry into the Origins of Cultural Change*. Oxford: Blackwell, 2000.

———. *The Urban Experience*. Baltimore: Johns Hopkins University Press, 1989.

Hasan-Rokem, Galit, and Alan Dundes. *The Wandering Jew: Essays in the Interpretation of a Christian Legend*. Bloomington: Indiana University Press, 1986.

Hegel, G. W. F. *Hegel's Philosophy of Right*. Translated by T. M. Knox. Oxford: Oxford University Press, 1967.

Hertenstein, Mike. "What Would Jesus Do? The Settlement House Movement and in His Steps." *Cornerstone Magazine* 26, no. 112 (1997): 39–40.

Heschel, Susannah. "The Exile of Redemption in Judaism." In *Religions of the Book*, edited by Gerard Sloyan, 3–10. Lanham, MD: University Press of America, 1996.

Hodkinson, Stuart, Paul Watt, and Gerry Mooney. "Introduction: Neoliberal Housing Policy—Time for a Critical Re-appraisal." *Critical Social Policy* 33, no. 3 (2013): 3–16.

Hombs, Mary Ellen, and Mitch Snyder. *Homelessness in America: A Forced March to Nowhere*. Washington, DC: Community on Creative Non-Violence, 1986.

Hopper, Kim. "A Quiet Violence: The Homeless Poor in New York City, 1982." In *Homelessness in America: A Forced March to Nowhere*, edited by Mary Ellen Hombs and Mitch Snyder, 61–68. Washington, DC: Community for Creative Non-Violence, 1986.

———. *Reckoning with Homelessness*. Ithaca, NY: Cornell University Press, 2003.

Horkheimer, Max. *Critical Theory: Selected Essays*. Translated by Matthew J. O'Connell. New York: Continuum, 1999.

Howells, William Dean. *A Hazard of New Fortunes*. New York: Modern Library, 2002.

Hubbard, Elbert. *The Philistine* 37, no. 2 (July 1913).

Hunter, Robert. *Poverty: Social Conscience in the Progressive Era*. New York: Harper Torchbooks, 1965.

Jencks, Christopher. *The Homeless*. Cambridge, MA: Harvard University Press, 1994.

Jusserand, J. J. *English Wayfaring Life in the Middle Ages*. Translated by Lucy Toulmin Smith. London: Ernest Benn Limited, 1950.

Kaplan, Amy. "Homeland Insecurities: Reflections on Language and Space." *Radical History Review*, no. 86 (Winter 2003): 82–93.

Katz, Michael. *In the Shadow of the Poorhouse: A Social History of Welfare in America*. New York: Basic Books, 1986.

Keats, John. *The Complete Poems of John Keats*. New York: Modern Library, 1994.

Kelling, George L., and James Q. Wilson. "Broken Windows: The Police and Neighborhood Safety." *Atlantic Monthly*, March 1, 1982. Accessed January 5, 2014. http://www.theatlantic.com/magazine/archive/1982/03/broken-windows/304465/.

Kerouac, Jack. "The Vanishing American Hobo." *Holiday*, March 1960, 60–61, 112–13.

Kertesz, Stefan G., Kimberly Crouch, Jesse B. Milby, Robert E. Cusimano, and Joseph E. Schumacher. "Housing First for Homeless Persons with Active Addiction: Are We Overreaching?" *Milbank Quarterly* 87, no. 2 (June 2009): 495–534.

Kingsbury, F. J. "Charity Organization a Necessity of Modern Conditions." *Lend-a-Hand* 14, no. 1 (1895): 3–9.

Kozol, Jonathan. *Rachel and Her Children: Homeless Families in America*. New York: Fawcett Columbine, 1988.

Kracauer, Siegfried. *The Mass Ornament: Weimar Essays*. Translated by Thomas Y. Levin. Cambridge, MA: Harvard University Press, 1995.

Kuo, David. *Tempting Faith: An Inside Story of Political Seduction*. New York: Free Press, 2006.

Kusmer, Kenneth L. *Down and Out, on the Road: The Homeless in American History*. Oxford: Oxford University Press, 2002.

Kyle, Ken. *Contextualizing Homelessness: Critical Theory, Homelessness, and Federal Policy Addressing the Homeless*. New York: Routledge, 2005.

Lane, James B. *Jacob A. Riis and the American City*. Port Washington, NY: Kennikat Press, 1974.

Lasch, Christopher. *Haven in a Heartless World: The Family Besieged*. New York: Basic Books, 1977.

Laubach, Frank Charles. *Why There Are Vagrants, a Study Based upon a Examination of One Hundred Men*. New York: Columbia University Press, 1916.

Law, M. W. "Our Ishmael." *American Journal of Sociology* 8, no. 6 (1903): 838–51.

Leo XIII, Pope. *Encyclical Letter of Our Holy Father by Divine Providence Pope Leo XIII: On the Condition of Labour*. London: "The Universe" Office, 1891.

———. *Encyclical Letter of Our Holy Father by Divine Providence Pope Leo XIII: On the Condition of Labour: Official Translation*. London: Westminster Press, 1891.

Levinson, David, ed. *Encyclopedia of Homelessness, Volume I*. Thousand Oaks, CA: Sage, 2004.

Lewis, Sinclair. "Hobohemia." *Saturday Evening Post*, April 7, 1917, 3–6, 121–22, 125–26, 129–30, 133.

Life 71, no. 1858 (June 6, 1918): 915.

Life 71, no. 1860 (June 20, 1918): 983.

Logue, Larry. *To Appomattox and Beyond: The Civil War Soldier in War and Peace*. Chicago: Ivan R. Dee, 1996.

Lubove, Roy. *The Professional Altruist: The Emergence of Social Work as a Career, 1880–1930*. New York: Atheneum, 1983.

Lukács, Georg. *The Theory of the Novel: A Historico-Philosophical Essay on the Forms of Great Epic Literature*. Translated by Anna Bostock. Cambridge, MA: MIT Press, 1999.

Mangano, Philip. "Abolishing Homelessness in Ten Years," interview by David Neff. *Christianity Today* 53, no. 5 (May 2009): 52. Accessed July 19, 2013. http://www.christianitytoday.com/ct/2009/may/30.52.html.

Marx, Karl. *Surveys from Exile: Political Writings Volume II*. Edited by David Fernbach. New York: Vintage Books, 1974.

McCook, J. J. "Charity Organization and Social Regeneration." *Lend-a-Hand* 13 (1894): 461–69.

McCulloch, Rev. Oscar C. *The Tribe of Ishmael: A Study in Social Degradation*. Indianapolis, IN: Charity Organization Society, 1888.

McDannell, Colleen. "Parlor Piety: The Home as Sacred Space in Protestant America." In *American Home Life, 1880–1930: A Social History of Spaces and Services*, edited by Jessica H. and Thomas J. Schlereth Foy, 162–89. Knoxville: University of Tennessee Press, 1992.

Merton, Robert. *Social Theory and Social Structure*. Glencoe, IL: Free Press, 1963.

Moynihan, Daniel Patrick. "The Negro Family: The Case for National Action." In *The Moynihan Report and the Politics of Controversy*, edited by Lee Rainwater and William L. Yancey, 45–124. Cambridge, MA: MIT Press, 1967.

Murdock, George Peter. *Social Structure*. New York: Macmillan, 1949.

National Alliance to End Homelessness. *Homelessness Counts*. Washington, DC: National Alliance to End Homelessness, 2007.

———. "Organizational Change: Adopting a Housing First Approach," August 24, 2009, 1.

Neale, Joanne. "Homelessness and Theory Reconsidered." *Housing Studies* 12, no. 1 (1997): 47–61.

Nye, F. Ivan. "Child Adjustment in Broken and in Unhappy Unbroken Homes." *Marriage and Family Living* 19, no. 4 (1957): 356–61.

O'Flaherty, Brendan. *Making Room: The Economics of Homelessness*. Cambridge, MA: Harvard University Press, 1996.

Olasky, Marvin. "Giving That Worked." *World Magazine*, 2009. Accessed March 2009. http://www.worldmag.com/articles/15070.

———. *The Tragedy of American Compassion*. Washington, DC: Regnery Gateway, 1992.

Park, Robert E. "Editor's Preface." In *The Hobo: The Sociology of the Homeless Man*, edited by Nels Anderson, v–viii. Chicago: University of Chicago Press, 1923.

Park, Robert E., Ernest W. Burgess, and Roderick D. McKenzie, eds. *The City*. Chicago: University of Chicago Press, 1925.

Park, Robert E., and Herbert A. Miller. *Old World Traits Transplanted*. New York: Harper and Brothers, 1921.

Philo. *Philo, Vol. 2*. Translated by F. H. Colson and G. H. Whitaker. Loeb Classical Library. London: William Heineman, 1929.

Putnam, Robert D. *Bowling Alone: The Collapse and Revival of American Community*. New York: Simon and Schuster, 2000.

Quinones, Ricardo. *The Changes of Cain: Violence and the Lost Brother in Cain and Abel Literature*. Princeton, NJ: Princeton University Press, 1991.

Reitman, Ben. "Following the Monkey, Unpublished Autobiography." Ben Reitman Papers, University of Illinois at Chicago, 1925–1940.

Reitman, Ben L. *The Second Oldest Profession*. New York: Garland, 1987.

"Review of 'American Charities.'" *The Dial*, August 23, 1919, 164.

Ribton-Turner, C. J. *A History of Vagrants and Vagrancy and Beggars and Begging*. Patterson Smith Reprint Series in Criminology, Law Enforcement, and Social Problems. Montclair, NJ: Patterson Smith, 1972.

Riesman, David. *The Lonely Crowd: A Study of the Changing American Character*. New Haven, CT: Yale University Press, 1950.

Riis, Jacob A. *The Battle with the Slum*. Mineola, NY: Dover, 1998.

———. *The Children of the Poor*. New York: Garrett Press, 1970.

———. *How the Other Half Lives: Studies among the Tenements of New York*. New York: Penguin Books, 1997.

———. *The Making of an American*. New York: Macmillan, 1925.

———. *The Peril and the Preservation of the Home: Being the William L. Bull Lectures for the Year 1903*. Philadelphia: George W. Jacobs, 1903.

———. "The Problem of the Children." In *My Brother and I: Selected Papers on Social Topics*, edited by A. J. F. Behrends, 261–76. New York: Hunt and Eaton, 1895.

Rooney, James F. "Societal Forces and the Unattached Male: An Historical Review." In *Disaffiliated Man: Essays and Bibliography on Skid Row, Vagrancy and Outsiders*, edited by Howard M. Bahr, 13–38. Toronto: University of Toronto Press, 1970.

Roosevelt, Theodore. *Theodore Roosevelt: An Autobiography*. New York: Charles Scribner's Sons, 1920.

Rossi, Peter H. *Down and Out in America: The Origins of Homelessness*. Chicago: University of Chicago Press, 1989.

Rousseau, Ann Marie. *Shopping Bag Ladies: Homeless Women Speak about Their Lives*. New York: Pilgrim Press, 1981.

Safire, William. "The Way We Live Now: ON LANGUAGE; Homeland," *New York Times Magazine*, January 20, 2002. Accessed July 19, 2013. http://www.nytimes.com/2002/01/20/magazine/the-way-we-live-now-01-20-02-on-language-homeland.html.

Said, Edward W. *Reflections on Exile and Other Essays*. Cambridge, MA: Harvard University Press, 2000.

Santorum, Rick. *It Takes a Family: Conservatism and the Common Good*. Wilmington: ISI Books, 2005.

Schlesinger, Arthur, Jr. "Introduction." In *A Hazard of New Fortunes*, by William Dean Howells. New York: Modern Library, 2002.

Schutt, Russell K., and Stephen M. Goldfinger. *Homelessness, Housing and Mental Illness*. Cambridge, MA: Harvard University Press, 2011.

Sheldon, Charles Monroe. *In His Steps*. Philadelphia: John C. Winston, 1937.

Shields, Charles Woodruff. *The Final Philosophy, or System of Perfectible Knowledge Issuing from the Harmony of Science and Religion*. New York: Scribner, Armstrong, 1877.

Shulman, Alix Kates. "Preface." In *Shopping Bag Ladies: Homeless Women Speak about Their Lives*, edited by Ann Marie Rousseau, 9–12. New York: Pilgrim Press, 1981.

Simmel, Georg. *Georg Simmel: On Individuality and Social Forms*. Edited by Donald N. Levine. Chicago: University of Chicago Press, 1971.

Sklar, Kathryn Kish. *Catharine Beecher: A Study in American Domesticity*. New York: W. W. Norton, 1976.

Smith, Neil. "Giuliani Time: The Revanchist 1990s." *Social Text* 57 (1998): 1–20.

Snow, David A., and Leon Anderson. *Down on Their Luck: A Study of Homeless Street People*. Berkeley: University of California Press, 1993.

Solenberger, Alice Willard. *One Thousand Homeless Men: A Study of Original Records*. New York: Survey Associates, 1914.

Sommerville, C. John. *The Secularization of Early Modern England: From Religious Culture to Religious Faith*. New York: Oxford University Press, 1992.

Sommerville, Maxwell. *A Wanderer's Legend*. Philadelphia: Drexel Biddle, 1902.

Staats, William. *A Tight Squeeze: Or, the Adventures of a Gentleman Who on a Wager of Ten Thousand Dollars, Undertook to Go from New York to New Orleans in Three Weeks without Money as a Professional Tramp*. Boston: Lee and Shepard, 1879.

Stiff, Dean. *The Milk and Honey Route: A Handbook for Hobos*. New York: Vanguard Press, 1930.

Stoker, Bram. "The American 'Tramp' Question and the Old English Vagrancy Laws." *North American Review*, November 1909, 605–14.

Strong, Josiah. *Our Country: Its Possible Future and Its Present Crisis*. New York: Baker and Taylor, 1891.

Sue, Eugene. *The Wandering Jew*. London: Dedalus, 1990.

Sutherland, Edwin H., and Harvey J. Locke. *Twenty Thousand Homeless Men: A Study of Unemployed Men in the Chicago Shelters*. Chicago: J. B. Lippincott, 1936.

Szasz, Ferenc M., and Ralph F. Bogardus. "The Camera and the American Social Conscience." *New York History* 55, no. 4 (1974): 409–36.

Tönnies, Ferdinand. *Community and Civil Society*. Translated by José Harris. Cambridge, MA: Cambridge University Press, 2001.

Trattner, Walter I. *From Poor Law to Welfare State: A History of Social Welfare in America.* New York: Free Press, 1989.

Tsemberis, Sam, Leyla Gulcur, and Maria Nakae. "Housing First Consumer Choice, and Harm Reduction for Homeless Individuals with a Dual Diagnosis." *American Journal of Public Health* 94, no. 4 (April 2004): 651–56.

US Department of Housing and Urban Development. *The Applicability of Housing First Models to Homeless Persons with Serious Mental Illness.* Washington, DC: US Department of Housing and Urban Development, Office of Policy Development and Research, 2007.

———. *Homelessness: Programs and the People They Serve, Findings of the National Survey of Homeless Assistance Providers and Clients Highlights.* Washington, DC: US Department of Housing and Urban Development Interagency Council on the Homeless, December 1999.

———. *A Report on the 1988 Survey of Shelters for the Homeless.* Washington, DC: US Department of Housing and Urban Development, 1989.

Vexliard, Alexandre. *Introduction a la sociologie du vagabondage.* Paris: Libraire Marcel Rivière et Cie, 1956.

Volunteer Special. *The Volcano under the City.* New York: Fords, Howard, and Hulbert, 1887.

Ware, Louise. *Jacob A. Riis, Police Reporter, Reformer, Useful Citizen.* New York: D. Appleton-Century, 1938.

Warner, Amos. *American Charities: A Study in Philanthropy and Economics.* New York: Thomas Crowell, 1894.

Webb, Philip. "Anti-Semitic Roots of Homelessness: Myth, Exile and Radicals in American Homelessness," In *Jewish Images in the Media*, edited by Martin Liepach, Gabriele Melischek, and Josef Seethaler, 39–60. *Relation: Communication Research in Comparative Perspective*, n.s., vol. 2. Vienna: Austrian Academy of Sciences Press, 2007.

———. "Discourse and Subjectivation in American Homelessness." *Queen: A Journal of Rhetoric and Power* 5, no. 2 (Fall 2009), special issue on the rhetoric of place.

———. "Family Values, Social Capital and Contradictions of American Modernity." *Theory, Culture & Society* 28, no. 4 (July 2011): 96–123.

Weber, Max. *The Protestant Ethic and the Spirit of Capitalism.* Translated by Talcott Parsons. Routledge Classics. London: Routledge, 2001.

Wiebe, Robert H. *The Search for Order, 1877–1920.* New York: Hill and Wang, 1967.

Williams, Raymond. *Culture and Society, 1780–1950.* New York: Columbia University Press, 1983.

Wilson, William Julius. *When Work Disappears: The World of the New Urban Poor.* New York: Alfred A. Knopf, 1997.

Wiseman, Jacqueline P. *Stations of the Lost: The Treatment of Skid Row Alcoholics.* Englewood Cliffs, NJ: Prentice-Hall, 1970.

Witte, John, Jr. "Ishmael's Bane: The Sin and Crime of Illegitimacy Reconsidered." *Punishment and Society* 5, no. 3 (2003): 327–45.

Wood, Margaret Mary. *Paths of Loneliness: The Individual Isolated in Modern Society.* New York: Columbia University Press, 1960.

Young, Terence. "Modern Urban Parks." *Geographical Review* 85, no. 4 (1995): 535–51.

Zukin, Sharon. "Gentrification: Culture and Capital in the Urban Core." *Annual Review of Sociology* 13 (1987): 129–47.

Index

Printed in the United States of America